The Director Within

publication of this book is funded by the

BEATRICE FOX AUERBACH FOUNDATION FUND

at the Hartford Foundation for Public Giving

The Director Within

STORYTELLERS OF STAGE AND SCREEN

PHOTOGRAPHS AND TEXT BY *Rose Eichenbaum*

EDITED BY *Aron Hirt-Manheimer*

WESLEYAN UNIVERSITY PRESS

Middletown, Connecticut

WESLEYAN UNIVERSITY PRESS

Middletown CT 06459

www.wesleyan.edu/wespress

© 2014 Rose Eichenbaum

All rights reserved

Manufactured in the United States of America

Designed by Richard Hendel

Typeset in Minion by Tseng Information Systems, Inc.

Library of Congress Cataloging-in-Publication Data

Eichenbaum, Rose.

The director within: storytellers of stage and screen /
photographs and text by Rose Eichenbaum; edited by
Aron Hirt-Manheimer.

pages cm

Includes bibliographical references and index.

ISBN 978-0-8195-7289-9 (cloth : alk. paper) —
ISBN 978-0-8195-7494-7 (ebook)

1. Theatrical producers and directors—United States—
Interviews. 2. Motion picture producers and directors—
United States—Interviews. I. Eichenbaum, Rose, author
photographer. II. Hirt-Manheimer, Aron, 1948– editor.

PN2285.D55 2014

792.02′32092273—dc23   2014013665

5 4 3 2 1

publication of this book is funded by the
BEATRICE FOX AUERBACH FOUNDATION FUND
at the Hartford Foundation for Public Giving

Contents

 Foreword

I have often wondered about the power of iconic film images to imprint themselves so indelibly upon our memories. My earliest is of Charlie Chaplin eating a bowl of spaghetti, each strand sliding up toward his mustache and then disappearing. The fact that I have remembered that scene so vividly while forgetting everything else I experienced under age three is a testament to creative talents of fine filmmakers to magically transform even the most mundane of activities into a memorable image.

Not only that, such images can even change the course of our lives.

The scene in *Flower Drum Song* of Nancy Kwan dancing gleefully in her bedroom singing "I Enjoy Being a Girl" inspired ten-year-old Rose to pursue a career as a dancer, and, in recent years, to study and document the creative world of choreographers, dancers, actors, and now directors—the fourth book in her series after *Masters of Movement* (choreographers), *The Dancer Within*, and *The Actor Within*.

In interviewing her subjects for *The Director Within*, Rose quickly found that most had themselves been captivated by certain films or stage shows they had watched in their youth that had led them to careers in the art of cinematic or theatrical storytelling. John Carpenter told Rose, "My drive to become a movie director goes back to when I was eight years old, after I first saw *Forbidden Planet* (1956). That's when I fell in love with cinema." Walter Hill was eleven or twelve when he first saw *Shane* (1953): "It made an enormous impression on me. I cried at the end." For Mel Brooks it was Cole Porter's *Anything Goes*: "I was about nine when I first saw it on Broadway and my whole world sort of lit up."

With few exceptions, directors, unlike actors, are rarely in the spotlight; they work behind the scenes. "Their presence," Rose tells me, "is embedded in their works." Rose's greatest challenge, therefore, was to convince them to step out of the shadows and shed some light on how they managed to enlighten, entertain, and inspire audiences through the magic of storytelling in their chosen media.

Somehow Rose succeeded in casting herself as a confessor to thirty-five directors, men and women who opened their hearts to a personable stranger bearing a tape recorder and camera. If the directors were initially guarded, they quickly opened up when it became evident to them that Rose had come prepared, having studied just about everything that had been written about their lives and having seen or screened most of their productions. Impressed with her understanding of their work — recurring themes, messages, storytelling style, and so forth — and her disarming personality, the directors not only described their inspiration and methodology but bared their souls, revealing everything from their inner ghosts and professional frustrations to their proudest achievements and future hopes. Rose's capacity to put people so at ease is no small feat in a fiercely competitive industry in which success — measured in box office receipts and viewer ratings — can be as fleeting as film credits scrolling up a screen.

Read on and you will see for yourself how this virtuoso interviewer combines her charm, skill, and knowledge to unlock the secrets of the directors' world. Learn how directors, in close partnership with screenwriters, actors, composers, and many other talented individuals, create those iconic images that endlessly enlighten, entertain, and continue to inspire countless individuals across the planet.

How do I know so much about Rose Eichenbaum? Not only have I been her editor and artistic collaborator for many years, I am her brother.

Aron Hirt-Manheimer
Ridgefield, Connecticut
April 2013

Preface

The thirty-five directors featured in this book are accomplished story-tellers who have created works on stage, screen, and television that have become hallmarks of American culture. I met with each of them for an hour or two, determined to learn how they breathe life into a script in such profound ways. Once these virtuoso storytellers saw that I had immersed myself in their oeuvre, they opened their hearts to me, providing penetrating insights into their creative alchemy—the elements that stirred their imaginations and determined their choices of subjects, their recurring metaphors or themes, and their desire to make political statements, or not.

My opening questions were designed to elicit answers that are more in the realm of psychology than methodology—Why did you become a storyteller? Why do you tell the stories you tell? I probed for answers that were unrehearsed, improvised—and then I took my cues from each director's narrative, hoping that he or she would arrive at new realizations in the process.

What drew action film director Walter Hill to cinematic storytelling? "It probably stems from my childhood and the fact that I was an asthmatic and not expected to make it. I missed a lot of school and became a voracious reader, immediately drawn to stories about adventure and survival. I guess I never got past it."

John Carpenter, master of horror, told me, "My drive to become a movie director goes back to when I was eight years old. I was different from the other kids and constantly bullied. I learned very early about how unfair and cruel the world was."

Television directors Jay Sandrich and James Burrows followed in their fathers' footsteps. Sandrich says, "There was that tradition that you did what your father did. Had I been born in Detroit, I would have gone into the automotive industry." Burrows agreed, "Had my father been a tailor, I would have known how to make a suit."

I began to see patterns in their responses. To find out why these individuals chose to become directors, I needed to probe their backstory.

Tim Van Patten revealed, "My mother died when I was twelve, and we found ourselves a family in crisis. My father was a highly literate man and understood that storytelling would take me and my siblings out of our misery and lift us up, which it did."

Broadway's Hal Prince said, "When I was a child, I had a cardboard theater and walked little model actors around on that stage. I liked the world of imagination and I escaped into that world, which was basically Broadway."

James L. Brooks told me, "My only ambition as a young person was survival. I came from a highly dysfunctional family. My father was an alcoholic and my hard-working guilt-ridden mother went hungry so we could eat. To cope, I read plays. I read for escape and I read for enjoyment."

Lawrence Kasdan explained that all his stories essentially have the same theme—finding a new family. "That's what *The Big Chill* was all about. One's own family is often difficult and unsatisfying or has left you damaged in some way. My stories are very explicitly about that search."

Many of the directors were motivated, often obsessed with themes that had social, political, ethical, or therapeutic messages. Mel Brooks, the son of Jewish immigrants, has made outrageously funny comedies, but the subtext of his stories invariably deals with racism and intolerance. "What drives *Blazing Saddles*," he told me, "is hatred for the sheriff because he's black. The best defense is to make *them* the joke. A lot of people thought I was just making fun of westerns, but there's a really big message there."

Taylor Hackford was the son of a single mother who made her living as a waitress. He told me that he's always been attracted to "stories about working-class people and their struggles to overcome obstacles and find their voices. Without a class pedigree, you have to struggle to get ahead. That was my ethos."

Julie Taymor explained that *The Lion King* has been seen by millions around the globe and continues to draw audiences because it makes them feel good. And then she relayed an incident: "The production helped a family get through the death of their daughter. It gave them an understanding that every time they looked into the sky, they felt her presence. *The Lion King* is the most gratifying thing I've done in my life."

Susan Stroman pointed out that a show needs to connect with where people are in their thinking and in their lives. "People flocked to the theater to see *The Producers* after the Twin Towers fell on September 11, 2001. They came for relief and to be uplifted in the same way that people went to see Fred Astaire and Ginger Rogers on the big screen during the Depression."

"The theater is immensely useful to society," explained director Doug Hughes. "We pay attention for two hours to this imitation of life that we hope might rehearse us a little bit for the life we're going to pick up when we leave the theater."

Directors understand the power of this medium to communicate emotions, ideas, and messages while at the same time they entertain, educate, inspire, and uplift us. In almost every case, the decision to become a director-storyteller stemmed from an inherent need to understand and explore issues and events they'd experienced in their own lives, as well as the desire to have a voice, a presence in our culture. Behind the curtain of slapstick, car chases, shoot-outs, love scenes, road trips, alien invasions, and mystery capers lay hidden their private narratives. If you watch very carefully and listen to their own stories, you'll see what drives their films and shows. You'll see their *within*.

Rose Eichenbaum
Encino, California
2013

# Acknowledgments

The Director Within became a reality thanks to the generous spirit of the thirty-five directors featured in this book. Their contribution to my ongoing research on the relationship of art making and human expression, this time in the form of storytelling, was invaluable. To each of them I extend heartfelt thanks for stepping out from behind the camera or stage curtain to share with me their personal stories and private thoughts on the director's life and craft.

I'd like to once again extend a special thanks to Suzanna Tamminen, editor in chief at Wesleyan University Press, for her encouragement and support and for embracing my vision for this book prior to seeing a single word or photograph. Trust like that is rare.

Thank you to Aron Hirt-Manheimer, editor, artistic collaborator, and big brother whose love, support, and guidance never wanes. His brilliance, intuition, and talent always bring out the best in me and in the material.

I am especially grateful to a number of people who were invaluable to this project, among them the many publicists, managers, and agents who delivered my requests and helped schedule my interviews: Andrea Scott, Gretchen Mitchelfield, Lisa Zeno Churgin, John De Simeo, Mari Bukofsky, George Segal, Lori Belilove, John Link, Christine Dobush, and Marcia Canazio. Above all, I am indebted to the following people whose kindness, support, and advice enabled me to complete this work: my mother, Adela Manheimer, and husband, Betzalel (Bitzy) Eichenbaum.

The Director Within

Peter Bogdanovich

*Author, screenwriter, producer, actor and director of such classic films
as* The Last Picture Show *(1971),* What's Up Doc? *(1972),* Paper Moon
(1973), and They All Laughed *(1981), Peter Bogdanovich is also an authority on the films of Howard Hawks, John Ford, Alfred Hitchcock, and
Orson Welles. So when we sat together in Los Angeles, he shared with me
a bit of cinematic history, commentary, and moviemaking techniques as
well as some sensitive moments about his own life.*

"You've been writing and commenting on cinema for decades. How do
you view the state of the art today?"

"Today, every time a movie is made it's like inventing the wheel. How
do you find an actor? How do you find a director? Everybody is independent. When I think back to the days of the studio system, I'd have to say
that it was actually a brilliant system that worked well for many years. It
operated much like theatrical stock companies, but instead of putting
on plays, they made movies. Everyone was under contract—directors,
writers, actors, producers—so it made sense as a business, and it also
produced some artistic work. Of course, there was a good percentage of
crap, but they did produce some great classic films. Today's pictures are
all about franchises and superheroes. You've got pictures being made for
hundreds of millions of dollars, which I think is a crime. Pictures today
cost too much. I knew when *Titanic* (1997) was a hit that we were in a lot
of trouble. Before it came out, everybody said, 'Oh, James Cameron is
spending a hundred and fifty million dollars and it's going to be a disaster. But it was a hit, so then everybody said, 'Oh, that's how you get a
hit. Spend a hundred fifty million dollars!' Independent filmmakers will
occasionally make good films, but that's occasionally. I hate to be negative, but I think we're in a period of decadence. I can't say anything good
about the industry today."

"What do today's films say about us as a society?"

"I think we're living in a very angry society right now, divided, terrified, confused; it's a mess, and movies reflect that mess. The novelist
Robert Graves had a great line and I'm paraphrasing: 'It's impossible not
to be part of your time, even if you're against it.' So every film that is

made is a part of our time. And what we want now are comic book heroes, escapism, and instant solutions through fictitious computer-generated fantasies. *Spiderman* (2002) proved you can do just about anything with computer-generated tricks. When people go to the movies today, what they see is fake and they know it. One of the greatest elements of movie-making has always been suspended disbelief. You believed it when you saw Douglas Fairbanks swinging from ropes and jumping all around, but he really did all those things. Buster Keaton did all his own stunts. He didn't resort to tricks. When he saved his father in *Steamboat Bill, Jr.* (1928), he lassoed a jailhouse and you're seeing it all happening. If somebody did that today, it would just be a trick—even if it was real, everybody would say it's a trick. So we've ruined it for the audience. The magic's gone. We have people going on Universal Studio Tours so they can see how it's all done."

"If movies are a mirrored reflection of where we're at now, are you saying that we're basically shallow and fake?"

"Yeah—pretty shallow and fake. That's how I see it right now. Occasionally, you'll find a few American and foreign filmmakers who make pictures well, have integrity and have something real to say about the human condition. Take a look at the films of the Golden Age like John Ford's *How Green Was My Valley* (1941) or Fred Zinnemann's *From Here to Eternity* (1953). No one's going to make films like that today."

"There also seems to be a lack of good women's stories being told and good parts for women actors. Why do you think that is?"

"Women once dominated films, back in the teens, twenties, thirties, and even in the forties with a last gasp in the fifties. By the sixties it was over for them; we saw fewer and fewer female stars because the men took over. The actors went independent when the studio system collapsed, leaving no one to promote and protect women."

"I read that silent films had a huge impact on you as a director and noticed that you incorporate many silent moments in your films."

"Yes, that's true. My father took me at a young age to see the great silent films at the Museum of Modern Art. I especially loved the movies of Buster Keaton, Charlie Chaplin, and D. W. Griffith. Silent films were the foundation of the medium—telling stories visually with moving pictures. They had a very hypnotic quality—the looks between people, the fine nuance of a gesture or facial expression. When I'm directing a scene, I try to imagine it without sound and see if we're still able to follow the story. The silent moments are usually the key moments, the best parts of a picture. I think it's the glory of the movies."

"Watching your films I also became aware of how you use the camera to show us the character's point of view on what he or she is seeing."

"That's based on the subjective use of camera. Hitchcock was so good at that. He liked to put audiences in the shoes of the characters so that they could identify with them much more strongly and see things through their eyes. In *Rear Window* (1954), Hitchcock reveals the story through Jimmy Stewart's point of view. We see what he's seeing through the binoculars as he watches his neighbor's apartment. But also there are scenes that are clearly not from Jimmy's point of view but from Hitchcock's. You'll see the camera pan from the temperature thermometer to Jimmy while he's asleep, and we know it's Hitchcock telling us the story."

"I've done that in all my pictures and pride myself on doing variations on it within a given scene. There's a way to do it, how you shoot it, so that it's subliminal for the audience. When you have a close-up of one character and a medium shot of another character as they're talking to each other, it automatically becomes the close-up's point of view. A lot of the time you'll see movies with cross-cutting. The director says, 'We want matching sizes,' and he or she is very particular that the sizes of the shot are the same. That's fine if you want to tell your story objectively, show two people talking without emphasizing any one character's point of view. There is an interesting scene in *Mogambo* (1953), a film that John Ford made in Africa with Ava Gardner and Clark Gable. It's Clark Gable's story; he's the lead. But the first time you see Ava Gardner, Ford switches it to her, and we see close-ups of her. And Gable is in a medium shot—interesting twist. It shows that Ford wanted to give the scene to Ava, and he's actually on Ava's side throughout the whole movie. You can tell that from the way he shoots it. That's a very important element in storytelling/filmmaking—whose point of view is this?"

"Close ups are also used to show heightened emotions experienced by the characters—correct?"

"Yes, but if you use them indiscriminately, they lose power when you really need them to make an effect. Look at a picture like Howard Hawks's *Air Force* (1943). There is no close-up until forty-five minutes into the picture. He gives you medium shots, long shots, two-shots, three-shots. When he needs it, he's got it. And you think, *Wow! Bang, bang!* Those close-ups really pay off. The grammar and the vocabulary of the cinema was established very early on by such great pioneers as D. W. Griffith, Ernst Lubitsch, King Vidor, Buster Keaton, and it hasn't been improved upon. There have only been variations of a theme, or it's been degraded."

"Is that because every art form is confined by the elements of which it is composed? For example, in dance, you have the elements of space, time, energy, effort-shape of the human body, and often music. It has what it has, and you can't make it something that it's not."

"Yes. That's true in film too. Filmmakers continue to do things that they don't need to do, like telling a story backwards or telling a story in jumbled time sequence. Those are all attempts to create something new or novel, but they are not telling the story better."

"Did you think that *The Artist* (2011) was well done? It was widely embraced by the public and won an Academy Award for best picture."

"It was a particularly good silent movie for anyone who has never seen a silent movie. But the original silent movies were a lot better than *The Artist*. It was fun, it was light-hearted and kind of a novelty—a black and white silent film in the twenty-first century. I think that's why it was popular. Mary Pickford had a great line after the talkies came in: 'Looking at the quality of the pictures, you would have thought the talkies would have come first.' What she meant was that many of the silent movies were so much more sophisticated visually, and their stories better told. Charlie Chaplin made a comment, 'Just when we got it right, it was over.' The silent era was a period of extraordinary work. You talk to young people today about silent movies, and it's like talking to them about Sanskrit. They don't want to know about it."

"How do movies stand the test of time?"

"Stories that are about human nature and regular people stand the test of time. These films don't get outdated because human nature doesn't really change much. A good example is King Vidor's *Crowd* (1928). I saw it when it was over thirty years old. When I saw it again, it was more than seventy years old, [and] it seemed more modern than ever because of its human theme, high quality of direction, and the actors' performances. When I make a picture, I think, *This is not just for this season. It's a picture that I'd like people to see in fifty or a hundred years and still get something out of it*. I'm very careful not to put in topical references unless it's a period piece and that reference is about that period. I wouldn't have a character say, 'Oh, I watched Johnny Carson the other night.' Things like that date a picture."

"You were part of the American New Wave cinema when filmmakers in the mid-1960s through the 1970s began exploring social issues, breaking with convention and taboos, and emphasizing realism. Were you aware that the art form was undergoing a huge change of which you were a part?"

"When you're in the midst of a big cultural-societal shift, you're not as aware of it. Twenty years later I looked back and thought, *Oh, that was happening then. Wow, I was in the middle of it.* Yes, I was part of that movement in cinema but my friends were not Francis Coppola, Billy Friedkin, and Steven Spielberg. My friends were John Ford, Howard Hawks, Orson Welles, Samuel Fuller, George Cukor. I hung out with them and Cary Grant, Jimmy Stewart, and John Wayne. These actors and filmmakers were still very much alive, and I felt kind of bad that I was working and a lot of them weren't. And so I talked about them in interviews and said things like, 'This was influenced by Hawks. This was influenced by Hitch or Welles or Ford.' What I had been doing in my work was using the grammar and vocabulary of movies that I'd learned from watching good films and from talking to them. They showed me the way. I put myself through the best film school anyone's ever been through. I didn't have some bum who never directed a picture giving me advice. I had Alfred Hitchcock telling me why he did a scene the way he did. I had Orson Welles explaining to me how he did a particular shot. Howard Hawks taught me that the audience doesn't know the geography of a place; they only know what you show them, so you can create your own world and this frees you up to make your own story. Sometimes I can hear their voices in my head and I remember their advice. I think about them often, and I always enjoy seeing their films. It's sort of like visiting with them again."

"You were extremely influenced by them, but your films were of a new age, especially a film like *The Last Picture Show* (1971), which in a way was like creating a new genre."

"When I was making *Picture Show*, which was my second picture, I did things that would not have been done in the golden age of movies that I had extolled and revered. Those filmmakers whom I admired wouldn't have done it the way I did it—the sex, putting his hand under her skirt, a nude swimming party. Looking back on it, I think *The Last Picture Show* was so impressive because I showed unusual things in a classic way. The technique of the film was not artsy—hand-held cameras, upside-down backwards storytelling. It was very much in the grain of good, classic American storytelling. But I was dealing with subject matter that would have been taboo in Howard Hawks and John Ford's time. I think it's the tension between the two—the formal way of telling it with material that wasn't formal—that made the picture work. I remember John Wayne calling me up after seeing *The Last Picture Show* and saying, 'Pete, I liked your film, but I can't show it to my family.'"

"The juxtaposition of classic storytelling with risqué material worked so well you could have done that in your future films. But you didn't do that."

"No, I didn't. I tried to make different kinds of pictures. It was a conscious decision on my part. I looked to challenge myself in new ways every time."

"You actually went a step farther, choosing to make genre films that were outside the normal fare in the 1970s, like *What's Up, Doc?* (1972), a screwball comedy; *Daisy Miller* (1974), a costume period piece adapted from the Henry James novel; and *At Long Last Love* (1975), a song-and-dance musical. You took big risks that audiences would accept these somewhat dated genres."

"Well, I was interested in exploring those genres. Someone once asked me, 'Why did you do the documentary *Tom Petty and the Heartbreakers—Runnin' Down a Dream* (2007)? Were you a big fan?' 'No, I didn't even know who Tom Petty was.' But I was interested for that reason—I could find out. My curiosity would be communicated to the audience, and they would find out things that I was finding out in the same way. People said to me, 'You grew up in New York City. How could you make a film so realistically about this small town in Texas?' That's why. To me Texas was a foreign country, so I was interested in inspecting the details of this place and showing them."

"You've said that when you worked on *The Last Picture Show*, it was one of the most creative periods in your life. How so?"

"I felt very inspired working on that picture and loved Larry McMurtry's story. I was focused on making the best film I could. I devoted myself to getting the best performances that I could out of these actors who were mostly unknown at the time. I spent all my time with them. And many things happened to me while on that film. I fell in love with Cybill Shepherd, and she became my muse for that film. My marriage to Polly Platt broke up and my father died suddenly, all while I was working on that picture. I was one person when I arrived in Texas and another when I left. My life changed entirely after that film."

"So many artists have told me that they can't separate their personal life from their artistic life, that when they're happy their art soars, but when things go badly their art suffers."

"Yes. I believe that's true. Working on *They All Laughed* (1981) was the most inspired I had been since *Picture Show*. Dorothy Stratten was my muse for that film in the same way that Cybill was with *The Last Picture Show*. I was falling in love with her. But when she was murdered, things became terrible. [Stratten was murdered by her jealous husband shortly after the film had wrapped.] I did a lot of reading after Dorothy was murdered. I read all those things you're supposed to read when you're in trouble — Francis Bacon, Montaigne, the Bible. And I didn't really get much out of those. But Robert Graves's work spoke to me. I think I was looking for a time in history when something like this wouldn't and couldn't have happened, and I found it around 4,000 BC. I dropped out and spent three years writing about Dorothy in my book *The Killing of the Unicorn*. I think it is the best thing I ever wrote."

"Artists, including filmmakers usually make work for self-expression or to deliver a message, but they don't just come right out and say it. They camouflage it through their artistic medium. Isn't this one of the artist's greatest challenges — to deliver their message indirectly but effectively?"

"Yes, my film *They All Laughed* is a perfect example of that. I wanted to cloak a personal story in the form of a genre picture, which is what all the great Hollywood filmmakers have done. Sometimes it's a gangster story or a western or a love story. I chose a detective story. I wanted to make a movie about personal relationships — falling in love, being in love, being promiscuous, being faithful — but I didn't want to make it about my own life, even though in this film John Ritter's and Ben Gazarra's characters were based on me — an older and younger me."

"Many of your films are about men falling in love with beautiful women — as in *The Last Picture Show*, *They All Laughed*, *A Thing Called Love*. Why?"

Peter smiled. "I guess it's something that interests me. I enjoy the company of women more than men. I feel like I can be more myself when I'm with a woman, and have felt most alive when I have been in love. Much of my life I've been occupied by love, falling in love, being in love, and sharing something with somebody you love. Being in love is one of the great glories of life."

Arthur Hiller

The Canadian-born director best known for Love Story *(1970) has spent much of his career making us laugh. Whether interpreting Paddy Chayefsky's brilliant social satires like* The Americanization of Emily *(1964) or hilarious comedies from Neil Simon like* The Out of Towners *(1970) or Collin Higgins's* Silver Streak *(1976), Arthur Hiller says that what he's always tried to do is to make his films "vastly entertaining with something worthwhile to say." Spending time with Hiller, now in his eighties and legally blind due to macular degeneration, was enlightening but at times very emotional. As I was leaving his Beverly Hills home, he turned toward me and said, "All this talk of directing has made me miss it terribly. I wish I could go on."*

"After watching many of your films I observed that most of your protagonists end up having a nervous breakdown, like James Garner in *The Americanization of Emily*, Alan Arkin in *Popi* (1969), Jack Lemmon in the *The Out of Towners*, and George C. Scott in *The Hospital* (1971). Is that coincidence or deliberate?"

"That's interesting. I'm not at all aware that I do that. I don't know why I've made the choices I have, other than the writing was good and I liked the story."

"I've asked a number of directors why they choose particular material or a particular genre, and most of them can't seem to answer the question."

"You haven't been able to get answers because what directors do much of the time is based solely on instinct and intuition. It's hard to define a passion and what gets to you. I think I'm drawn to characters who find themselves in difficult situations and how they come out of them. All I know is that I want to be on a high with the material, and I want to excite the audience in the same way that I'm excited. That's it!"

"What's the first thing that usually turns you on when you read a script?"

"Great writing! I drop to my knees in front of the writer who sits alone in a darkened room somewhere, gets an idea, and then creates a screenplay or adapts a work. They work from their imagination. The rest of us have a floor plan—the screenplay. I loved Paddy Chayefsky's writing, and I directed two of his screenplays: *The Americanization of Emily* and *The Hospital. The Americanization of Emily* was a first draft, a perfect script. If we changed six lines, it was a lot. It challenges you when you're working with this kind of genius. You don't want to impair such brilliant writing. Chayefsky was only fifty-nine when he passed away, and with him that great talent."

"I've heard you say that you want audiences to see your films not just with their eyes but with their gut. How do you achieve that?"

"By getting people to feel as enthusiastic about the story and the characters as you are. That's the goal of the director. One of the hardest parts of directing is creating an atmosphere where everyone on the production end is excited about what they're doing so they give their best effort. It's up to the director to engage everyone, not just the actors, but the dolly grips and the gaffers too. You have to give everyone involved the feeling that they're doing good work and that you appreciate them. I had a silly way of making everyone on the set feel comfortable. I'd loosen them up by coming to work everyday wearing another one of my crazy ties. I own around sixty crazy ties. I have one made out of denim material with its own pocket where I can put my pencil. I even have one made out of wood!"

"Is the director the person who establishes the vision for the film?"

"Yes. There can only be one vision on a film, and that's the director's vision. If you have more than one vision, you're going to confuse everyone. Which vision do they follow? This doesn't mean that the director is smarter than the writer or the producer. It's just that the director is in touch with every aspect of the moviemaking process."

"How do you define *vision* in this context?"

"Your vision is a compilation of all the feelings you have about the material and all the emotions that you want to convey. That's what you're reaching for."

"Is it difficult to hold on to your vision when there is input from so many other creative minds working on the film—the producer(s), the cinematographer, the actors, the editor, set designer, the wardrobe people, etc.? Don't they all want to bring their vision to the film?"

"I find the more prepared I am, the more secure I am in my vision, and the more open I am [to] suggestions from the people I'm working with—it doesn't frighten me, and I don't panic when I'm listening to what's being offered. Often they come up with terrific ideas that I end up incorporating into the picture and consequently taking credit for. I want to be able to answer any question about the film two weeks before shooting, whether it's from an actor or the prop man. I want them all to have a feeling of confidence that I know what I'm doing and what we're after."

"Your films are typically labeled comedies—romantic stories or dramatic satires—but they're really socially relevant message movies. *The Americanization of Emily*, for example, is an antiwar film."

"Well, that's what a film is: telling a story through a visual medium and trying to make it vastly entertaining with something worthwhile to say. In *The Americanization of Emily* I was telling the story of a handsome coward played by James Garner who unintentionally becomes a hero. The message in the film is saying, Let's not glorify war so that young boys will want to enlist and become soldiers."

"*The Hospital* was another one of your films with a strong social message."

"Chayefsky's original title for the film was, *You've Got to Piss Right Smack into the Wind*. The picture was saying you've got to get in there and do something about the problems we face in society—in this case the health-care system and the medical profession. I didn't want to rehearse scenes from *The Hospital* because I wanted it to be, how shall I say, *messy good*. I had the cameraman shoot it a little off-base because I wanted the audience looking around the corner to see what's coming. It was meant to be confusing."

"*Love Story* was one of your most commercially successful films, earning seven Academy Award nominations including one for you for best director."

"When I was first approached to do *Love Story*, I thought it might be too simplistic. I had to really think long and hard before deciding to direct it. When the movie came out, it had the biggest first-weekend box office in history. To this day, its return for dollars invested still ranks among the highest."

"Its most famous line is 'Love means never having to say you're sorry.'"

"Those words came from Erich Segal's novel. What I thought that line meant was, if it's a great love that you have for one another, then you don't have to apologize if you've done or said the wrong thing because it's already understood that you're sorry. I wanted to express that it's okay to have disagreements and still love and respect each other and, above all, stay together. If you can't, then it's not the great love. I felt that people needed this film, and that it was the right film for its time."

"Why is that?"

"We were ready for a film about the heart, about people caring for one another. We had been going through a period of individuality in the 1960s, what I call the 'biker films,' like *Easy Rider* (1969). If *Love Story* [had come] out a few years earlier, it would have been run over by the motorcycles. A few years after, it would be lost to special effects. Movies have their time of why they work and why they don't."

"One of the most powerful scenes in the film is when Ryan's character, Oliver, learns that his wife, Jenny, is going to die from a rare disease. Distraught, he runs from the doctor's office out into city traffic. The scene is shot slightly out of focus with lots of camera movement. You bring us inside his frantic emotional state against a soundtrack mixing of the *Love Story* theme with traffic noise—car horns and truck engines. It's very powerful and emotional."

"Remember, Rose, you're telling a story through a visual medium. Why does the cinematographer create a particular lighting for a scene? Why put a diffusion filter on a lens? You do what is best for the telling of your particular story. For this scene with Oliver I used a long lens so that everything around him would be a little out of focus—which is how he felt. And these were the days before the Steadicam, so we purposefully shot that scene so the picture would be somewhat shaky. In his grief, Oliver has lost contact with the world around him; he is only present in his own thoughts of despair, and this is what I tried to show."

"Many of the actors who appeared in your films, like Ryan O'Neal and Ali MacGraw and George C. Scott, received prestigious nominations and awards. Do you take any credit for their giving such noteworthy performances?"

"No. I don't. I've worked with many gifted actors. Most did their own backstory that led them into their characters. The director's job is only to give his actors faith in themselves and the feeling that they're doing a good job. Actors tend to be insecure. That's why directors are often thought of as parent figures or as psychiatrists—pulling something out of them that they didn't know they could do. Sometimes I'd challenge actors psychologically without them knowing it, like set up a situation that makes it easier for them to come through with what I need. You can't make up general rules for all actors to follow. Every actor is different."

"Have you ever felt insecure in your role as director?"

"Yes. All of the time! But directors must hide their own insecurities because everyone else depends on him to be confident. Creative people need others to tell them that what they're doing is good. I call that 'creative insecurity.' I'd get panicky after every film and ask myself, *Did I really get what I wanted? Was it really good? Will I ever work again?*"

"I imagine that directing can be very stressful. Did it ever interfere with your ability to sleep at night?"

"I'd sleep at night because I was usually utterly drained by the work. Directors typically work up to eighteen hours a day, and then there's all that thinking they have to do in preparation for the next day's shooting. I've had days when I've come home and gone straight to bed, without dinner, washing up, or saying good night to my wife."

"Has there been any one director whose work you really admired and [who] influenced your filmmaking?"

"David Lean's pictures just bowled me over. He could do small but brilliant films like *Brief Encounter* (1945) and *Hobson's Choice* (1954) and then something of the magnitude of *Lawrence of Arabia* (1962) and *Dr. Zhivago* (1965). These were very different kinds of films, and yet he could do them all. He inspired me to risk trying different things. This reminds me of a funny story. Many years ago the Academy held a luncheon for a group of foreign-nominated directors. And who walks in but David Lean. I thought to myself, 'Oh my God, my hero!' I wanted to jump up and run over to him and tell him how much I admired his films. But then I thought, *No I can't do this. It wouldn't be proper to behave like a groupie.* A bit later I see him get up and walk around to the side of the table to where I'm seated. He leans over and whispers in my ear, 'I just have to tell you how much I loved *Silver Streak*.' Here I was hesitant to tell my hero how much I loved his movies, and yet he says this to me. I'll never forget how much that meant to me."

"Have you had films that were critically disappointing?"

"Yes. When we did *Man of La Mancha* (1972), I thought we'd really made a good movie. But the critics didn't agree. After the film opened and the reviews were in, I got a letter from Arthur Krim, the head of United Artists just to say, 'Arthur, that's the film we were looking for. I'm sorry it didn't work out better.' He wanted me to know that he wasn't mad at me. It was very nice of him. Here I had this great story, coming from a great play, and basically I did the movie I was trying to do. It was about eight months later before I realized that that picture should have had more fantasy or less fantasy, one or the other. I realized that when you're sitting in the tenth row watching a theatrical production and Quixote says, 'That's not a kitchen scullery maid, that's a princess,' you can imagine it. But when your star is Sophia Loren and she's twenty feet tall on the big screen, it's too hard for people to make that mental shift. After the film came out, I got very depressed and for about eight months I second-guessed myself about what I might have or should have done differently.

There are some pictures that you ask yourself what you did wrong. You never find out. Sometimes it's because you didn't get a tight grip on it, and maybe you shouldn't have taken it on in the first place."

"Overall are you satisfied with what you've achieved as a filmmaker?"

"No, I don't think so. I'm satisfied with some of what I achieved, but I don't think I achieved enough. You'd like to do more, more, more. And the truth is that once you make a film that doesn't work and you're over fifty-five, chances are you won't get another offer. *Oh, he's too old*, goes the phrase. When *The Babe* (1992), my film about the life of Babe Ruth didn't take off financially, my offers just went flat. It happened to Frank Capra, Billy Wilder, and John Ford—despite their incredible bodies of work."

"Do you plan to continue directing?"

"Well, I can't. I haven't been able to work for seven years. I have macular degeneration. It's taken away most of my sight. Something like this hits you hard. When I first started to lose my sight, I could still watch television and see movies if they were well lit, but not dark movies like a Scorsese film or action pictures. But now the macular degeneration has gotten worse, and I can hardly see at all. I can see that you're sitting there, but not any details like if you were to wink at me. I wouldn't see that. Not too long ago I was offered to direct a film, but I turned it down. I said, 'I can't see the actors up close.' They said, 'Sure you can. We'll get you another director to assist you.' But I told them, 'No, it wouldn't be fair to the picture. It wouldn't be fair to the actors.' That's just not the way I work."

Mark Rydell

Mark Rydell had a quick rise as an actor in a number of films and on television's popular soaps The Edge of Night *and* As the World Turns. *In the late 1960s he turned to directing and proved an accomplished storyteller with such films as* The Reivers *(1969),* Cinderella Liberty *(1973),* The Rose *(1979), and* On Golden Pond *(1981), for which he earned an Oscar nomination for best director. Today, Rydell shares his vast knowledge and experience with students at the Actor's Studio West where he and Martin Landau serve as co-artistic directors. Following our interview, I took Mark's photograph inside one of the venerated theaters at their Sunset Boulevard location.*

"I understand that you were a professional musician before becoming an actor and then subsequently a director. Why did you make the change?"

"I loved being a musician, but in the fifties musicians were heavily into drug use. Drugs frightened me because I knew I had an addict's personality, and so I began looking for another way to perform. A friend of mine, Marilyn Bergman, who would later become a successful songwriter, suggested that I become an actor. She told me about the Neighborhood Playhouse where I could study acting. I enrolled in class with the great acting coach Sandy Meisner."

"Did it take long for you to get acting jobs?"

"No. Sandy nudged me through, and I assumed leading roles on Broadway, in movies, and television fairly quickly. I was never one of those actors to suffer the humiliations of trying to make it."

"What inspired you then to move into directing?"

"Some people are followers and some are leaders. I've always been inclined towards leading. Even when I was a musician, I'd lead the band. I've always been more comfortable in the role of leader, nurturer, and benevolent father figure. Even while I was an actor, I knew I was moving toward directing. I understood that directing was about distilling a concept and leading people toward and having one's vision realized."

"I've heard you say, 'Art doesn't read unless it moves you.' What's necessary for art to move us, to transport and elevate us?"

"Truth! There are some truths that we all relate to, the universal truths,

and there are truths for each individual. To say one is in pursuit of the truth sounds a bit flowery. But isn't truth what art should be about—revealing the truth about something or someone? Art executed in a way that's attractive and exciting can really move people."

"How does one find truth?"

"Analysis! For me, it's been analysis. I've been in analysis for sixty years! I think Woody Allen and I win the prize for having had the most therapy. It has become for me a way of life. The first thing analysis does is put you in touch with the truth. There's no lying in analysis, not if you're committed to gaining a greater understanding about your life. You get to confront all sorts of things about yourself and the more significant issues of life. It allows you to eliminate anything that impedes you from full expression. We all have neurotic behaviors to a greater or lesser degree. And all those are impediments to the full expression of your self. When you remove them, you find that you're in touch with your own truth and the deeper parts of life. There's nothing like insight."

"It's been said that filmmakers are our culture's premier storytellers. Why is storytelling so important culturally?"

"People have been telling stories since we were first able to express ourselves. Maybe we need stories because everyday reality is not satisfying enough. So we need to stimulate our imaginations, and movies do that for us. Human beings have yearnings, desires, and curiosities that art especially in the form of storytelling enables us to mine."

"When we go to the movies or the theater, do we instinctively compare our own lives to those we observe on the stage and screen?"

"The first obligation of the director is to capture people's interest, find something in the material that the audience can identify with so that they can take the journey that you're taking them on. You want to say to them, 'This could be you. You'll understand this because what I'm talking about is in you as well. You give them a character—*Oh, yeah, I understand what that guy's feeling. He's like me.* When that happens we drop our resistance and we're willing to take that journey. It's the fun of art."

"In *Intersection* (1994) you take us on an emotional rollercoaster ride with the film's three main characters played by Richard Gere, Sharon Stone, and Lolita Davidovich, who are involved in a love triangle. As the teller of this story did you also go for that ride?"

"Yes, of course. This is critical. If you can't identify with the dreams of the characters, you're just photographing them. You're not illuminating human yearning, which is what makes art universal. What makes directing compelling is the ability to dig into people's hungers and drives.

You're dealing with issues that everyone understands, and it's identifying with those needs that hook us."

"I've heard you compare filmmaking to climbing Mt. Everest. Is this because you have to fully invest yourself mentally and physically, ratchet up all your skills and knowledge and commit yourself for an extended period of time?"

"Yes. You have to invest all of yourself and sometimes for as long as eighteen months to two years. Then six months after the film's release you're either basking in its glory or sitting all alone depressed. Every time I read a script, I have to ask myself, *Is this something I'm willing to invest myself in?* Once I find something that matters to me I know I can pour all of my being into it without any reservation. I recognize its validity—where it can be exciting and where I can tell the truth. But it's very hard to find material like this. Regardless of the hard work and endless hours, these are the kind of hours I love spending. It's like being in bed with a great lover. You don't want to get out of bed. You want more and more and more. Well, I'm getting old for that now, but I remember that I used to want more," he said laughing.

"How do you make a story your own when you're not the story's author or screenwriter?"

"I can best respond with a story. Every time the famous director Frank Capra made a film, the critics called it *his* film. He would receive all these accolades, and his writers went ignored. Finally one infuriated writer complained to Capra, 'I'm sick and tired of everyone talking about the 'Capra Touch.' I wrote the damn thing. Why is it your film? What do you do that gives you the right to call it a Frank Capra film?' Capra replied, 'Bring me your best script.' So the writer dutifully left and came back with a heavy stack of pages. 'Okay,' he said to the writer. 'Very good. Now run that through a projector.'"

"How do we recognize a 'Mark Rydell' film?"

"If you laugh and cry, there's a good chance that it came from me. What directors do essentially is tell the world, 'This is how I feel, and how I relate to the yearnings of people or the folly we recognize in humanity.' Directors expose themselves through their direction. Their interpretation of the material and its presentation is what makes it theirs."

"What's your process for developing the look and sound of a film?"

"The look and sound of any film have to serve its message. You cast your crew the way you cast your actors. Who's right for this? When considering your cinematographer you ask, 'What kind of photography does he do? Does he like to move his camera a lot or is he more interested in the depth of portraiture with intense close-ups?' So I assess what's needed to tell this particular story and move through it that way. Above all, I always ask, 'Does this person have the heart for this material?'"

"*On Golden Pond* was beautifully photographed by cinematographer Billy Williams. How did you know that he was right for this film?"

"I first went to Vilmos Zsigmond, who I had used on a number of pictures, but he was tied up. He recommended Billy Williams. So I sent him the material and later flew to London to meet with him. We sat down together to have dinner, and within two minutes I knew he was perfect for the job. He understood the depth of what we were after, which was the telling of a story about aging and the crisis of mortality. For the music I turned to the brilliant pianist and composer Dave Grusin. I knew that he had the sensitivity for this picture. The first thing he said to me was, 'Let's go look at the lake.' So we got on a plane and flew to our New Hampshire location. We rented a boat and rowed around the lake for hours, just the two of us, taking it all in. Dave went back to his studio and came up with the beautiful theme you heard in the film."

"What was it like working with such an extraordinary cast—Henry Fonda, Katharine Hepburn, and Jane Fonda—and what were the dynamics like among them?"

"Jane Fonda was ill every day before she acted with her father. They hadn't spoken to each other in years, primarily because of their opposing political views. But what happened in the story between them was real; we witnessed a real reconciliation and their true emotions. Henry Fonda was a very private man, very close-to-the-vest type of guy. During rehearsals Kate kept telling stories about Spencer Tracy. And I could feel Henry pulling back, not wanting to expose himself. Finally one day I took Kate aside and said, 'I think you should stop talking about Spencer Tracy. You should engage Henry Fonda, get to know him, and get close to him. Your relationship with him needs to be nourished.' The next day she brought in one of Spencer's old hats and gave it to Henry and said, 'I'd like you to wear this.' He put it on and wore it throughout the film. What she had done was transfer her allegiance to him right in front of all of us. She heard what I was saying and did the right thing. This helped facilitate the performance you see on screen. I've always felt very good about how I handled that. And after we finished shooting, Henry said to me that he was very proud of what he had done."

"I noticed that in all of your films you draw us in within the first few minutes. In *On Golden Pond* we were lulled in by the tranquil scenes of nature and the beauty of the film's outdoor landscape. In *The River* (1984) we observe the force of nature, a powerful rainstorm and subsequent flood that nearly drowns Mel Gibson's character, Tom Garvey. Why are the openers so important to the telling of a story?"

"It's the director's job to seduce the audience, to make it so arresting and attractive that they'll want to stay with you. Sometimes you hook them slowly and gradually, and after only ten minutes they're in. In other instances, like with *The Rose*, it can be immediate—the wildness of Bette Midler's singing, the intensity and rawness of that performance, her hair flying. It grabs you instantly. I knew that when I shot the first tight, tight close-up that it would hold everyone and not let go."

"Mark, you must really love women. I say that because I noticed in so many of your films your female characters are shown with tremendous sensitivity. It's as if you can see into their souls. How are you able to express so well the needs and desires of women?"

"Analysis, Rose."

"Analysis taught you how to understand what women feel?"

"Yes. Because in psychoanalysis you're examining among other things, your relationship with your mother, how your relationships with women were formed, how you relate to women and how they relate to you. So you become more attuned and aware of their way of seeing and thinking. I've been very influenced by Ingmar Bergman's films, and his treatment of women. Bergman had wonderful women in his films, and while his attention was on the more neurotic aspects of their lives, he portrayed them with realism and truth. Bergman loved and understood women and was intensely curious about how they felt about things and what mattered to them. I paid careful attention to this. Over the years I had the opportunity to meet many of his leading ladies, with whom he had had romantic relationships. All of them told me that they worshipped him even after he left them, because he understood them."

"How are you able to get compelling performances out of your actors, like you did with Marsha Mason in *Cinderella Liberty*?"

"Getting a good performance out of an actor often comes from words you have with them during the shoot. But in an odd way, to be a good director you have to relinquish control. People think of directors as the controlling element, and in a way he or she is, but you have to plant the seeds of a performance in an actor and then let those seeds grow. You have to provide a safe environment for them, nurture and provoke them to have the experiences that you want them to have. And if you see them going in the wrong direction, you nudge them one way or the other. Much of directing is having an understanding of the sensitivities and sensibilities of the people you're working with. It's helpful to know where they're coming from and what matters to them. It's scary being an actor. They have to reach inside themselves to experience moments of agony, yearning, and pain—not just to pretend to do it, actually go there. I'm convinced that my being psychoanalyzed for so long made me aware of how to help people reveal themselves with impunity: *It's not going to hurt. I'll take care of you. You'll be all right.* I admire actors because they're willing to reveal intensely personal secrets through their performances. Whenever you see a great performance like Marsha's, it's because she revealed something about herself that she hadn't planned on. When an actor does that, it's gold."

"I understand you were reluctant to cast John Wayne in your film *Cowboys* (1972). Why was that?"

"When the producers asked me to consider John Wayne to star in *Cowboys*, I said, 'No way!' I knew he was an icon in the industry, but I didn't want him. I abhorred his politics. But because the studio had optioned the book, I had to go and meet him. He seduced me immediately. He said to me, 'Sir, I'd really like to be in your film. I promise I'll give it everything.' Well, how do you say no to that? Suddenly I was producing and directing a film with John Wayne! Boy, was I wrong about him! I ended up really admiring him, and he gave a wonderful performance, even insisting on doing most of his own stunts—and he was no longer a young man."

"Looking back, do you feel good about the career choices you've made?"

"Yes. I've had a great life. It's been rocky at times, but I've never been bored. I was born to do what I'm doing, but really for me the most difficult time is when I'm in between pictures—like right now. I'm in agony when I'm not directing. Now I spend most of my time reading screenplays and books that I might turn into a movie. I always hope that when I read a script that the hair stands up on the back of my neck. That's what I wait for."

Rob Marshall

Rob Marshall choreographed Tony-nominated Broadway musicals—
Kiss of the Spider Woman *(1993),* Damn Yankees *(1994),* Cabaret
(1998), and Little Me *(1999)—before leaping into feature-film directing.
His first,* Chicago *(2002), won an Oscar for best picture and a nomination for best direction; his second,* Memoirs of a Geisha *(2005), received
three Academy Awards. Penelope Cruz went home with a best supporting actress Oscar for* Nine *(2009), and* Pirates of the Caribbean: On
Stranger Tides *(2011), starring Johnny Depp, was a worldwide hit. I met
Rob at the Carlyle Hotel in Midtown Manhattan for a drink. It had been
several years since I had photographed him during the run of* Cabaret.
*He greeted me with the warmth of an old friend and opened himself to
my many probing questions about his life as a movie director.*

"You've had an extraordinary Broadway career as a choreographer and
director. What made you decide to switch to films?"

"I was very happy working on Broadway and had never planned on
making movies. Then, suddenly, I got an offer to direct the film version of
Chicago. It came while I was developing the show *Hairspray.* After spending two years working with its writers and composer and just before we
were about to go into production, I got the offer. I had to make a decision.
I felt I couldn't turn down such a great opportunity."

"What was it like to transition from the narrow parameters of the pro-
scenium arch to the much wider scope of filmmaking?"

"The transition was not difficult because I had learned from Bob
Fosse, Michael Bennett, and Hal Prince how to make live theater more
cinematic. They employed techniques of cross-cutting and dissolves, as
well as continuous seamless action that avoided blackouts and clunky
scenic transitions. With movies, you can shoot from anywhere and tell
stories with multiple layers, create time sequences and add special effects.
You practically have to create your own limitations so as not to be over-
whelmed by the wealth of possibilities."

"Has your storytelling approach changed as you transitioned from
theater to feature films?"

"Even when an audience is sitting in the dark watching a screen, I still

want them to have an intimate experience, something that feels immediate. The films that I've always loved are those that gave me the feeling that I was seeing something unfold for the first time. And I'd like to create that in my work. With *Chicago* I wanted to take audiences into the exciting era of the 1920s. With *Memoirs of a Geisha* the audience peered into a lost and forbidden world. With *Nine* they're in 1960s Italy as the story slowly unfolds inside Guido Contini's head. And with *Pirates of the Caribbean: On Stranger Tides* they're immersed inside the swashbuckling world of Captain Jack Sparrow."

"It must be challenging to have actors perform for the camera in the same way they do in front of a live audience."

"You always want to keep the blood and guts of a performance, because this tells the story in a most immediate way. So when I'm in the editing room, I'm always looking for the take that's going to look the most real, even if it's got a rougher edge to it. Because with film you have the ability to do multiple takes, I have to resist trying to perfect an actor's performance; making it flawless takes the life out of it. Even when an actor is at the height of his or her emotional moment or the cameraman has captured a great visual image, I'll go with the take that feels most alive."

"Film is often thought of as a vehicle for actors, but isn't it really a director's medium?"

"Yes. My good friend Anthony Minghella, who wrote the screenplay for the film adaptation of *Nine* and sadly passed away before the film's release, once told me, 'You're hired as a director for your taste, your likes, and your point of view.' Coming from the theater, which is highly collaborative, I like to hear what others have to say, but I never work by committee. I follow what I feel in my gut."

"I imagine your dance and choreography background has been very helpful when staging scenes and moving actors around."

"Choreography is all about movement. So I understand how to create fluidity of movement from scene to scene, how to move actors around and through their scenes, and [how] to tell the story with the movement of the camera. For example, in *Chicago*, when we did the scene with Renee Zellweger and the use of mirrors, it started with the idea that this character is a narcissist and in love with herself. She wants to be a star—Roxy up in lights. So the narcissism grew into the idea of having mirrors everywhere. I was looking for a way to show many different images of her imagined self. We rehearsed it with the camera running. I like to have the cinematographer with me in rehearsal so we can create the musical numbers together. The camera work informs the staging, and the staging informs the camera. You work back and forth until you find your shape. I try to do my creative thinking in advance because on a shooting day the clock is running and you get locked in."

"Are you ever conscious of putting yourself in your films?"

"I prefer to make it look and feel as if I'm not there, not draw attention to myself. I try not to show my hand, but I think it happens anyway, organically and unconsciously. Viewers should be immersed in the story and surrender to the characters without having to think about how it's being put together. I always try to make sure that the subtext of the story is grounded in the emotional life of the characters. What's really exciting in storytelling is to explore who they are beneath the surface. In *Chicago*, Renee really understood her scene with the mirrors. We sat down together prior to shooting and discussed her character's intention. Renee disappears and Roxy, who has a desperate need to feel special, beautiful, and unique, takes over. We see her practically make love to herself in her mirror's reflection."

"Did you have a similar conversation with Johnny Depp in *Pirates of the Caribbean: On Stranger Tides*?"

"Yes, absolutely. This film was the fourth in the series, so we talked at length about the danger of Jack Sparrow becoming too much of a cartoon character. We didn't want him winking at the camera continuously and crossing that line. Once the character becomes a caricature, the audience no longer cares about him or the danger he faces; they have no emotional investment in the story. I spent a lot of time talking with the cast of *Pirates*, and that's rare for a spectacle. I expect actors to play their characters fully, so it's not unusual for me to say, 'It was almost there. I didn't quite believe it. Let's go one more time.'"

"How do you balance the story line with the visual aspect of a film?"

"It's difficult to achieve both; you can easily get caught up in the part that you favor and lose sight of the other. My instinct is to favor the seductive part of storytelling, which is the visual, how things look. I am constantly reminding myself, *Think about the story, think about the story. Don't forget to think about the story!*"

"I felt that in *Memoirs of a Geisha* you blended story and presentation beautifully—a young girl is sold by her father to a geisha boarding house, where she yearns for a better life. It's a clearly drawn survival story told through a prism of stunning visuals that reveal an exotic and distant culture."

"We were very aware that we were exposing a segment of Japanese society that was private and hidden. And so we shot scenes as if you're peering in on a forbidden world—through silks, bamboo, running water, doors, and windows. Even though the story takes us into this protected world, it's really a universal story. It's about not being allowed to do what's natural—experience love."

"How do you convey to the crew your cinematic vision of a project?"

"I work very closely with the cinematographer/director of photography—the person who really needs to understand the story you're telling and how you want to tell it. I'll also invite the costumer, set designer, sound designer, and line producer to join us. I try to involve everyone so that we're all on the same page and telling the same story and clear about what we're trying to accomplish. Working on movies like *Pirates of the Caribbean*, which had a $250 million budget, is like working with a huge circus. The most important thing is to keep the circus under the tent."

"How do you challenge yourself artistically?"

"By trying different genres. I'm not trying to reinvent myself each time I make a film; I just want to travel different roads, grow, and learn. My next two movies are different from anything I've done before—a *Thin Man* with Johnny Depp, which is a murder-mystery film noir; and a film version of Sondheim's *Into the Woods*, which is in the fairytale genre."

"The actors you've worked with sing your praises. What do you do to endear them?"

"My greatest joy is to bring out the best in actors, to protect and support them. With me they can make as many mistakes as they need to, so that they're free to grow and do their best work. I'm a director [who's] *with* the actors, not against them. I don't play tricks on actors. I tell them, 'You can do this. You'll be great.'"

"You got Richard Gere to perform a dance number in *Chicago*?"

"Yes, exactly. I had him believe that he could, and so he did."

"In 2009 you directed the screen adaptation of the Broadway show *Nine*. It was a unique tapestry of dramatic scenes and musical numbers shown through the vehicle of Guido's moody fantasies and thoughts."

"*Nine* was the most personally challenging work I've ever done."

"How so?"

"As the director you have to become your characters, understand them in order to bring them out. This story is about Guido Contini, a famous Italian movie director who is juggling—lying to and deceiving the many women in his life while having a personal and professional breakdown. I found Guido's character, as played by Daniel Day-Lewis, very intense and disturbing. He is completely derailed by his own ego. By nature I'm very different from him—a glass-half-full kind of a guy who looks for the joy in life. So being immersed in this moody persona forced me to draw on everything I had. For me it was a cautionary tale about how destructive the abuse of power can be: *Don't ever go in that direction. Don't follow that road, because you'll end up alone with no one to care about you.*"

"Guido lost his passion for his art. Do you think that could ever happen to you?"

"Guido becomes a broken person who eventually has nothing to say. I work very hard every day to never be like him. My greatest hope is that I'll always have passion for my art."

Kathleen Marshall

Kathleen Marshall has brought her talent as a director-choreographer to a string of Tony-award-winning shows: Wonderful Town *(2005),* The Pajama Game *(2006),* Grease *(2009), and* Anything Goes *(2011), and her latest,* Nice Work If You Can Get It *(2012), which premiered just days before our meeting at the Imperial Theater. With two shows running on Broadway and two-year-old twins at home, she still found the time to share her insights and expertise on what it takes to keep theatrical audiences coming back for more.*

"How does one become a director-choreographer?"

"Most director-choreographers begin as dancers then move up to dance captain or associate choreographer, to choreographer, and finally director-choreographer. Bob Fosse, Michael Bennett, Gower Champion, Tommy Tune, and Susan Stroman, to name a few, all began like that, as did my brother, Rob Marshall, and I. I never thought that I would become a choreographer, let alone a director-choreographer. I just wanted to dance, but I've also always been interested in the bigger picture. Whatever the project I was working on, I'd always want to become familiar with the depth of the story we were telling. I'd read the entire script, not just the parts that featured dance, and I also studied the score and lyrics. When I became assistant choreographer on my brother's shows *Kiss of the Spider Woman* (1993), *Damn Yankees* (1994), and *She Loves Me* (1994), I got to see the creative process of these shows unfold. I also got to watch great master directors at work, like Hal Prince, Jack O'Brien, and Scott Ellis."

"What important lessons did you learn from these masters?"

"It's all about proportions. How much focus and time are we going to apportion to that scene, this dance number, that song? When you're the choreographer, you might want to create a dance number that runs twenty minutes long, but the director has to say, 'No, no, no, you can't take that much time.' When you're both director and choreographer you have to be your own editor and find the right balance. A dance number, a song, a dramatic scene, all have to work in proportion with the entire show."

"Fascinating Rhythm"
"They All Laughed"
NICEWORKONBROADWAY.COM
STANDI

"I imagine the choreographer also has to be a bit of a dance historian, understanding the dance styles and trends of a particular time and place as you did in *Wonderful Town*, which takes place in the 1930s."

"I love doing research, so whatever show I'm working on, particularly a vintage show, I always pay careful attention to the dance styles of its era. What you're doing as a director, aside from telling the story, is creating an illusion of what that time period looked and felt like. In *Nice Work If You Can Get It*, the audience gets to peek into what life might have been like for a wealthy young man in the 1920s. In *Wonderful Town*, two sisters arrive in New York City during the Depression looking for jobs. In *Pajama Game*, which takes place in the 1950s when labor unions had gained a good deal of power, two people fall in love but are on opposite sides of a union issue. Even if the details aren't entirely historically accurate, you want an audience to feel as if they've been transported back to an earlier time and place."

"Theatrical stories are usually about the character's circumstances, personal relationships, and emotions. Isn't that what draws audiences in?"

"Exactly! *Oh, that's what it's like to fall in love. Oh, that's what it's like to have your heart broken. That's what it's like to find your joy.* It's about recognition of a human experience, and that's what every theatrical play or musical is trying to achieve."

"It's what makes theater useful."

"I think people come to forget about their life for a couple of hours. Some like to see shows that are silly or sexy or glamorous. Some want to be provoked into thinking about serious issues and the human condition. Some come to have a collective experience—to share with others a great laugh, a collective gasp, a moment of revelation. You enter the theater and find your seat. The house lights go down, the audience slowly hushes up, and whether it's a play that starts with silence or a musical that begins with the downbeat of an overture, there's that sense that we're all about to go someplace together. You don't get this from watching a DVD alone on your sofa."

"How do song, dance, and music work on an audience to intensify the storytelling experience?"

"In a musical that's well written, the song or dance comes in when words no longer suffice. The obvious example would be when someone sings a love song. A man and a woman declare their feelings for each other, but ordinary words can't fully express their emotions, so they take it to another level—they sing. When lyrics and music no longer suffice, they dance. That's what happens in *Nice Work If You Can Get It*.

When Matthew Broderick and Kelly O'Hara's characters reveal how they feel about each other, they sing Gershwin's, *'S Wonderful*. The lyric 'It's marvelous, you should care for me' is basically a declaration of love between Jimmy, a wealthy playboy, and Billie, a tough-talking bootlegging gal. They are alone in his big, beautiful Long Island mansion and have this wonderful romantic moment together that turns into a song and a dance—because ordinary words won't do. It's actually one of the longest dance duets I've ever created. Jimmy and Billie are experiencing such joy that they get up and dance around the living room and up and down on the furniture. Musicals require heightened emotions like joy, anger, or confusion for a song and dance to work. Another good example is in *Sweeny Todd* (1979) when Todd sings his epiphany, grabs a knife, and says, 'I'm going to have my revenge not just on the people who have done me wrong, but on everybody.'

"Watching *Wonderful Town* I felt as if I were on Christopher Street in Greenwich Village. Using such a minimalist set, how do you get the audience to suspend disbelief and go there with you?"

"As a director what you have to do is figure out what you want the audience to experience and when. George Abbott said, 'You've got about seven minutes at the start of a show to establish the style of the show.' I think audiences accept what they see. When the curtain is up and you're looking at a bare stage with four chairs, you think, *Okay, they're going to leave everything to our imagination*. Or the curtain is down and then it goes up to expose a fully realized living room—sofa, coffee table, lamps that look like you could live up there. You think, *Okay, they're going to tell this story with a very realistic setting*. My feeling is that if you root your characters in some kind of reality at the beginning, the audience will take the journey with them even if they end up in some crazy or absurd situation. Once you're with them, respect them, and view them as real people with real problems, you suspend disbelief about all the other things."

"You've done a number of revivals: *Grease, Pajama Game, Two Gentlemen of Verona*, and *Nice Work If You Can Get It*, which is loosely based on *Oh Kay!* from the 1920s. How do you freshen up older shows so that they appeal to contemporary audiences?"

"I try to make something modern without being anachronistic. You don't want audiences to feel as if they're watching a museum piece. One way to update shows is to employ newer stagecraft methods that get us more quickly from set change to set change. In the past, the curtain would come down between scenes, the crew would come in and move everything, and then the curtain would go up. Today, it's fairly common to see sets being assembled and disassembled right in front of the audience, which becomes part of the theatrical experience. Also many of the revivals I've done have had new orchestrations and dance arrangements. With most shows the musical arranger takes the melodies from the composer and creates dance music specifically for the choreographer. Musical arranger David Chase, who I've worked with on many of my shows, will put his own spin on the music, and that makes it fresh. *Wonderful Town* was an exception because Leonard Bernstein wrote both the orchestration and the dance music.

"The other very important element in making a show feel up to date is choosing the right cast. I love working with actors [who] take their comedy seriously, know how to land a joke, create rhythm in a scene, but also treat their characters as real people and not cartoons. When you have *real* actors giving believable performances, the audience can't help but come along. And one of the things I love about working with actors is creating behavior, behavior that's believable and recognizable—private moments that are shared with the world. So it's all about how a show looks and moves and behaves."

"How do you balance the story's plot line with the show's staging?"

"I try to build a show where everything's moving along until we settle down for an emotional moment. Many directors don't lock into the blocking until later in the process because the actors are still finding their way through the story. But in musicals we talk with the actors about their characters and read through the scenes for a week before we even get on our feet. If you're working with an ensemble and performing dance numbers, you've got to know where everyone is on the stage physically. I've worked with set designer Derek McLane a great deal, and together we'll create a model for each show by laying out how we're going to get from one event on the stage to the next. I'm always asking where the main events in a scene are going to take place. If, for example, a singer sings a song in the first act and she's standing stage left, to achieve balance I'll make sure that when she sings again in the second act, that she's either center or stage right. I'll also vary entrances and exits to keep things looking interesting."

"With a live show you have the advantage of seeing how well audiences resonate with the work and can make changes accordingly."

"Yes, the advantage of being a stage director is that we get to sit out there and see if the audience is fidgeting or engaging with the story and the characters, understanding the humor, etc. Sometimes what happens is, *Oh, I thought that was going to be funny. But the audience doesn't think it's so funny. Better change that.* It's much more difficult for the movie director because by the time they're putting their film in front of a preview audience, they've already shot it and sent the actors home. Changes on a film can be made in the editing, such as reordering scenes, taking things out, or shortening or lengthening things, but the director has a finite amount of material at that point and would have to go back and reshoot, and that's difficult and a big expense."

"What do you want your audience to come away with after seeing a show?"

"A theatrical evening should be a series of delights and surprises. Some of those surprises can be dramatic, visual, or comedic: *Oh, wasn't that a beautiful song or dance* or *Wasn't that absolutely hilarious?* My job as the director is to figure out what those treats are. Sometimes the treats are unexpected, like in *Wonderful Town.* The police force in the 1930s is heavily composed of Irishmen. When Eileen gets arrested, the police officers serenade her with 'My Darlin' Eileen.' It turned out that our show ran during the 1990s *Riverdance* craze, so we had the policeman perform Irish step dancing. Everybody in the audience got that we were doing—a *Riverdance* parody. It fit the characters, the scene, and the story. I always want to have moments in the show that are unexpected that people will love."

"How do you continue to remain inspired and creative?"

"I love that I get to play 'let's pretend' for a living. My profession enables me to remain a kid in a playground. I think as long as I can continue to tap into that inner child, keep that sense of wonder alive, I'll be able to continue creative work. Typically after opening a show, I feel like I have no more ideas left in me, no more dance steps, nothing left to say. So I try to replenish myself, fill up and cleanse my artistic palette by going to see other shows and other forms of art. Once the exhaustion fades away and another story comes my way, I get very excited. I love working with good people on material that we can sink our teeth into. Whether I continue to do musicals or branch out into plays, I know that my job is to help actors, dancers, and singers, give them the tools and support they need to deliver shows that soar."

Doug Hughes

Doug Hughes is a perennial stage director. The Tony Award winner for Doubt *(2005) has pleased audiences and critics year after year since the 1980s. He was in rehearsals on Theresa Rebeck's* Poor Behavior *(2011) when I caught up with him at the Mark Taper Forum in Los Angeles. He permitted me to shoot a few photos while he worked out a pivotal scene in the final act. Afterward we moved to his dressing room for the interview. I returned the next evening as an audience member, bringing with me the insights I had learned about Hughes's creative process and how it reflected his life and philosophy.*

"Your parents were both respected New York actors—Barnard Hughes and Helen Stenborg. How did they influence your choice of career?"

"I was always infatuated with what they did. When I visited them backstage or on movie sets, I'd become intoxicated and exhilarated by the foxhole camaraderie of the folks who put their shows together. That was really magnetic for me. When I got older and headed off to college, I began thinking about doing other things—*Maybe good to avoid the family business.* I attended Harvard, which had no theater degree program, and enrolled as biology major. But I became intensely interested in starting a theater on an extracurricular basis. The idea was to present new staged works. I thought I was going to be its impresario, very Joe Papp, but because nobody wanted to direct, it fell to me. I was around twenty when I began to have second thoughts about becoming a research biologist. I finally decided that I had better radar for the stage and learned how to direct by apprenticing with a number of directors. By twenty-four I was doing some of my own productions."

"What was it specifically about directing for the stage that so interested you?"

"Theater gives me the opportunity to draw attention to human behavior and aspirations, and to illuminate life at its most exhilarating and humiliating. The theater is a place where people, if they're searching for something, can be more open and alert. An audience witnessing something from either literature or a great piece of staging articulated well can potentially become more humane and better citizens."

"How does directing inform you about yourself and serve you personally?"

"Directing gives me the ability to discipline my mind, to focus on *this world* for a given amount of time. If I were left to my own devices without the privilege of having all these little worlds to fiendishly focus on, I might be just gibbering in a cell somewhere. I need it. I just love wandering through these little environments that you make onstage, dreaming them up for months and months, and working with colleagues who've gotten to know me and who I've gotten to know. The world is most lucid for me in the theater. There is so much noise outside, so much discord, such a surfeit of information that I just crave the focus I experience when working on a production. For me, the experience can last for many months—for an audience a few hours, but in that brief time I hope I furnish them with some of that focus in a concentrated dose that lasts. I think of myself also as a member of the audience who gets to talk back without being hauled off the premises. I have a certain privilege of speaking about what I want to see and choosing the people I'd like to be part of it. I adore such privileges as an extraordinary luxury."

"Once you've decided to take on a play, what are the next steps?"

"I take a look at the script, the world, the actors, and try to create some kind of blank slate in my mind so that I really have the great privilege of filling it up with the things that would compel my attention and fill me with delight. I love to prepare, that solitary aspect of the job, the constant reading of the play and then rereading it out loud. I keep a blue notebook that I fill up with my ideas for the production. It's in no schematic order. I don't organize these thoughts. I just let them come to me. And I'm diligent about writing down in notebooks everything that might be useful or have some hip-pocket value to me, including mental images, poetry, citations from other plays, or my own thoughts about a moment or an association in my life that might be useful to those onstage. My decisions are very intuitive, and writing helps me reveal to myself what I'm thinking. When I was sent the script for *Doubt*, I read the first line—'What do we do when we don't know?'—and I knew I wanted to do that play, that it had great dramatic potential. Next comes the less solitary preproduction phase that has to do with casting. Can we attract this star or that star, or can we be brave enough to attempt to take part in the making of a star? Then there is the delightful phase of working with my set and costume designers, imagining things visually. Those collaborations are focused conversations about the lives of characters for the play and what environment will be a great playpen. I use that silly term, playpen, even on plays that have darker, rugged subject matter, like *Doubt*, *Frozen* (2004), and *The Grey Zone* (1996), because you are at play in those environments. If you can honestly say that you're at play with frightening, dangerous, and lethal experiences, you've reduced your fear of them."

"How can theater be useful to us as a society?"

"We live in a fairly heedless society, barreling through life without much pause. So I find the intense commitment that it takes to go to the theater—getting in your car or taking a bus or subway or walking downtown and entering a room with your fellow citizens to hear what another fellow citizen, the author, has to say is an expression of respect for humanity. I find something sacred and humanizing about it. I think it has something to do with ritual that doesn't have an ideological or religious axe to grind. It is simply about a communion that does not have a super agenda. We are going to pay attention for two hours to this imitation of life that we hope might rehearse us a little bit for the life we're going to pick up when we leave the theater."

"When does telling a story become art?"

"When the result is both surprising and inevitable and when the familiar seems strange and the strange seems familiar. We're doing this play here, sort of an old-fashioned marital sex comedy infused with danger. It's defiant of the usual comic curve. It doesn't restore everything to order or bring harmony back after the events of a midsummer night. It is seductively comic with components of dislocation and chaos. An audience of largely married people would feel that the challenges and patience of marriage are affirmed and honored by the author's message. But the author keeps going into a realm of our greatest fears—humiliation, abandonment, and betrayal. So you have a healthy dream in which certain fears are given shape in front of you, and that can be empowering in helping you to work out something that's going on in your life. Life is hard, so in order to get through it we kid ourselves and deny things. We pretend that we're unaffected by the things that affect us deeply. We are not one hundred percent in touch with our feelings. We lie to ourselves. Society lies to us. Our politicians lie to us. Our parents lie to us. So we love coming to see these events on the stage because it is here where we hear the truth. We have an affective, powerful moment in the theater that is honest. Nobody's sparing us or shaving off the jagged edges. The experience can be dangerous, and yet we're still safe and we come through it. I like to think that the experience of seeing a great production might improve our vision, acuity, and aptitude for getting through the next twenty-four hours of our lives."

"Do you believe that a theater is in a sense like a house of prayer in that its environment predisposes people to be more sensitive, perhaps even more spiritual?"

"Yes, I think one experiences an altered state. The audience enters a theater and there is a measure of awe. I'm not a religious man. But if by 'a house of prayer' you mean some place that promotes greater focus and surrender to the present moment, why yes, I do think of the theater as such a place. Of course, these days the devices we all carry with us persistently invite us to be elsewhere. And there isn't one director, actor, playwright, or audience member alive who hasn't been maddened by the ring of a cell phone in the middle of performance. But the theater remains a bastion of the here and now, even if the purity of the moment is often challenged by a marimba ringtone."

"What makes a play a Doug Hughes play?"

"I strive to make things look more like organisms and not like machines, and I try to refine myself out of the process so that I'm invisible to the audience. Maybe this comes from my biological training."

"Do you ever forget how to direct?"

"I'm forgetting all the time because I feel as though my technique needs constant readjusting to different circumstances. What have I learned about the actors with whom I'm working? What's best dealt with publicly? What's best dealt with privately? I think the job is a constant act of forgetting. I'm trying to stave off for as long as I can the deadly phenomenon of being a pro. I will say that over time the anxiety with which I meet my ignorance has really decreased. But to declare that I know what I'm doing would be to declare the end. I'm content to live in a state of *I don't know. Here's what I propose.* What's really necessary in rehearsal is to commit to a decision, but only after having prepared an escape route—and if that escape route doesn't work, have five or six other plans waiting in the wings. I find that I'm preparing more fiendishly for a production in my fifties than I did in my twenties. I have no idea why that is. I find myself more fluid and less frightened, but still constantly starting from zero."

"So much of the material in your plays deals with deeply emotional material—internal conflict, good and evil, hate, doubt, illness, identity, death. Why do people go to see plays with disturbing themes, and why do actors want to play in them?"

"I think we're drawn in the theater to a realm where we might have some power for a brief time over the things that scare us. That I think is of profound value to this work. I look for material in which a character is placed in an impossible situation and has no painless way through it.

We want these characters sacrificing for us and brought into a very controlled environment to a place of the impossible and unthinkable moment. And I think those moments are the most riveting for an actor on the stage with an audience as witness. It happens in *Frozen*, in *Doubt*, and in *Poor Behavior*."

"When you take on plays with dark themes such as *Grey Zone*, which takes place in Auschwitz, is it difficult not to become emotionally enslaved by them?"

"I used to pretend that I could be detached and distant, but that was pure pretense. You can't do these things without being affected. And you need it to a degree. There's a difference between immersion in the material for the concerns of the play—giving it energy, inspiration, and endurance—and falling in love with the material to the degree that you lose your critical perspective and become sentimental. So it's a balancing act. You have to be completely enthralled with the material, but a part of you needs skepticism."

"You said earlier that in the early stages of your process you read the script out loud. Does that give you the opportunity to play all the characters and release some hidden actor lurking within?"

"Yes. I think anyone who works in the theater—the stage manager, set designer, even the janitor would have to admit that their initial impulse is to act, to perform. They all secretly desire this. We all want to be the actors!"

"How are your opening nights?"

"I hate them. I hate them! There's a lot of celebration with the opening of a play for me, but the great celebrations are the impromptu ones that happen when a production has found its legs and after the curtain comes down everyone goes across the street to the diner for a drink. That's the merriment that's part and parcel of the opening of a play. But waiting for a critical judgment, a photo op, and press event—all of those seem to me to bleed a bit of the joy out of it. I never sit and watch the play on those occasions. And there's that reality: I won't be able to go to work on it the next day. It's done. I'm at that point comparatively obsolete, and that isn't a good feeling. What I'm always after in the role of director is the intense pleasure of getting a play assembled and getting it up and running. I crave that immersion and focus, which I haven't been able to find anywhere else in my life. And that's probably why when it's over, I dash quickly off to the next play."

Julie Taymor

Julie Taymor is a visual artist working in multiple mediums—puppetry, mask making, mime, dance-drama, painting, and sculpture. Combined with her interest in storytelling, mythology, folklore, and the adaptation of literary works from Shakespeare and other sources, she has become one of the most accomplished and respected directors on the theatrical stage, in opera, and in feature films. Her production of The Lion King *(1997), for which she won two Tony Awards, continues to enchant audiences in cities across the globe and has been seen by millions. Her films—* Titus *(1999),* Frida *(2002),* Across the Universe *(2007), and* The Tempest *(2010)—have been critically acclaimed for their stunning originality. During our interview in her Manhattan apartment, Julie confessed that what's most important to her is respect for artistic integrity and the originality to which she has devoted her life.*

"Your creative path seems to have been as unique and original as your theater pieces and films."

"I'm a visual artist and always have been. I sculpted and painted my whole life. I acted and danced, studied mime and mask movement. As a visual artist I was interested in putting these various mediums together and finding a form of theater that combined the visual with the theatrical. My Watson Fellowship [proposal] was on visual and experimental puppet theater in Eastern Europe, Indonesia, and Japan. I was supposed to spend three months in Indonesia and stayed four years from the age of twenty-one. There, I created a theater company that combined traditional theater forms with new ones that I invented to tell stories based on books, literature, or original ideas."

"How did you come to understand so well the use of theatrical storytelling in cultural settings?"

"I had studied the origins of theater and shamanism at Oberlin College. The shaman was the first theater director as well as the religious healer and spiritual leader of the community. You can go back and talk about Plato's cave as the beginning of theater, but the first artists were the shamans in every community, and therefore theater wasn't really about entertainment. It was about spiritual balance—physical and mental health in a community. Theater was created to ensure balance and to celebrate births and tooth filings, coming-of-age ceremonies, weddings, and funerals. All of those things were marked and celebrated, but also if an illness happened in the community, a shaman would be called upon to do a spirit journey and to right that wrong. I really got to see this ancient custom in practice in a very fundamental way. The knowledge and experience I gained in Java inspired me to create *Way of Snow* (1974). This piece about transitions, modernization, and sanity in culture was based to a great extent on someone who was very close to me and had gone through psychological turmoil—what we would call mental illness. It was completely visual and musical with no words, and was told through imagery, puppetry, dance, and the use of masks. I felt that it transcended differences in culture. It was the first piece that I created completely from scratch from my personal ideas."

"How did that first directorial experience inform you about your future path as a theatrical director and filmmaker?"

"I knew I wanted to find a form of theater that was highly visual. It was unlikely that I would do straight dramatic plays—four-character dramas in kitchens, living rooms, and bedrooms. There were enough people doing that. I was interested in how the audience perceives art. When they see something that's familiar, they view it as natural and they are intrigued by it. What intrigues the artist is an abstraction of reality. Abstraction gives you a potentially new way of looking at something that's familiar. And that's what interests me in the theater, film, opera, and in all the other mediums. You can tell familiar stories, whether it's the *Ramayana* or the *Mahabharata*, *The Iliad* or *The Odyssey*, but it's *how* you tell the story. The method of telling the story is equal to the story itself."

"Doesn't telling a story in an entirely new way require that the audience be willing to go there with you?"

"Audiences have a very hard time stepping away from the familiar. It's jolting for an audience to take a ride they haven't experienced before, but when they're willing to go there, that's usually what creates an extraordinary trip. So that's what I wanted to do from my earliest work—take people to places [where] they didn't know they wanted to go. It means that once you're there, the experience should be such that it's fulfilling, illuminating, and challenging. It's not that you say, *Hey, I don't want to go there. I thought I was going here.* This is where we get into trouble in the commercial world, because a lot of the time producers want the audience to get what *they* think people want. I think that's a mistake and knocks the work down a level. I'm there to create a new experience, and it has to be a new experience for me as well."

"How does one step into the creative unknown?"

"That is always the artist's gamble. I never know exactly how it's going to work out when I begin a project. If I did, then it wouldn't be a challenge and it wouldn't be fresh. Okay, I have these ideas. I'm the director, and that means I'm also pulling together all the elements, including my collaborators. Directing is not a solo art form. It's not like when I paint or I sculpt. When I do that, it's just me and the paint and the clay or paper. And I love to do that because there's no talking, there's no convincing, there's no psychological manipulation. But the director has to be very savvy on how to have an actor go to a particular place without manipulation, yet it is manipulation. But it's the kind of manipulation in which the actor feels that they are also being creative and contributing to the experience. I expect a lot to come from my performers, but my goal is to be a guide or an editor. It's my responsibility to pick and choose and put into a form that which will work out best for the piece."

"How do you remain true to your own creative vision and at the same time satisfy the needs of an audience?"

"If I don't feel moved or challenged intellectually, and don't have a good time doing it, then I haven't succeeded. If it's boring to me or I have nothing to say, I don't want to do it. If it's been said already, then who cares. I had to find in *The Lion King* something—what would thrill, excite, and move me: *Where is the pivotal moment? How do I get there?* It had already been done as a successful animated film, so how do I take it to a place that's fresh and new for me as well as the audience?"

"Are your project choices based to a good degree on their visual potential, ideas or stories that lend themselves to artful exploration and interpretation?"

"Yes. My choices have to have a cinematic raison d'être. There has to be an original world created. What I often do in my works is juxtapose real worlds with heightened worlds, like I did with *Frida*. I knew that Frida Kahlo's paintings were autobiographical and that they would have to come alive. I wanted to show what drove her as an artist. So I created all of those live moments in the film. Being able to do that is why I agreed to do the film. Music is another very important component to me. The film's composer, Elliot Goldenthal, who is also my other half and with whom I mostly work—when I'm not working with Mozart, Strauss, Stravinsky, Wagner, the Beatles—helped me tell this story musically."

"How does visual presentation—choice of color palette, over all design, scenery, costumes and lighting, props, etc.—deepen the experience for the audience?"

"I think that visual and musical expression are much more potent than words. Because they are slightly abstract, they have a power that people can't explain or rationally understand, or even talk about it. There is something very potent about the visual image. You can try to describe what happened to the Twin Towers on 9/11, but nothing will inform and move you as much as a photograph or a film of the event or the expression of misery etched on the face of someone who experienced it. We respect visual arts but people don't quite understand how to talk about it in terms of live theater, movies, and opera. They call it visual effects or spectacle. They don't quite get that that is the story, and the look of the work and the story are in equal balance."

"Seeing Frida Kahlo played by Salma Hayek, lying unconscious covered in shattered glass, gold glitter, and debris after she's been impaled in the streetcar accident, says more than any verbal description can. Its vividness conveys the depth of that experience and imprints it on your psyche."

"Yes, exactly. It's like an ideograph—says so much with so little. That's the basis of how I work when I work with designers, actors, and in my mind: taking a concept or image and reducing it to its essence. Ideographs have a beginning and middle and end, but they're brush strokes; they're the most minimal way to tell a maximum story. Ideograph of *The Lion King* is the circle, the circle of life, the circle of Mufasa's headdress, the circle of the way Pride Rock comes out. You'll see it all the way through *The Lion King*. It's a motif that comes from me having to ask, 'What is this about?' He goes away as prodigal son, but he comes home again. And so when I come to a work, I ask, 'What is its essence and how can I make it as simple as a Haiku poem?'"

"Is it difficult working ideographically with Shakespeare's material?"

"Shakespeare is a great inspiration for me in my films and theater works. What's hard is finding a balance with the material because he's difficult to understand the first time out. It's a foreign language, and it gets better the more times you see it and hear it. In *Titus*, I felt that the visual imagery was always there to support the dialogue.

"The line 'Who is my niece who is locked of body bare who made of these two branches?' gave me the idea to replace her cut-off hands with tree twigs. I never try and lay an idea on top of the language. I try to support the dialogue with imagery."

"Shakespeare did not give stage directions, allowing artists great freedom in their portrayal and staging of his plays."

"Yes, that's correct. When I did *Titus Andronicus* on the stage, which was a very minimalist production, only ten to twelve actors, I put Livonia on a pedestal, wrapped her hands in black, and replaced them with twigs. And then when I did the film, I had to find the cinematic equivalence, so I put her into a tortured, burned-out swamp, which is representative of her violated womanhood. Because Shakespeare didn't put the actual rape onstage, I didn't put it onscreen. I don't ever put more violence in a production than he would."

"What is your process to establish a story's visual concept and aesthetic?"

"I begin with research. Doing research often sparks my imagination, so in the case of *Spiderman* (2010), I read hundreds of comic books and then went to their origins stories, the myths. I also looked at the comic-book art from a number of eras. With my designers I found a vocabulary we liked and came up with the concept of the spider web and the wires. The visibility of that presentation was very important. With *Tempest*, I happened to be on the island of Lanai in Hawaii on a holiday with Elliot when Harvey Weinstein asked me to do the film. I saw Lanai as the island of *The Tempest*. The volcanic rock and sand, the nature and the corral, [it] was the perfect place to film it. It had all these different landscapes in one. Each landscape could be used for a particular metaphorical scene. For example, the labyrinths of trees were where the conspiracy would happen. The kind of Hansel and Gretel ramble forest was where the drunken clowns were, and the wild black-lava landscapes on the Big Island were where the men went mad."

"What I find most fascinating about your work is that you combine an imagined reality with a familiar, contemporary reality."

"Yes. I blend and collide time periods. In *Titus* you ask, 'Is this really happening in Mussolini's period or in ancient Rome?' We have chariots next to cars and motorcycles, modern-day men's suits with senator's robes from ancient Rome. One can't really identify the period. I do this also because Shakespeare blended time. He had Elizabethan Christian morality and design in an ancient Roman setting. I've never completely updated Shakespeare because that seems belittling, but that doesn't mean that his characters aren't contemporary. In *Titus*, the court players are very Velasquez conquistadors, but their clothing is designed with zippers, which were not invented until the nineteenth century. Each character's clothing is meant to reflect who they are and what they're about."

"What do you think your creative choices reveal about you to yourself?"

"I have noticed that the stories I'm drawn to are about outsiders—people walking on the crater's edge: Hop-Frog in *Fool's Fire* (1992), Grendel in *Beowolf*. Peter Parker is an outsider in *Spiderman*; Frida Kahlo and Diego Rivera, in *Frida*. I don't think I fit into a very neat place for people in our culture."

"How do we identify or describe your work?"

"I've noticed that my work doesn't really fall into a particular genre. It's not avant-garde in the sense of movies that come out and are hip and cool with a certain kind of edgy violence. That's not what I do. When *Frida* came out, people said, 'Oh, it was too colorful.' And to them I said, 'Well then, you didn't understand Frida. She wore bows in her hair. She wore those brightly colored costumes. She didn't wear morose black and sit around moaning about her life. And if you've ever been to Mexico, you'd understand that.' But in our culture we tend to think colorful things are not deep. People don't know how to put their finger on what I do. 'Oh she does puppetry.' No. I don't always, unless it requires a puppet. The story determines the method and the medium. I'm attracted to stories about people, but I've done lots of work about animals and monsters through mythic tales. There is great power in myths, and I think that's where I get to be much more artistically expressive. I often bring myths into the present or juxtapose them to a present-day situation. I did that with *Spiderman*, which I consider a contemporary myth."

"There's been a lot of media and controversy over your *Spiderman: Turn Off the Dark*. What happened?"

"I always referred to *Spiderman* as a circus rock-and-roll drama. I never called it a musical. People tried to squish it into this form called the Broadway musical. And once they did that, they said, 'There are rules.' And I said, 'There are no rules.' A Broadway musical is not what I wanted to do and not what we started out doing. What I said was, 'I'm going to create a form of entertainment that will tell a story, that will be visual and musical, and we're going to do it in a way that I haven't seen yet. Therefore, yes, we'll make mistakes; yes, it will take longer; but that's what we're trying to do.'"

"You ended up leaving the show before you saw your vision realized."

"Well, yes. I was fired, let go. But it's still my work. The most disappointing thing is that the part of *Spiderman* that was most critical for me was its spiritual aspect. *They* think it's just about putting on a suit and having the children get that theme-park experience, but that was only part of my job. I was the one trying to raise the bar. I'm not the one who is selling out the audience. I'm not the one pandering or dumbing down. I'm the opposite.

"I didn't want to be a celebrity over this, but this experience this year pushed me out in a way that I loathed. The enjoyment for me is always the process. It's very critical for me. When the process becomes nasty or unpleasant, which obviously the end of this one did, it starts to ruin it for me because the making of it, the doing of it, is every bit as important as the result. Making a lot of money with a Broadway musical can't be the reason for doing it. That could be the outcome, but what you should really be thinking about is giving as many people as possible a great experience."

"The artist's path can be a very difficult and challenging one. What motivates you to keep on going?"

"The greatest satisfaction is knowing how many people are affected by the work. Presently, fifteen productions of *The Lion King* are touring around the world. And this brings me back to the role of the shaman. There is a very moving true story that was told to me about *The Lion King*. Tickets were very hard to come by, so this family with two young children bought tickets six months in advance. And during that time, their daughter, who was about ten, died of an illness. Distraught, the parents didn't want to attend the performance, but everybody said to them, 'It's not fair. You have to take your son to the show.' So they went. Well, there is a point in the story when the child says to Mufasa, 'Will you always be there for me?' And the father says, 'Look at the stars. The great kings from the past look down on us from those stars. They live in you. They live in me. They are watching over everything we see.' When that happened in the show, the little boy turned to his parents and said, 'Sarah's with us isn't she?' And that is enough for me. That is everything. That's my role, like the shaman of the old days. If this theatrical production helped this family get through the death of their daughter and give them an understanding that every time they look into the sky, they feel her presence, then I've done my job. That is the most gratifying and important thing in my life."

Gary Ross

Gary Ross's first two screenplays, Big *(1988) and* Dave *(1993), earned Academy Award nominations for best original screenplays, as did his directorial debut,* Pleasantville *(1998). In 2003, he wrote, produced, and directed* Seabiscuit, *which was nominated for seven Academy Awards, including best picture. I met with Ross at his Sunset Boulevard office just after the release of his blockbuster hit* The Hunger Games *(2012), which he adapted for the screen with the book's author, Suzanne Collins. He shared with me the deeper motivation behind his films.*

"I read that your father, Arthur A. Ross, had been a successful screenwriter with credits that include the horror film *Creature from the Black Lagoon* (1954), *The Great Race* (1965), and *Brubaker* (1980). What was it like being the son of a screenwriter?"

"My dad worked at home in a room above our garage. I remember the soothing percussive sound of the typewriter keys clacking in the background. So for me to go into the arts was not a massive leap out of the culture in which I was raised. Cinema, art, and literature were part of my orientation, as was my parents' progressive politics. As a kid I was taken to see foreign films and, as soon as I could read, was reading subtitles. My mother worked for Stella Adler as a speech coach and ran the speech department at Stella's conservatory."

"Did your father mentor you in writing?"

"He did, but only a vestige of what I learned has stayed with me. He had offered guidance, wisdom, and experience, but with that came a certain degree of tension between us. It's very important to have mentors, but at the same time you need to break free and find your own voice. When that happens it's a very significant moment for an artist."

"What was that moment for you?"

"In my mid-twenties, when writing *Dave*, I felt adrift, lacking a sense of purpose and the confidence to complete the work. I thought to myself, *I've really messed this up.* So I showed the draft to my mother, and she gave me some phenomenal advice, recognizing that *Dave* was very Capra-esque in style. My mother said, 'All of Frank Capra's movies had a political point of view. You've backed away from the political point of

view here. You can't write this without being for something or against something. You can't write a neutral movie about politics.' What was significant was that I had gone for advice to my mother, not my father. Because of my feelings of guilt for my early success and a rivalry between us, I turned from him to my mother. Ironically, that shift would ultimately help me find my independence and my own voice."

"What influenced your decision to become a director?"

"I'd been interested in photography, so the technical aspect of making films appealed to me. When I was a student at the University of Pennsylvania, I took a history of film class and every day saw another phenomenal classic movie that immersed me in the world of great cinema. Before taking that class and eventually becoming its [teaching assistant], I viewed movies from the perspective of the screenwriter, which I had inherited from my father. That college course allowed me to see filmmaking more from the director's perspective. I followed up by studying acting with Stella Adler, but with an eye toward directing. Stella was an amazing influence on my life. She was an incredibly wise lady who gave me a deeper understanding of the playwright's intention and point of view—and as expressed through the prism of the actor, with implications for directing."

"How did you learn the director's craft?"

"I had been preparing and apprenticing for a long time. I spent every day of shooting *Big* and *Dave* on the set. And Ivan Reitman, who directed *Dave*, allowed me access to the editing room so I could learn. Until you cut a movie you're not really comfortable directing. Now when I direct a film, my head is also in the editing room, thinking how I'm going to edit scenes and imagining the finished film."

"How has your screenwriting changed since becoming a director?"

"Before I was a director, I didn't fully understand the process of translating my scripts to the screen. Now I write more cinematically. I'm conscious of things like sound design and rhythm. I don't see things in three-page scenes anymore. I'm much more comfortable driving the narrative forward as paragraphs within a chapter. That chapter may be seven, eight pages of screenplay, but I'm seeing it more as moving pictures."

"That was evident in *The Hunger Games*."

"I think you see that in *Seabiscuit* as well. I'm no longer locked into the rhythm of that three-page metronome."

"How do you ascertain if a story is worth telling?"

"It has to have themes or ideas that sustain my interest and characters that feel real and engaging. I can't just make a piece of entertainment unless I find it personally meaningful, especially if I'm going to spend a year and a half working on it. And I need to feel connected to it emotionally, as I did with *The Hunger Games*. The story is about preserving one's humanity in an inhuman system, finding the courage to separate oneself from the norms of their own culture, and standing for a moral principle. If Katniss Everdeen is going to die during the games anyway, why be complicit? The moment she refuses to be complicit and opens her heart to her own humanity with compassion for Rue and her ability to trust Peeta, she's found a personal truth. What moved me was how she arrived at that moment of humanity in the face of such inhumanity. That's the story I'm telling in the writing, acting, and the cinematic choices I make. That makes it worth it to me."

"Were you attracted to Katniss Everdeen's character and circumstances also because you identified with her in some way?"

"No, it's not like *This character is me*. Expressing Katniss's compassion, individuality, and desire to live an ethical life doesn't mean that her character is analogous to me and my life. I can, however, find aspects of the character that I care about and that interests me. What interested me in *Seabiscuit*, for example, were how the central characters evolved in a cruel, harsh universe to find a place of love for one another, and how they healed one another through acts of generosity and kindness. That's a pretty brave thing to make a movie about — kindness, gentleness, and sensitivity at a time when cynicism passes for naturalism in modern cinema."

"In *Pleasantville*, an Edenic allegory set in a homogenized 1950s universe in which there is no conflict, pain, despair, struggle, grief, [the setting] is a false utopia, because that's ultimately what makes a life's journey complete. You can't know joy in life without pain. You can't know love without loss. I aim to express the full scope of life and the untidiness of human existence. That was a really complex idea that sustained me."

"Your films are so often about people struggling to exercise their independence, yearning to fulfill some deep-seated wish or satisfy an innate calling. This is perfectly illustrated in the scene in *Pleasantville* when David, Tobey Maguire's character, says to Bill Johnson, Jeff Daniels's character, 'You can't stop something that's inside you.' What can we take away from a scene like that?"

"The moment David tells Bill Johnson to do things out of order — 'You can make the fries and then the burgers' — that's the big bang in the story. When Johnson does that, he has an epiphany: 'You know, I like that.' What happens, ironically, is that his life turns from an unexamined life to an examined life, and he begins to question himself. Once he starts the process of questioning, it leads to self-awareness. He discovers that what he really loves is to paint the Christmas decorations on the windows—and then realizes that he loves art and wants to be a painter. Once you find your own truth, once you know it, you can't unknow it."

"How can we as viewers recognize the meaning or subtext of a story when it's so often camouflaged in allegory, plot line, or character development?"

"That's the question of all literature. How do you get the point of it if you're pulled out of it? As the storyteller you don't necessarily want everyone to understand everything as if it's a legal argument. You want to engage the audience so that they leave with lingering questions. Storytelling is at its best when you can stimulate a kind of questioning process, which is both cerebral and emotional. The emotional one is obviously a more resonant one, and that means you can't afford to create too much aesthetic dissonance in the experience. So if I stimulate a kind of questioning process which is cerebral, and I stimulate an emotional process which is engaging, then that's really good for the audience."

"Why is an emotional response more resonant and engaging?"

"The moment you are able to engage emotionally, that's the moment of change because you recognize the truth in the emotional response."

"Is this also true for the art maker—being more emotionally engaged leads to greater truth?"

"An artist by definition is someone who seeks or questions the deeper truth and wants to look inside themselves for a personal subtext or motivations or what it is that makes them tick, and to express those emotional dynamics. So yes, I think it's an integral part of the artist's process."

"Is it necessary to have read the book *The Hunger Games* to grasp the film's deeper meaning or message?"

"Well, I don't know, because I've read the book. But I think the film is a stand-alone work. I don't think that you need to have read the book to understand that the 'tributes' are being exploited and sacrificed in this harsh universe. Why did they willing participate in someone else's spectacle? How does one break from conformity to become a rebel? Katniss's compassion and protectiveness makes her stronger, not weaker, and that's what gives her the power to stand her ethical ground. That's the irony that I find in the story and I think that comes through in the film. I don't think there is any danger of anyone watching this film and not identifying with Katniss. It's her character that makes it a young adult story with such pop-culture appeal."

"Does it matter to you if the viewer gets the ethical message behind the story?"

"There is a subtext if you want to dig. If you don't, I don't mind if somebody takes in the movie at face value. It's not for me to say how an individual should experience the film."

"What do you look for in the actors you cast?"

"A lot of this job is recognizing something special in an actor when they walk in. With some people you know their body of work and you're dying to work with them. I felt that way with Joan Allen, Jeff Bridges, Chris Cooper, and Stanley Tucci. Often with kids you go through an audition process, and I felt there was something special about Tobey Maguire the day he walked in. The same applies to Jennifer Lawrence, Josh Hutcherson, and Reese Witherspoon. When you connect collaboratively with an actor, you feel the process of invention. It's almost as if the script never existed, and when they speak you're hearing the lines for the first time. I get very excited when I see them give voice and interpretation to their characters with their own wrinkles, nuances, and subtleties. I imagine it's very much like being a composer when the musician stands up and plays the piece with virtuosity, the way he had imagined it in his head. At such moments of connection you feel gratitude and love for that person. I tend to bond strongly with my actors and am humbled by their ability to bring storytelling to life."

"Do you think that cinema has the potential to make us more compassionate, empathetic, and thoughtful human beings?"

"I sure do. I think film is the most provocative and viscerally engaging medium, which is something that gives it great impact. There's a reason that propaganda flourished with the advent of filmmaking. It's such an immersive experience. From its inception, art has provoked us to question our culture and allowed us to see deeper truths beneath the surface."

"As one who has the capability of reaching a broad audience, do you see yourself in some fashion as a messenger of truths?"

"I'm not a messenger at all. I'm an artist who hopefully investigates, examines, and exposes ideas, themes, and emotions that may not be accessible in everyday life. I think that's the function of an artist. These are not messages, but engaging, provocative, emotional experiences that provoke people to ask their own questions."

222

BATTLEPLAN
PRODUCTIONS

Rod Lurie

The son of internationally respected political cartoonist Ranan Lurie, Rod Lurie graduated from the United States Military Academy at West Point and served in the army before becoming one of Hollywood's most provocative and thoughtful filmmakers. Bursting on the scene with his critically acclaimed political drama The Contender *(2000), he has continued to write, produce, and direct films and television shows of social and political relevance. They include* The Last Castle *(2001),* Commander in Chief *(2005–2006),* Resurrecting the Champ *(2007),* Nothing but the Truth *(2008), and* Straw Dogs *(2011). I met with Rod at his production office, Battleplan Productions, on the old Samuel Goldwyn Meyer studio lot in Hollywood.*

"What led you to become a filmmaker?"

"When I was in the fourth grade, my parents went out one night and left me with a babysitter. *Ben-Hur* (1959) was being shown on television for the first time. The babysitter sent me to bed when Ben Hur was on the slave ship. I protested, 'He's got to escape. I can't leave now.' 'You go to bed right now!' she insisted. So I went, but I couldn't fall asleep. I wanted to know what would happen to Ben Hur. I snuck back and, through an open crack of the doorjamb, watched the chariot race. I was so enthralled by that scene that I knew then that this was the business I wanted to be in: *I want to make movies!* Even to this day, I think it's the best action scene ever filmed. *Ben Hur* is the movie that led to my becoming a filmmaker."

"Before directing, you were a film critic, and a rather controversial one. Why was that?"

"To be honest with you, I purposefully created controversy. I wanted to become a famous film critic because I saw film criticism as an entry to making movies. I would often write very viciously. I look back on it with regret. I hurt some people's feelings in ways that were unnecessary. It did make me well known and create a curiosity about me, although I'm not sure it actually contributed to my being able to make films later on."

"The film that catapulted you into the mainstream was *The Contender*. What motivated you to write that story and how did it come about?"

"In 1998, while working as a film critic for KABC I was asked to present

Joan Allen the Los Angeles Critics Award for best supporting actress in *Pleasantville*. I really admired her. So when I get up onstage I said, 'You know, I should write a movie for Joan Allen. If she makes it, it'll be a good movie.' When I sat down, Joan said, 'You know, if you write that screenplay, I'll definitely read it.' So I tell my wife, 'I'm going to write a screenplay for Joan Allen!' When I got home, I turned on my computer and sat there staring at that horrible view so many writers face—a blank screen and a blinking curser. I had no idea what it would be about. After a while I got up to kiss my little girl Paige good night, and she asked me a question: 'Daddy, why don't women ever run for president?' 'I don't know why,' I said. And she said, 'Maybe Mommy can run for president. Or maybe Grandma can run for president.' 'Mommy's probably too young to run for president, and Grandma is selling real estate in Connecticut.' So Paige says, 'Okay, I'll be the first woman president!' And as I'm walking down the stairs back to my computer, I'm thinking about the obstacles women face in attaining high elected office. That's it! I sat down and typed the words 'The Contender.' This was what I was going to write about—a woman attempting to attain high political office, but more importantly, I understood that the films I should make would present a world in which Paige could be the president. I started writing and didn't stop for two days and nights until I had it finished. I sent the screenplay to Joan Allen. She called me from Ireland to tell me she was in. That ignited the process and was enough to get Jeff Bridges and Gary Oldman into the film, which is what got the movie made."

"I've heard you reference *All the President's Men* (1976) a number of times as a major influence on your filmmaking. What's so significant about that film?"

"That's my *Moby-Dick*. *All the President's Men* is the film I'll forever be tracing qualitatively. I saw that film by myself when I was thirteen years old at the Landmark Cinema in Stamford, Connecticut. It really would normally fly above the head of most children my age, but it didn't for me because I grew up in a political household where Watergate was discussed on a daily basis. The greatness of that film was that it was completely realistic and yet suspenseful, even though we already knew the details of how Bob Woodword and Carl Bernstein broke that story and what happened subsequently. And yet there was this extraordinary tension created by its director, Alan Pakula, and actors Redford and Hoffman. The film had an exquisite screenplay by William Goldman and brilliant cinematography by Gordon Willis. It has over the years been cemented more and more in my mind as the apex of filmmaking. I don't think it really gets better. It's still a movie that profoundly affects me."

"I find it interesting how often directors will visually reference or borrow from the films that inspire them. Have you done that as well?"

"I can find moments in each of my films that were influenced by other movies, and sometimes it's simple, uncreative grand-theft larceny. In *Resurrecting the Champ*, the newsroom scenes were filmed in accordance with how Gordon Willis filmed *All the President's Men*. We have Josh Harnett who plays the reporter crossing the newsroom exactly the way Redford traipsed across the newsroom at the *Washington Post*. In *Straw Dogs*, I took a lot from Peckinpah's original film, but I was also influenced by a scene in Joel and Ethan Coen's *Blood Simple* (1984), when Dan Hedaya's character is crawling in the street. I also took from *The Vanishing* (1993), when the female protagonist is doing her lipstick in the car, flips over the visor, and we see her face. When you're able to reference certain films, it's easier to tell your DP [director of photography] what you're after. I'm not trying to say I'm in the same league with these directors, I'm not, but they do have an artistic pull on me."

"There's an important line in *The Contender*, when Gary Oldman's character, Shelley Runyon, says to Christian Slater's character, Congressman Reggie Webster, 'People *want* us for our opinions, our subjectivity, not our objectivity.' Do the films that you make serve as a vehicle for you to express your social and political views?"

"Yes. Absolutely. The kind of movies I make definitely reflect my politics, the values I was raised with and the West Point in me. Let me tell you an interesting story. *The Contender* was made as an independent film and bought by DreamWorks. We had many offers, but I wanted to get in the editing room with Steven Spielberg. I wanted his wisdom and experience. There is a scene in the film when Joan Allen, who plays Lane Hanson, explains what she's all about in a very liberal speech: 'I'm for the right of choice, I want to get a gun out of every house.' She also talks about living in the chapel of democracy—the U.S. Congress—and reveals that she's an atheist. I did that scene dry, without music. And Steven said to me, 'You really should have music there.' 'But Steven,' I said, 'then people are going to think it's my point of view that I'm pushing.' I'll never forget him crooking his head and saying, 'What's wrong with that? We're not reporters. We're not documentarians. We're filmmakers. What we do is present a point of view.'"

"Do you sometimes take heat for your politics?"

"Yes. I am known as a very liberal filmmaker, and sometimes it has hurt me. For example, *Nothing but the Truth* is about a Washington reporter named Rachel Armstrong, played by Kate Beckinsale, who is a mom, loves her boy, but goes to jail because she will not reveal a source who identified a CIA operative. The story is very much like the Valerie Plame situation. She appears to be protecting her source beyond any sanity and spends hundreds of days in jail. She is beaten and possibly raped. So is protecting a source a First Amendment issue, a Republican position, or a liberal position? Both sides have taken up that flag, and I don't know if it's liberal or conservative. But when I was reviewed in the *New York Post*, which is a very conservative paper, the film was referred to as 'liberal hogwash.' The reviewer assumed that it's liberal because I made the film. I am a liberal and my protagonists are often liberals, so maybe the shoe does fit, but I'm perceived in this way regardless of what I do. I can make a movie about the heroism of George W. Bush, and it would still be labeled liberal just because I did it."

"That's interesting, because I think you actually present both the conservative and liberal points of view fairly convincingly in that film."

"*Nothing but the Truth* may be the most objective film I've made because the right of the journalist to protect a source is not in and of itself a liberal or conservative issue. So it was easy to present both sides. Matt Dillon's character plays the special prosecutor and the film's antagonist, who believes that Rachel Armstrong has committed a criminal act. By the end of that film, it's clear that what motivated her may not necessarily have been what everyone else thought it was. So you're left with a real question mark about what was the right thing for her to do."

"I think your films are more about making ethical and moral decisions than siding with partisan platforms. Your films ask us to put ourselves inside the character's shoes and think, *What would I do?*"

"That's absolutely right. *What would I do? Did that person do the* right *thing?* One of my greatest fears is that at the end of one of my movies the husband will turn to the wife and say, 'Where do you want to go for dinner?' What I want him to say is, 'What would you do?' Joan Allen has a line in *The Contender* that is not just that film's theme but one that has permeated a lot of what I've done: 'Principles only matter when you stand by them when they're inconvenient.' She was standing up for the principle of privacy, even if meant that she would be destroyed in the process. My films often deal with how people live by their principles and how doing that can destroy them. But at the same time, it's what defines their greatness."

"Are the protagonists in your films reluctant heroes—pushed by circumstances to take a stand and adhere to it?"

"I don't think of them as *reluctant* heroes. Rachel Armstrong is not making a decision; she's simply doing what she must. It never occurs to Rachel, the lead character, to reveal her source. She doesn't have the arc; it's the supporting characters that have the arc. The story dealt more with how she affects and shapes the opinions and decision-making processes of those around her. The person who has to make a big decision in *The Contender* is not the Joan Allen character, but the president, played by Jeff Bridges. Is he going to support her to become his vice president or not? In *Nothing but the Truth* will Matt Dillon's character decide to prosecute Kate Beckinsale's character to the full extent to the law? People often ask me, 'Do these characters in your films represent you, Rod Lurie?' The answer is no, they don't. They represent who I want to be. What I really admire about these characters is how they embrace certainty. This is what makes them heroic. In many ways these films are about the DNA of greatness."

"What was the impetus for your doing a remake of Sam Peckinpah's violent 1971 film *Straw Dogs*?"

"Peckinpah's *Straw Dogs* was a very right-wing depiction of human nature. What Sam seemed to be saying is that all human beings are coded to violence through genetics—sociobiology. I wanted to see if I could make a liberal version of the same story to demonstrate that violence comes from how we are nurtured and the environment we live in. I thought it was an interesting exercise to see if the same story could be told from different political points of view."

"Were you successful?"

"I'm very proud of *Straw Dogs*. I think I achieved what I set out to do. But it was a career miscalculation. It was doomed because generally women simply do not go to movies that have rape scenes in them. It's a woman's worst nightmare, so why would she want to see that. But the other miscalculation was making it for a genre studio that was not in the business of putting out intellectual films. It became thought of as a violent genre film instead of a thought-provoking story, and therefore it did not do well at the box office."

"My sense is that you want audiences to engage intellectually with your films and contemplate how we as human beings make choices about our lives."

"That's right. The decision-making process of the human being is really what interests me. I do like to put the audience into that center of gravity. I'm not sure when or why the kinds of movies I try to make, with the emphasis on *try*, have gone out of favor. You look at some of the films that were made when you and I were growing up, like *Taxi Driver* (1976), *Kramer vs. Kramer* (1979), or *All the President's Men*, and you see that these films were hell-bent on intellectualism and, in fact, did extremely well at the box office. I believe that intelligent filmmaking is still absolutely viable. Look at the success of *The King's Speech* (2010), *Black Swan* (2010), or *Argo* (2012), which very much reminded me of the films made from 1969–1977, a time when people evidently did go see films that asked them to think."

"How important are high production values, compared to narrative and message in making a successful film?"

"Best-picture winners like *Rocky* (1976) or *Kramer vs. Kramer* had limited or unimpressive production values, but their narratives were very strong and impactful. Some films with state-of-the-art production values do poorly. In the end, it's about character, story, and message. That's the beating heart of a movie."

"What makes a great cinematic story?"

"It depends on the audience. I would rather boil my eyeballs than see one of Merchant Ivory's movies, but other people watch them and are on the edge of their seats. So the answer is that I don't know."

"What makes a great cinematic hero?"

"A great hero is either someone who you are or someone who you want to be. Dustin Hoffman's character Ted Kramer in *Kramer vs. Kramer* is a man that lots of men could identify with. He's going through a tough experience and making decisions that a number of men wish they would have made. So he becomes a great cinematic hero. Then there are the people who you want to be, like James Bond or Indiana Jones. And who doesn't want to be those guys?"

"What makes a great cinematic villain?"

"A great villain is one who has his reasons for doing what he's doing. In *The Last Castle*, James Gandolfini plays the warden in a military prison. He has his reasons for keeping order and discipline the way that he does, which happens to be very extreme. And because he has his reasons, he continues to do what he's doing and that makes him dangerous and therefore a great villain. Great villains are also usually very charismatic, and so we root for them until the end of the movie. In *Flight* (2012), Denzel Washington plays an alcoholic who's dangerous because he's an airline pilot. He flies airplanes when he's drunk and stoned. He's the bad guy, and yet throughout the entire movie you don't want him to be found out and caught. After all, it's Denzel Washington! But he's not a hero, even though we treat him like one. He's really the villain of that film."

"What makes a great film?"

"That is the greatest mystery of them all. The great film critic Judith Crist once said, 'Tomorrow I may see the best film ever made, but what is that?'"

"Do you think you could give up filmmaking, leave the pressures, the criticism, the high stakes, the rollercoaster?"

"No. Once you start directing, there's nothing on earth you'd rather be doing. Directing isn't really working. You're only working when you're *not* directing—when you're in between projects and trying to figure out what you're going to do next. That's when the suffering comes in. Directing is better than eating. Directing is better than sex. It's better than just about anything you can think of."

Robert Benton

I met Robert Benton, the Oscar-winning screenwriter and director of Kramer vs. Kramer *(1979) and such notable films as* Places in the Heart *(1984) and* Nobody's Fool *(1994), at his New York office in the fall of 2011. His sensitive stories deal with human relationships and the power of love. I wanted to know what drew him to storytelling and how he got his first big break. Benton began our conversation with an interesting confession.*

"I have to preface my story by saying that I am seriously dyslexic. For a long time it was very hard for me to read. Till this day I still can't spell or punctuate. And while it's very hard for me to read, less so than it used to be, I loved reading. I was always at the bottom of my class and spent every summer in summer school. I never would have made it through high school if my mother hadn't played bridge with my high school teachers. If they failed me, it would have broken up the bridge game. In college I took a creative writing course and flunked it.

"An enormous amount of my life has been spent going to and thinking about movies. I learned narrative from movies, not from books. It's a different kind of narrative—conveyed more by images than by words. For me, movies functioned in the way books do for someone who wants to be a novelist or short story writer."

"Can you recall a particular movie that really captivated you?"

"When I was in high school I went to see *Asphalt Jungle* (1950), directed by John Huston. The first five minutes were shot on the streets of downtown Los Angeles in the style of the neorealist cinema. I believe it came from Huston's experience of shooting documentaries during the war. I had never seen anything like it, except newsreels. The film's sense of immediacy and truthfulness was utterly new to me. When the movie ended, my father said, 'Okay, let's go,' and I said, 'No!' I don't know why, but I had to see it one more time. I stayed and watched it again.

"A number of postwar European films, like *Children of Paradise* (1945), which I consider one of the greatest of all time, also captivated me. And the Japanese film *Rashomon* (1950) was like stepping off the edge of the world without a safety net. In *Rashomon*'s world there was no such thing as absolute truth. I walked out of the theater into a bleak world where all

truths were provisional at best. The power that movies had over me was enormous. They taught me what life was about. I never got that feeling from a book."

"Could you imagine yourself a filmmaker in those years?"

"No, I couldn't even dream of doing that for a living. I grew up in Waxahachie, Texas, during the Depression. My parents had no idea about this thing called creativity, but they knew the desperation of their dyslexic child who could not read. So they encouraged me to draw. The walls of our house were covered with my drawings. If you do something day and night for ten years, you get to be pretty accomplished. I don't mean to say that I was a genius or anything. I've never been that good of an artist, but I learned enough to be taken seriously. I was accepted at the University of Texas as an art major. The university was a godsend for me because I did better there than in high school. I needed only to show my teachers some imagination. They didn't care if I could spell or punctuate. They gave me better than passing grades, and I gained there a sense of confidence. At the University of Texas I met people with whom I could have long discussions about art and film. They took movies seriously like I did. These people transformed my life. They were like a life raft for me, like drawing had been a life raft. In my senior year I wrote a short story. My girlfriend at the time helped me put it into readable language, and it was published in a student magazine. The story was about a boy who belonged to the Assembly of God College in Waxahachie, whose members were not permitted to go to the movies. He finally went to see *one* movie and responded as I did to *Asphalt Jungle*. He went back and saw it again and again an again. When it moved to the next town he followed it. I was like that boy, tethered to movies in that way."

"When did you begin studying filmmaking?"

"After I graduated from the University of Texas, I moved to New York and attended Columbia University, hoping to study with the great art historian, Meyer Schapiro. In my spare time, I would go to Brentano's bookstore on Fifth Avenue and in the center well in the basement came upon the book *Film, Form and Film Sense* by Sergei Eisenstein. I couldn't afford to buy it, so I'd [go] there every day and read portions of it. At about the same time I bought a book of screenplays for a quarter at a local library. I began to study how screenplays are structured and written, though I wasn't yet thinking about becoming a screenwriter. After one semester at Columbia I ran out of money and had to drop out. I stayed in New York and worked different jobs. In the spring of 1954 I did an illustration for *Esquire* magazine and got hired as its assistant art director. Shortly thereafter, I was drafted into the army. After I got out, I returned to *Esquire* and became its art director for five years."

"Meanwhile your infatuation with movies continued?"

"Yes, that's right. I would go to movies all the time, seeing great films like *Bringing Up Baby* (1938) and *Citizen Kane* (1941). I saw my first Stanley Kubrick film, *Killer's Kiss* (1955). I wanted so badly to see George Cukor's *A Star Is Born* (1954), I went AWOL, leaving the base without a pass. Fortunately, I didn't get caught. I must have watched George Stevens's *A Place in the Sun* (1951) fifteen times. I had the film memorized. With George Stevens, for example, I realized that he was an incredibly literate filmmaker. He respected the form and the nuance of the form. He was concerned not just with the narrative but with the layer underneath the narrative that gave the picture a kind of power I didn't find in Theodore Dreiser's novel that it was based on."

"Who were among your favorite directors at that time?"

"Elia Kazan, Arthur Penn, Bob Mulligan, and John Sturges. I would see and study their films over and over again just for the love of it. I also took notice of the movies coming out of Europe directed by Truffaut, Godard, Fellini, Bergman, and Lindsay Anderson. Those films were alive and exciting in a way most American films weren't. It was also around that time that a community of people began discussing cinema. Peter Bogdanovich was writing about movies for *Esquire* and gave talks. Andrew Sarris of *Village Voice* wrote about the auteur theory—writers, directors, and cinematographers whose voices were uniquely strong and consistent from film to film. I began to look at Howard Hawks (*Rio Bravo*, 1959) and Sam Peckinpah (*Ride the High Country*, 1962). The narratives of Hawks and Peckinpah were character-driven. In contrast, Otto Preminger's characters were shaped by the narrative. Film excited me more than any of the other art forms, such as painting, sculpture, and theater. But I still wasn't thinking about becoming a filmmaker."

"What was the turning point?"

"In 1964, at the age of thirty I was eased out as the director at *Esquire*, and I didn't want to work for any other magazine or go into advertising. Instead, I decided to write a screenplay. Now remember, I was seriously dyslexic and couldn't spell or punctuate. So I turned for help to a friend at *Esquire*, David Newman, who was a wonderful writer. I convinced David to work with me by regaling him with stories about the glamorous life of screenwriters—a total lie. Together we wrote a treatment for *Bonnie and Clyde*, which took us about three months. We wrote it in the style of the French New Wave films, specifically in the manner of Truffaut and Godard. Our idea was to create a new American cinema. We arranged for a public reading of the script to make sure it made sense. It was attended by Helen Scott who worked in the French Film Office in New York and was a trusted friend of François Truffaut. She translated the script into French and sent it to Truffaut. He wrote to us and said, 'I'm very interested in this.' We arranged to meet at the Regency Hotel in New York and spent two days going through the script. Two young producers, Elinor and Norton Wright, gave us twelve hundred dollars, and we turned it into a screenplay. Truffaut said that he loved it, but he was about to do *Fahrenheit 451*, and he didn't want to commit to another film, especially in English. He gave the script to Jean-Luc Godard, who came to New York and told the Wrights that he wanted to direct the film. Now what happened next was nobody's fault. Godard thought American producers were like European producers—they give you the money and you go make the movie. But the American system was different. In America, you start with a script, then you get a director, and then you get a star, and once you've created a package, you go to a studio for money to make the film. Because our producers didn't have the experience or the money, Godard walked out. Then in 1967, Warren Beatty read the script and offered to buy it. He became the film's producer and asked us who we wanted to direct. We told him Truffaut and he said, 'You've written an American story; you need an American director.' He was right about that. He suggested George Stevens, but I thought Stevens, though a great director, was not right for this. David and I thought the only American director who would understand the style of this movie was Arthur Penn. Arthur joined us and Warren, and that's how I got started in the movies."

"Why do a movie about Bonnie Parker and Clyde Barrow, bank robbers from the 1930s?"

"David and I got the idea to do *Bonnie and Clyde* from a book we were both reading about John Dillinger. There was a footnote about Bonnie and Clyde that read that they were not just outlaws but outcasts, and that's what caught our attention. I grew up listening to stories about Bonnie and Clyde and Pretty Boy Floyd and Ma Barker. These people were talked about as though they were folk heroes in their off-center way. On Halloween, the kids in our town dressed up as Bonnie or Clyde. My father, who was a law-abiding man, attended their funeral. He's the one who told me where they're buried."

"What makes a story worth telling?"

"If the people you are talking about are worth spending time with. I ask you to give me an hour and a half or two hours of your time with the promise that I won't waste it. I remember seeing Hitchcock's *To Catch a Thief* (1955) and thinking, *I want it to be five minutes longer.* In the same way I want people to say about each of my films, 'I wish it would have been five minutes longer.'"

"Virtually all of your films are about love. Why?"

"Probably because I've failed at it so many times. My films are not only about romantic love. They are about empathy or affection for another person—a parent for a child as in *Kramer vs. Kramer*; a woman in Depression-era Texas for a black workman as in *Places in the Heart*; a freelance construction worker for a semi-retarded co-worker as in *Nobody's Fool*. What thrilled me most the first time I was in love was the intimacy, not the sex, because nothing is shut out from one another. There is a kind of trust and risk in intimacy that I find heroic. When I can find in a script the thread of love in that way, I know I have my story. I know I have my characters. I know I'm onto something."

"To what degree do your films reflect your own life?"

"A lot of my work does. For me, *Kramer vs. Kramer*, which I adapted from Avery Corman's novel, is not about separation or divorce. My wife and I have been happily married for almost forty-two years. It's about the relationship between a father and a son, the intimacy between them. It's about being so close that you can get up in the morning and make French toast together without even having to say anything to each other."

"The characters in so many of your movies find themselves in crisis like Dustin Hoffman's character Ted Kramer in *Kramer vs. Kramer* after his wife abandons him and their son and then wants custody of their little boy. Or Sally Field's character, Edna Spalding, in *Places in the Heart*, whose husband is killed and she must keep the bank from foreclosing on her farm. Your characters go through this arc—confusion and fear, acceptance and personal growth."

"I feel sympathy with these characters because of my own personal travails. I don't have the temperament to write or direct a cold and chilly thriller. In fact, I don't think I was the right person to do *Billy Bathgate* (1991). I loved some scenes and the performances of Nicole Kidman and Steven Hill, but I'm not the right person for that type of story."

"Why do movies have the power to affect us so profoundly?"

"I don't make movies to teach. I make movies to describe. I don't know what there is to take away from them. I'm interested in the people. I want to know what happens to them, and I just want to spend some time with them. You go to movies to lose yourself. Movies are not like literature. They stem from our oral culture. When I was a young boy in Waxahachie, families would get together for dinners on summer evenings. After eating, the women would go inside, do the dishes, and gossip. The men would stay outside, smoke, and tell stories. One story was told over and over again. A stranger came to town, rented a room, and was found dead the next morning. So they put this man in the back of a wagon and took him to my grandfather's furniture store. In those days furniture makers also built coffins. Then they put him in a coffin and propped him up in the window of the furniture store. There was so little to do in the town, people lined up around the block to get a glimpse of the dead stranger. This wonderful story has always remained with me. The oral storytelling tradition I grew up with is gone now. Instead, we've become a visual culture where stories are told on a screen. But there will always be storytelling in one form or another."

"What would you do if you had to stop directing?"

"I'd write screenplays or produce. If I couldn't do that I'd teach. If I couldn't do that, I'd take photographs or draw. My life has been about making things. To make something is to be given a huge gift. There is great joy in making art. If you do it long enough, sooner or later you'll make something really good. In those great moments I feel something in me come alive. Oh . . . oh . . . what a feeling!"

Paul Mazursky

The director of such popular Hollywood films as Bob & Carol & Ted & Alice *(1969),* Harry and Tonto *(1974),* An Unmarried Woman *(1978),* Down and Out in Beverly Hills *(1986) had me laughing so hard during our photo session I could hardly operate my camera. A born comedian, Paul Mazursky regaled me with some of his favorite jokes and Marlon Brando impersonations. Just an hour earlier Mazursky had been stone serious as he answered my questions about his career and the future.*

"In *Harry and Tonto*, Art Carney's character, Harry Combs, calls his son from a roadside phone booth and tells him, 'Life is confusing. We're just trying to get on with it.' Those words seem to echo a recurring theme in many of your films—the idea that we as human beings are all trying to make sense out of our lives. Is your intent to tell universal stories?"

"I never start out saying, 'I'm going to tell universal stories.' I just see things and say, 'That's a movie!' A good example is when one of my wife's friends, Carolyn, came over after her divorce was final. She was elated because she had with her a document that showed she had purchased a home in her own name. On the document next to her name was written 'An Unmarried Woman.' Out of that I saw a movie. I made up a story about a woman named Erica Benton whose husband leaves her for a salesgirl he meets while buying a shirt at Bloomingdale's. Erica starts a new life and discovers her independence. The idea behind every one of my films has come from a different source. When I wrote *Bob & Carol & Ted & Alice*, for example, I got the idea from a *Time* magazine article about the Gestalt therapist Fritz Perls, who at the time was conducting workshops at the Esalen Institute up in Big Sur, California. He was pictured sitting in a hot tub with four or five other people, all of them naked. So I said to my wife Betsy, 'Let's go up there. Maybe there's a movie in it.' We drove up and spent forty-eight hours in an emotional marathon. Betsy started crying, and out of that I wrote the first pages of the script. Natalie Wood and Robert Culp would play that scene in the movie. I showed what I had written to my writing partner at that time, Larry Tucker, and together we wrote the rest of the film based on my fantasies about marriage. There was very little conscious thought that about

telling a universal story. All I'm hoping for in any film I do is that people will *get it* and be entertained."

"People did get *Bob & Carol & Ted & Alice*, and it put you on the map as a screenwriter and director."

"After *Bob & Carol*, Larry and I felt we could do anything. But we became blocked. We didn't know what to do next. So we decided to imitate the Fellini's film *8½* (1963). Ours is about an American movie director who is so blocked that he dreams in the style of other directors. I based the character in great part on myself. He had a wife and two kids like I did. He took LSD like I did. We called it *Alex in Wonderland* (1970) and cast Donald Sutherland and Ellen Burstyn in the lead roles. It was a flop, so when I wanted to make *Harry and Tonto*, a story about a retired New Yorker who goes on a cross-country road trip with his cat, no one would back it. Depressed, I retreated to my office and in six weeks wrote *Blume in Love* (1973). I didn't know that I could write my own scripts, but it turned out that I could. It just flew out of me. I got the idea for that film after I heard the story of a very famous movie star who kicked her husband out after she caught him in bed with his secretary. He was desperately in love with his wife, but because of that one mistake she would not forgive him. In my story she does. I gave the script to my agent and he showed it to John Calley, one of the big shots at Warner Brothers. Calley read it in my agent's office and said immediately, 'It's a deal!' *Blume in Love* starred George Segal and Susan Anspach. It was a big hit and that enabled me to make *Harry and Tonto*."

"What most compelled you to become a director?"

"It was ambition. I wanted to be successful. I never thought about the artistic side of things. I started out as an actor then moved to writing and then to directing, always desperate to have the next thing."

"How did you get your start as an actor?"

"I read for Stanley Kubrick, and he hired me to be in his first movie, *Fear and Desire* (1953). Kubrick had never made a movie before and knew nothing about acting. But for me, getting hired to be in his film was validation: *Maybe I do have something.* So I decided to pursue an acting career and changed my name from Irwin to Paul. A couple years later, I got a role in *Blackboard Jungle* (1955), playing one of the juvenile delinquents, opposite Sidney Poitier and Vic Morrow. But then the acting jobs stopped coming, so I partnered up in a comedy act with Herb Hartig, a friend from my Brooklyn College days. We called ourselves 'Igor and h' and performed in nightclubs and hotels around the country. It was an alternative to being offered crappy acting parts, but I found the comedian's life rough. Audiences screamed insults at me, and I, lacking a clever retort, would yell back, 'Fuck you!'

"In 1959, I decided to move out to California with my family. I got parts in a couple of plays and directed one. In the span of a couple of years, I went from being a mostly out-of-work actor to a hot comedy writer for Danny Kaye's television variety show with my buddy Larry Tucker. When the *Danny Kaye Show* entered its final season in 1966, Larry and I decided it was time to do something on our own. We rented an office on the Sunset Strip and in about two months wrote *I Love You, Alice B. Toklas* (1968) about a middle-class Jewish lawyer named Harold Fine who runs out on his own wedding and becomes a hippie. I had my heart set on directing it. We were trying to raise money for the film when one of my agents asked, 'Would you mind if we gave it to Peter Sellers to read?' I said, 'Great!' The next day I get a call: 'Sellers read it, wants to do it, I can make a deal tomorrow.' 'But I direct,' I told him. 'Hold off on that,' he said. Sellers wanted Federico Fellini or Ingmar Bergman to direct. But they weren't interested, so it came to me. But then Peter Sellers accused me of sleeping with his wife, Britt Ekland, which I hadn't. I was out as the film's director. So it wasn't until 1969 with *Bob & Carol & Ted & Alice* that I directed my first film."

"What about the actor within you? Didn't you want to play Harold Fine?"

"The actor within me was frustrated. I could have played Harold Fine in a minute, but there's no way we would have gotten the money to make the film. We needed a star, and Sellers, who had done *Dr. Strangelove* a few years earlier and was on top."

"*Next Stop, Greenwich Village* (1976) was based on your own life, wasn't it?"

"Yes, it's my most personal film. I exposed something very raw. I get very emotional every time I see it. I wrote it after my parents had died. I had a terrible relationship with my mother, Jean Mazursky. Shelly Winters gave an accurate portrayal of my mother, even though she'd never met her. She brings to life a lower-middle-class woman who says to her son as he's leaving to make his first Hollywood film, 'If you ever meet Clark Gable tell him your mother loves him.' It's a great line and my mother really said that. The tragedy of my mother's life was that she was probably bipolar and could have been helped with pharmaceuticals. She would go through black depressions and severe mood changes. It was because of her that I grew up with a very rich fantasy life. She let me cut school to go with her to see double features starring actors like Clark Gable,

Humphrey Bogart, Marlene Dietrich, the Marx Brothers, and Edward G. Robinson. And, we'd see the great foreign films like *Grand Illusion* (1937) and *Children of Paradise* (1945). She took me to the Metropolitan Opera House and to Harlem's Apollo Theater to see the great black performers like Billie Holiday, Billy Eckstine, Count Basie, and Cab Calloway. Imagine. I experienced all that as a kid. That's what made me an artist, if you want to call it that."

"I read that you based one of the characters in *Alex in Wonderland* on your mother."

"That's right. When the film came out, my mother was furious with me: 'How dare you portray me like this? At least you could have gotten a great actress like Betty Davis to play me.' She threatened to picket the theater. My therapist asked me, 'Why are you always putting down your mother? You're happily married. Your mother must have given you real love. You're exaggerating.' So I said, 'Maybe you're right. Would you like to meet her?' 'Yes,' he said. So I had her come in for a session with him. When I came to pick her up, the door opened and the doctor was there, white-faced and shaking. When I saw him next, he said to me, 'Paul, you're a miracle! You're a walking miracle. You've proven that all our theories are wrong.'"

"You cast your films brilliantly. In *Next Stop, Greenwich Village* Shelley Winters as Faye Lipinsky and Lenny Baker as Larry Lipinsky were amazing. Jill Clayburgh received an Oscar nomination for her role in *Unmarried Woman*, and Art Carney won best actor in a leading role for *Harry and Tonto*. How do you know when someone is right for a part?"

"If I write the part, I know what I want even if I can't verbalize it. If I didn't write it, I really have to talk to the writer and ask, 'What did you mean with this character?' Shelley Winters should have gotten the Oscar, at the very least been nominated. She gave a devastating performance. But sadly, they rarely give Oscars for comedic roles. I had a very hard time casting the Larry Lipinsky part. I auditioned just about every actor in L.A. and New York, but no one seemed right to me because I kept seeing myself as a young man. Finally, this young theater actor, Lenny Baker, came in, and I knew he was right. Sadly, he died a couple years later.

"I have great respect for actors. They're naked on the screen and because of that I excuse their egos and paranoia, their demands and excuses—not all, but much of it. Most directors or casting agents see parts based on the actors they're familiar with, not on real people: *I'm looking for a Leonardo DiCaprio type. I'm looking for a Marcia Gay Harden type.* They're talking about actors, not characters. I think the character will appear more real if the person chosen is not like a particular actor or actor type."

"Who would you say most influenced your way of storytelling?"

"Federico Fellini. When I first saw his *I Vitelloni* (1953) and *Nights of Cabiria* (1957), I admired his ability to mix humor with tragedy and irony with pathos. Just as the person is falling on the banana peel and you're starting to laugh, something touches your heart. I tried to do the same thing with my films, although they are completely different from his. Fellini became a good friend of mine after I sought him out to appear in my movie *Alex in Wonderland*, which he did. He later told me that he considered me like a younger brother. I can't make light of it. It meant an awful lot to me. When we would get together, we didn't talk about movies and directing. We talked about women, magic, and our love for cheese. Fellini was so human, accessible, and funny. I've also been influenced by Vittorio De Sica, Preston Sturges, Billy Wilder, Stanley Kubrick, Orson Welles, Bernardo Bertolucci, François Truffaut, Ingmar Bergman, Akira Kurosawa, John Ford, Charlie Chaplin and Buster Keaton."

"Your films often deal with personal crises—divorce, aging, infidelity, sexuality . . . and many have become part of the cultural conversation: *Bob & Carol & Ted & Alice* on partner-swapping, *An Unmarried Women* on divorced women. Was it your intention to get people talking?"

"I don't set out to get people talking. I see something and think, *Oh, this could make a good movie.* I've made a lot of movies about marriage. It must be an obsession of mine. Betsy and I have been married fifty-eight years. I've written a number of stories about the middle class and the lower middle class and their struggles. But I've also written stories about the nouveau riche—like *Down and Out in Beverly Hills*—making fun of the characters and of myself, because I'm nouveau riche now. I am Dave Whiteman, the Richard Dreyfuss character in the film. Often when you're writing, you don't realize that you're writing about yourself to some degree. I got the idea for *Down and Out in Beverly Hills* while taking out the trash in the alley behind my Beverly Hills home. I saw this bum pushing a shopping cart with a dog and remembered Jean Renoir's *Boudu sauvé des eaux* (1932), a film I had seen at the age of about twenty. Years ago vagabonds were romanticized. They dropped out because they had had enough of society. In the film the vagabond named Boudu goes to a Paris bridge to kill himself. A shopkeeper saves him and brings him to his home, where the vagabond turns everyone's life upside down. The Renoir movie ends with the vagabond, disgusted with bourgeois life, returning to the streets. I decided to do a modern version of it in Beverly Hills with a homeless person played by Nick Nolte. Nolte's character, Jerry Baskin, tries to take his own life by throwing himself into the private swimming pool of someone's Beverly Hills home. He is saved by the homeowner, a wealthy clothes-hanger manufacturer played by Richard Dreyfuss. Baskin ends up seducing everyone in the family and decides to leave with Dreyfuss's daughter and go back out on the streets.

"I wanted to end the film with him changing his mind and going back into the house. He's had a taste of the good life and really doesn't want to go back to eating out of garbage cans. My producer on that film wanted Baskin to go back onto the streets with the girl. I said, 'I can't do that.' I couldn't end my story like Renoir did because the homeless today are not heroic figures, but tragic ones. I moved the picture to another studio so that I could maintain the integrity of the story as it had been written. I can be flexible about a million things, but not about what I write."

"You are a real artist."

"I find it pretentious to call myself an artist. I love art, and I know I have artistic tendencies, but what does it mean to be an artist? While Michelangelo was lying on his back painting the Sistine Chapel, he wasn't thinking to himself, *I'm being an artist*. He was probably thinking, *My back hurts!*"

"What has success meant to you?"

"It certainly satisfied my ego. I met great, great human beings, traveled the world to make movies, enjoyed nice homes and had the luxury of making enough from *Bob & Carol* at the beginning that I never again worried about money. I never did anything especially for money, and so I made a lot of money. It's a paradox. But the truth is that the more successful I got, the more nervous I got that I'd be able to come up with another movie. I'm still always asking about what am I going to do next."

"What have you learned about life from telling all those human stories?"

"You've got to live life one day at a time and in the moment. Don't speculate too much about the past or worry too much about the future. Love is the best thing you can have in your life—love of family and what you do. Value your health and try to enjoy every day. Know that whatever your troubles might be, you're better off than lots of other people. All the rest is bullshit."

Reginald Hudlin

Reginald Hudlin rose to prominence when his first feature film, House Party *(1990), which was based on his Harvard University student film, appealed to a broad segment of America's youth and won big at the box office. He has directed and produced a number of films—including* Boomerang *(1992), starring Eddie Murphy, and* The Great White Hype *(1996), with Samuel L. Jackson—and several popular television series.* Django Unchained *(2012), directed by Quentin Tarantino and produced by Hudlin and others, was a runaway hit. I met with the filmmaker at a Beverly Hills restaurant where he told me his thoughts on the power of cinematic storytelling.*

"When did you first feel the desire to tell stories?"

"As far back as I can remember I've had this primal impulse to make up and act out stories. I am the youngest of three sons and so our house was filled with toys—all kinds of blocks, vehicles, and different kinds of army men and action figures. And so I was constantly creating elaborate stories complete with action sequences and dialogue between the good guys and the bad guys. I always had some narrative going on in my head. And so when my friends came over and wanted to play I'd say, 'How can we play together? You don't even know the story. How can you be a part of this?'"

"So storytelling in the movie industry was a natural career choice?"

"Yes. Filmmaking was a way for me to tell my very personal stories, and I thought if I told them well, the world would connect with them. I also always loved art and understood that cinema embodies most of the other art forms—dance, theater, literature, music, and architecture. And from a practical perspective, it paid the best and lasted the longest."

"How did you first learn the director's craft?"

"I don't know if directing can really be taught, but one experience in my senior year at Harvard Film School stands out. I was checking out some camera gear from the department's equipment rental office, and when I picked up the heavy case with camera and lights, the guy checking me out called to me and said, 'You'd better look inside to see if you have a light meter.' I looked in the box and there was no meter. At that moment

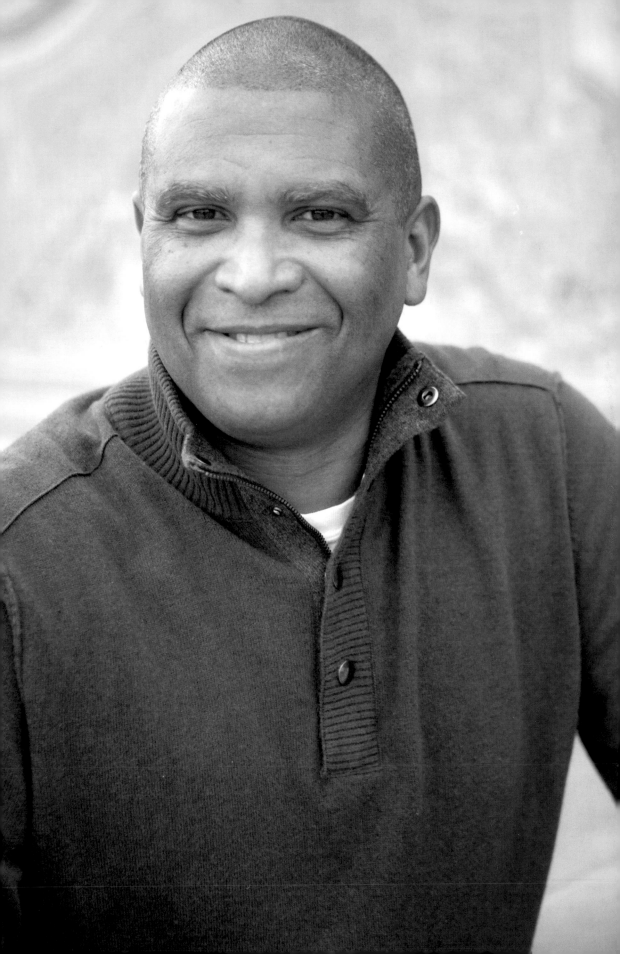

I had this incredible moment of clarity: *If I was not organized enough to check for a light meter, then I was going to be an abject failure. I had spent four years studying film and had wasted my parents' money. I should have picked another major. What was I going to do with the rest of my life?* But now it was too late to change my major, so I finished making the movie even though I felt like a complete incompetent."

"All that from just forgetting your light meter?"

"Yes. What it meant was, *You're not on it.* There are a million little details that could be the end of you as a filmmaker. It is right to take it very seriously because you can shoot a movie and [if] the lamp is wrong, it can ruin the scene. You have to be incredibly detailed and you have to question everything all the time. You have to know what's going on in every frame, every line reading, and know if there are better ways to do [those things]."

"How did you get past that feeling that you would be a failure as a filmmaker?"

"I learned an important lesson from that experience: even if you screw up, things can work out. When I made my first movie, I realized very quickly that all the years leading up to it were preparation. All those years of being broke and sitting around with my artist friends debating some minute aesthetic topic for hours had not been a waste of time. When you're on the floor making a movie, you have to make split-second decisions and you don't have the time to think them through. Your instrument has to be so fine-tuned that you're making decisions practically subconsciously. You have to trust your gut. All that early thinking about it goes into the gut, and you either have a well-tuned gut or you don't."

"Who were some of the filmmakers that most influenced you?"

"I've always had a very broad appetite with regard to movies. I loved the films of Howard Hawks, Woody Allen, and Akira Kurosawa. And I was influenced by the best of the black exploitation films that captured the language, style, and music of what was happening all over America in the 1970s: *Shaft* (1971), *Super Fly* (1972), *Foxy Brown* (1974), *Bingo Long Traveling All-Stars & Motor Kings* (1976). They were incredibly entertaining films but weren't inside mainstream cinema. But probably the most singular primary influence came to me not from a filmmaker but from a musician. It was George Clinton and his funk/soul/rock collective Parliament-Funkadelic. He continues to be my most inspirational artistic influence, and my goal is to make films like he makes records. He makes music that is incredibly playful, but if you examine it lyrically and musically, it's very profound and it has political and cosmological implications. It works no matter how you choose to engage with it. And that holographic accessibility was very inspiring to me. His music reflected black intellectualism, but it wasn't somber or self-important. In fact, it was the opposite. He was like the fool on the hill, the Zen master saying, 'I'm just kidding,' but he was totally not kidding. He delivers profound messages in a brightly colored package."

"How is that reflected in a Reggie Hudlin Film?"

"I think my films are probably a mix of humor and politics. Generally, I have an optimistic view of life. I like people and I like making people happy, and that mood is pretty consistent throughout my work. I never forget the audience. People work hard, and when you take forty bucks or whatever it is to see some entertainment, you'd better deliver at least sixty dollars' worth of entertainment in return. I always have this image of a taxi-cab meter running in the theater and feel like forty-five minutes into the film you should get your money back and the last half should be cash back. Like, 'I got my money back plus some!' That's the covenant I keep as an artist."

"*House Party* really launched your filmmaking career. This film was a huge success that resonated with young people regardless of race or ethnicity. What inspired this story, and how did it come together for you."

"I was blown away by *American Graffiti* (1973), *Animal House* (1978), and *Risky Business* (1983). I thought, *Why can't I make movies like those?* The exploitative films about hip hop in Los Angeles and New York being made at the time were just terrible. I thought, *I don't want to make movies about any of that. I want to make a movie for the rest of America—middle America. I want to tell their story. Their story isn't about being cool or tough. It's about being a kid and the vulnerabilities that come from that.*"

"Was it your intention with *House Party* to deliver some moral behavior messages for young people, particularly with regard to sex? In the car when the main characters Kid and Play, rappers Christopher Reid and Robin Harris, are driving home at the end of the night, Play chastises Kid for not having had sex with Sidney just because he didn't have a condom. Play tells him, 'That's the girl's problem if she gets pregnant.'"

"I thought it would be an important film about unprotected sex because it was just at the time when HIV was breaking nationally. I wanted the movie to be so much fun that kids do not perceive the message to use a condom, which comes two-thirds into the film, as preachy. I hate cod-liver-oil movies. I didn't know its real impact until I was given an award from a health organization in New Jersey. At the awards ceremony the presenter, a doctor, told me that young people were referencing *House*

Party as the reason they were using condoms when having sex. That was a huge day for me. It's gratifying to hear from a guy on the front lines that the arrow you shot in the air actually hit its target."

"How did you come up with the story for *House Party*?"

"The summer before my senior year at Harvard, I was working on a movie script for my senior thesis. As I was packing up to go back to school, the Luther Vandross song *Bad Boy Having a Party* came on the radio. I had this habit at the time of creating music videos in my head, so I started working through the visual of that song in my mind. It was then that I realized that it would make a great movie. I ended up writing the script for *House Party* that night, abandoning the screenplay I had been working on all summer. *Bad Boy Having a Party* was the first song you hear in the film."

"Is cinematic storytelling for you a way of serving society and having an impact on our culture?"

"Yes. My parents were hard-working people and huge on education, both having received degrees in higher education. They spent a lot of time dedicated to social causes. Doing that was assumed [to be] normal behavior when I was growing up. In my view, movies must have utility if they're going to be successful entertainment that also offers something of substance. People want protein in their diet. I try not to exaggerate my ability to change the world. With all the great love songs out there, we still have a fifty percent divorce rate. If Stevie Wonder can't keep you together, if Al Green can't do it, then who knows if there is hope for change. So yes, I think I can make a difference, but I have to keep it in perspective."

"How do you avoid stereotypes in capturing the zeitgeist of the culture?"

"I make art and not propaganda. You have to be ruthlessly honest. I remember reading a review of Richard Wright's book *Native Son*. The critic called it a great novel but faulted the author for having created a world in which he did not exist. That was a powerful critique. I think when you are honest about the world, as honest as you can be, you paint a picture that most people can relate to. When you twist and manipulate truth for the sake of propaganda, your effort is futile. The black community doesn't need propaganda, good PR, because that's not their problem. The assumption is, 'Oh, if they understood us they wouldn't treat us this way.' Black people are treated the way they are for economic reasons. So propaganda in films is not the cure for the problem. If, on the other hand, you create a great piece of art, it will touch more people, it will be more resonant, and it will change more people both inside and outside the black community. Too often 'black films' are judged on the basis of two criteria: propaganda and profit. How much did it cost, and did it make money? Is that a good look for black people or is that a bad look for black people? Unfortunately, artistic merit is not in the equation, but it is the essential factor in the best movies."

"Is there such a thing as 'black films,' 'white films,' 'Asian films,' etc.?"

"No, but I think there are specific audiences. Michael Bay makes his movies for a very specific audience. Woody Allen makes his movies for a very different audience. I think it's a mistake to label films, like saying, 'Oh, this is for young people. Oh, this is for old people or blacks or whites. I'm sure Woody Allen wasn't thinking of me as his target audience, but I love his films. So those labels are too crude to describe movies."

"I think it's accurate however to label your films comedies. Why are your films usually comedies?"

"Maybe it's because I come from a small, very poor, very corrupt town, and so I developed a kind of black humor—and I mean that in both senses of the word—along with a sense for the absurd. Things were just so messed up when I was growing up. All you could do was laugh to keep yourself from crying. That was my family's attitude toward life. They never stopped fighting to make a difference, but took life with a sense of humor. I think humor always wins. Of the two great films *Dr. Strangelove* and *Fail Safe*, which do you remember better? Both came out in 1964, were about the same subject matter, and were both great films."

"*Dr. Strangelove.*"

"That's right. It's the one that's more resonant over time. Why? Because, of its humor. If you can pull if off, humor almost always wins."

"Your films *The Ladies Man* (2000) and *Boomerang* were hilarious comedies but contained real moments of sentimentality about romantic love. What's the most immediate way for a movie to touch an audience?"

"First I want people to *feel*; thinking will come later. If they're not feeling, they're not going to be thinking. You have to hit them at their core—their emotions. If you feel something, then I probably have your attention, and if I have your attention, then I can tell my story. And once I can do that, then I have a chance to do all my little arty tricks. But it starts with feeling."

"How do you get them to feel?"

"You start with a dilemma that makes people care about the characters. Years ago I went to see Woody Allen's *Husbands and Wives* (1992) with my good friend Chris Rock and that film literally ripped our heads off because we identified with every character. One of the couples is getting divorced, and it reverberates throughout the other couple's lives. We identified with and cared about all the couples and we never stopped caring."

"There's the power of the medium!"

"Yes, it's an extraordinary medium. I always think of the famous line by Woodrow Wilson at the White House screening of *Birth of a Nation* (1915). He said, 'This is history written in lightning.' That's an incredibly powerful lie. It was not history. It was in fact propaganda, a distorted view of the South after the Civil War glorifying the Ku Klux Klan. Wilson did have the 'lightning' part right. To see something come to life on a screen is very exciting, but representing historic events inaccurately is a problem. The truth is that a lot of people get their history from movies. If in the public mind movies serve as the conduits of what happened in the past, that's pretty powerful. It's also terrifying to think of movies as the primary source of people's knowledge of history. Movies are actually stories set in historical periods."

"Do you worry much about what other people or critics think about your films?"

"You can't live for other people or spend time worrying about what they might think. Fear is a great manipulator, right? And this is very much a fear-based business. You have people who try to manage you with threats, implied or otherwise, about what you need to do. And there is the element of vanity at play—what you need to do to look cool. The way I see it, you have two choices. You can eternally be on a quest for the coolness you lacked in junior high, or you can say, 'I don't care.' My not caring, it got me here, and I will continue not to care. That's been my approach to life."

"If there is one central theme that runs through your films what would that be?"

"It's all about love. Love early on immunizes you as much as breast milk does. Love is more important than money. I think everything comes down to whether or not one was loved as a child. One of my favorite scenes in *House Party* is when Kid's father comes home late and falls asleep in the bed still dressed. Kid unlaces his boots and takes them off. It's the unrequited gesture that says what their relationship is all about. I'm always thinking about humanity, and the essence of humanity is love. Love is always at the heart of it."

KINGS ROW 1942
NOW, VOYAGER 1942
YANKEE DOODLE DANDY 194
CASABLANCA 194
PRINCESS O'ROURKE 19
MILDRED PIERCE 1945
A STREETCAR NAMED DESIRE 1951
HOUSE OF WAX 1953
A STAR IS BORN
THE F.B.I. STORY
ROBIN AND THE SEVEN HOOD
HARPER
SEARCH
HARRY O
WONDER WOMAN
ROOTS
ROOTS: THE NEXT G
THE THORN BIRDS
THE WEST WING
GILMORE GIRLS

JAGGED EDGE 1985
ART II 1986
1987
1987
1988
CKS 1988
1988
ION 1989

James Burrows

Seeing the words "directed by James Burrows" on your TV screen usually means "get ready to laugh!" After forty years as one of television's most respected producer-directors, James Burrows shows no sign of slowing down. His smart, hip, quick-witted sitcoms have dominated prime time since the mid-1970s, with shows like The Mary Tyler Moore Show *(1970–1977),* The Bob Newhart Show *(1972–1978),* Laverne and Shirley *(1976–1983), and* Taxi *(1978–1983). In the 1980s and 1990s, he brought us* Cheers *(1982–1993),* Fraiser *(1993–2004),* Will and Grace *(1998–2006), and* Friends *(1994–2004). I sat down with Burrows at his Warner Brothers studio office, where he was about to begin rehearsals on his latest sitcom,* Partners. *In front of my camera he demonstrated his instinctive wit by making a gag out of our photo shoot.*

"How did you get started in the entertainment business and who most influenced you?"

"I came to Hollywood in 1974 at the invitation of Grant Tinker. I knew him and his former wife Mary Tyler Moore from an ill-fated musical that my father, Abe Burrows, had written based on *Breakfast at Tiffany*'s character Holly Golightly. I was the show's second assistant stage manager. Mary was its star, but it was a miserable failure. Later when I was working in summer stock and dinner theater, I saw *The Mary Tyler Moore Show* on television and wrote Mary a letter. She and Grant brought me out here to work on their show with its director, Jay Sandrich. He was my real mentor. I watched how he worked with the writers, dealt with the actors, and how he empowered them. *The Mary Tyler Moore Show* had been on the air for four or five years before I arrived. Jay taught me to play by the house rules, but also how to subtly slip in my own ideas. He would teach me a lot of things, but not how to be funny. One can't teach you how to be funny."

"How do you become funny?"

"You're born that way. My father was funny, and I was like him. Had he been a tailor, I would have known how to make a suit. I like to tell the story about the day my stepmother came home with a new tennis racket made in Italy. By the time I drew a breath to say 'strung with spaghetti,' my father had already said it. I inherited a lot of his humor. He was a successful playwright and director with many credits to his name, among them *Guys and Dolls* (1955), *Silk Stockings* (1957), *Can-Can* (1960), *How to Succeed in Business without Really Trying* (1967), and *Cactus Flower* (1969)."

"Sounds like you were destined for this sort of work?"

"The truth is that I never had the drive or the creative impulse people need to succeed in the entertainment business. I didn't have to knock on a lot of doors. I just had an in. When I graduated from Oberlin College in 1962, my father got me into Yale School of Drama as a playwright, even though I had never written before. After I graduated, I started working in the theater. Stage managing and directing are the only things I've ever done. I have no other skills. When I wrote that letter to Mary Tyler Moore, I knew that I was ready for directing. After directing my first episode of her show, the offer to direct other shows started flooding in. And it's sort of been like that ever since."

"Today you're like the Hal Prince of television sitcoms. You've directed more pilots and created more hit shows than probably anyone in television. To what do you attribute your ability to spot good material and turn it into a successful television show?"

"I look for scripts that have a certain sense of humanity in them. And the most important thing to me is that they are well written. I also like to create shows with unknown actors. An audience that is unfamiliar with an actor has no preconceived idea as to whether that actor is funny or not. Humor is ninety percent surprise. So if you cast a famous actor like Bill Cosby, you know he's going to be funny, and you lose a bit of the surprise. I believe that if you cast great, you can only get better than great. If you cast mediocre, you can only get to good. So I try to always cast great actors. Those are the things that define my work."

"How important is a show's premise for success?"

"I'm not a high-concept kind of guy, so premise doesn't matter. Virtually all of my shows are about people. *Cheers* is about people in a bar in Boston. *Friends* is about six people sitting around a coffeehouse. *Night Court* (1984–1992) is about a judge and his urban night court. *Fraiser* is about a guy who lives with his father and works as a radio psychiatrist. I go for low-concept shows that focus on a group of people who are empathetic toward each other. My shows are not issue-oriented and do not take a political stand. I never proselytize. I'm the opposite of Norman Lear, who is very political and opinionated. I'm a big fan of his, but I don't think that way. *Will and Grace* is my only show that may be perceived as having made a social statement by making audiences feel okay about gay people, but we never set out to do that. It just happened."

"So how do you hook viewers?"

"I do not cater to any particular demographic or ethnic group. I'm after people who want to laugh. That's it! The actors on my shows will walk the comic plank for me. That means that they're willing to take creative risks, go to the edge just before it drops off and becomes ludicrous. When comedy goes overboard we say, 'The show jumped the shark.' That's a phrase that has become a part of television lingo. It's based on an episode of *Happy Days* when Fonzie goes too far. He *jumped the shark*. It typically means that the show has taken a turn for the worse. I can get people to walk the comic plank and do things that they ordinarily would be afraid to do. The director is a manipulator. His job is to get an actor or writer to do what he wants without overtly coming out saying, 'What you just did was shit.' A lot of directors say to their actors, 'You have to do it my way. It's the only way.' I don't do that. I'm a guy who manipulates."

"You're known for having great ensemble casts. How do you blend talent so well?"

"I have the ability to gel a cast, and I think that's why I get hired so often. I do it by infusing my cast members with love for one another. I tell them, 'If you bring the love you feel for each other into the work, it will come across on the screen.' What the audience sees is real love and friendship among the actors, who don't need to act out of fear or ego. That's really at the core of what I do."

"Does a television director maintain complete control of the show's vision, as in the case of feature films?"

"What I do is different from the movies. It's not a singular vision, but one of four or five different people. I may have an idea that the writers don't agree with, and I'll push for it, but I'm not a traffic cop. I function more like a theater director. Every week I direct a twenty-five minute play in front of an audience. We record it every Thursday night, and every Thursday night is its opening night. The difference between seeing a show in a theater and what we do is that the audience hears me say 'action!' and 'cut!' Sometimes, if an actor screws up a line just before a joke, I have to intervene. I'll back it up because you're going to get the best reaction to a joke when you hear it for the first time. And with comedy you've got to protect the joke."

"If sitcoms are filmed before a live audience, why do they use a laugh track?"

"The only time we use a laugh track is if we need to make an edit—

like if you're cutting out lines in a scene and there's a joke, you have to bridge that gap from where you cut to where you come back in the show. There's not a lot of canned laughter in my shows. I know people like to accuse sitcoms of using canned laughter, but what you're hearing is genuine laughter."

"The situation comedy has been a staple of television broadcasting since its inception, but its popularity tends to go up and down. Why?"

"The television sitcom has actually been dying for decades, but it never does; it just keeps bouncing back. You can't kill it because comedy always works. We all have to laugh. Comedy is necessary for people who don't appreciate their own lives, but for those who do, comedy makes them even happier. Comedy is important during the good times, when we want to celebrate our prosperity, and in depressed times to help us get us out of our misery."

"How is entertainment generally beneficial?"

"It takes us out of our reality and offers us relief. I remember when I was living in New York City and eager to see my girlfriend, who was coming in from college to spend time with me. I was on my way to meet her when I saw her walking down the street with another guy. I was devastated. I saw my life flash before my eyes. That night I went to see the play *A Thousand Clowns*, and it really helped get me out of my funk. That's my definition of entertainment."

"Do sitcoms accurately mirror real-life concerns and behaviors, or are they idealized versions of reality?"

"Every story you see on a show is a derivative of stories that have come before. As far as dramatic or comedic plots go, there are only so many stories you can tell. All we're doing in television is plugging new characters into old stories and telling them from that perspective. Our stories are about real human emotions — sadness, happiness, embarrassment, disappointment, sympathy, loss, joy. You felt sad when Coach died in *Cheers*. In *Mike and Molly* (2010–) you felt happy when they got married. Audiences can relate to real life experiences and corresponding human emotions."

"How do you explain the success of reality television shows over sitcoms?"

"Hollywood is based on shadenfreude, which means enjoyment at the ill-fortune of others. Reality shows show real people tripping over bicycles and falling down, getting hit over the head with an inflatable hammer, or being humiliated. These shows are popular because viewers sitting at home think, *Wow, we're not as pathetic as them. We don't do stupid things like that*. I think they would rather see a real person on a reality show have that happen to them than a fictional character trip and get hurt. When a fictional character falls down, you laugh not from shadenfreude, but because it's funny."

"Many of today's network shows come with warnings—'coarse language,' 'highly suggestive,' 'explicit sexual references.' We've come along way since *I Love Lucy* (1951–1957), when words like *pregnant* were not allowed to be spoken on television."

"Yes, that's true. On the *Mary Tyler Moore Show*, Mary Richards could not be divorced, so she had to break up with her boyfriend. Television today pushes the envelope to see what it can get away with. The one thing I like about network over cable television is that we have to use euphemisms. The greatest euphemistic show was *Will and Grace*. The names we had to come up for the human anatomy or the act of sexual intercourse made it more interesting and funnier. I remember an episode when Karen once called the female organ a 'kagina.' But I predict that pretty soon there will be curse words on network television."

"Who can ever forget the great characters that populate your shows: *Taxi*'s Alex Rieger, Louie de Palma, and Latka Gravas; *Cheers*'s Sam Malone and Diane Chambers; *Fraiser*'s Fraiser and Niles Crane; *Friends*'s Rachel, Monica, Phoebe, Chandler, Joey, and Ross. They're like family to viewers, part of our popular culture and collective memory. We've developed emotional attachments to them."

"I wish I could take all the credit for that. So much of it has to do with the writing. I am very good at protecting a writer's vision, contributing to the stories and casting, but there's a lot of luck involved. You have to be able to get on a good network and cast the right actors in a slot where they don't have to prove themselves right away. It takes time for your characters to take hold with viewers. When you're making a new show, you don't have any history or track record to rely on. I always try to pick scripts with characters that have real human attributes and then cast actors who will embody those attributes. We really hit it right with *Cheers* and *Fraiser*, which were each on the air for eleven years. *Friends* lasted ten and *Taxi* five. Viewers identified with the characters, and the shows entertained them. But the underlying reason that these shows you mentioned stood the test of time is that they were funny, really funny. And that's a tribute to the writers."

"How do you contribute *your funny* to the writer's stories?"

"When I first read a script, I don't have many ideas. It's when I combine the actors with the writer's words and get it up on its feet that ideas come to me. I'll understand when some physical comedy or a gag is needed; it'll just come to me. Sometimes I overdo it and sometimes we crash and burn, but my experience is that often you have to fail in order to succeed. I once did a show called *Free Country* (1978) starring Rob Reiner, about Jewish immigrants on the Lower East Side. There was a scene where Rob's wife was afraid to go out of the apartment. Several times she tried to muster up the courage to step out the front door, but turned back. It occurred to me that I needed something funny right there, so I said to her, 'Steel yourself on that chair, and as you try to go out the door, take the chair with you.' She did it and it got a big laugh. When the producers saw that bit, they called Rob and asked, 'Who thought of that with the chair?' It was that gag that led to my being hired to direct *Taxi*."

"Why haven't you made the big move to features?"

"I tried it and didn't like the experience. I directed a film called *Partners* in 1981 and hated having to shoot the same scenes multiple times with different angles, and then do close-ups. Coming from television, I was content when I got the shot the first time. The shooting schedule lasted forty days, and I couldn't wrap my head around it."

"How do you view your future?"

"I love what I do in television. I don't want to ever lose that in my life. I feel that it keeps me mentally sharp and makes me feel thirty years younger. I'm clearly ten to fifteen years older than everyone in the sitcom world, but I'm still being offered to direct every pilot. They all still want me for their shows, and that's very gratifying. When you do a sitcom and people laugh at it, it gives you *naches* [pride]. The adulation is important to me. It's good for every human being to feel appreciated."

Jay Sandrich

In a career that spans more than fifty years, Jay Sandrich has left an indelible mark on television comedy with classics such as Get Smart *(1965–1970),* The Mary Tyler Moore Show *(1970–1977),* Soap *(1977–1981),* The Cosby Show *(1984–1992),* The Golden Girls *(1985–1992), and dozens of others. I met with the veteran director at his Marina del Rey home, where he shared with me how he rose from second assistant director on* I Love Lucy *to director of America's most-watched sitcoms.*

"Your father, Mark Sandrich, was a very successful movie director known for some of Hollywood's most popular musicals starring Fred Astaire and Ginger Rogers. Did he influence your work as a director?"

"I was thirteen when my father died, and I remember very little about his professional work. The only memory I have is when he took me with him one day to the set of *Holiday Inn* (1941), starring Bing Crosby and Fred Astaire. The entire set was blanketed with snow, and being a California kid, I'd never seen snow before. My father said, 'Go over there and play in the snow.' So I went running over to the snow only to discover that it was made out of plastic! I really can't say that his career had an influence on mine other than the tradition of doing what your father did. Had I been born in Detroit, I would have gone into the automotive industry. I really had no great drive to go into the entertainment business, but what else was I going to do? So I majored in theater and film at UCLA. In my junior year, I got a call from the Director's Guild informing me that this was the last year that the guild would automatically be accepting sons of directors. So I joined."

"Did you know how to direct?"

"No, not at all. My early education came from working with director George Stevens when I was in the service during the Korean War. Stevens had been in the signal corps, and I knew that he had known my father. So I wrote him a letter and asked if I could work with him. I got transferred to his unit, which was making training films. When I got out of the army, I wrote a letter to the production manager at Desilu Productions, mostly because I liked their shows—*I Love Lucy, The Danny Thomas Show, Our Miss Brooks*—and got an interview with a man named Argyle Nelson.

After ten minutes he asked, 'When can you start?' I thought to myself, *I must have given a really good interview*, but I found out later that he had been one of my father's assistants and that Lucille Ball's first speaking role was in one of my father's pictures. She was very fond of my father because he had been kind to her. So although I didn't learn how to direct from my father, being my father's son was a big advantage. I was twenty-five when I began working at Desilu as a second assistant on *I Love Lucy* and other Desilu-produced shows."

"What was it like working on such a groundbreaking situation comedy show?"

"While it was a tremendously creative experience, it was a terribly difficult time for me. Going in, I had very little real experience. I didn't know how to run a set or do process; it was all really over my head. But Jack Aldworth, the show's assistant director, was wonderful and wet-nursed me through, telling me what needed to be done and often doing things for me. By the time I got there, the show had been running for several years, and America's favorite couple, Lucy and Desi, were not at all getting along, and William Frawley and Vivian Vance were not talking to each other."

"Did you aspire to move up from assistant director to director?"

"I had no real desire to be a director because I found it very intimidating and I didn't have great confidence in my ideas. I thought I was going to be an assistant director all my life. I had never studied acting like a lot of good directors do. I had never worked on the stage. Gradually I learned as I worked and eventually trusted my ideas, but that took a lot of years. I learned a tremendous amount from watching Jerry Thorpe direct *I Love Lucy* and Sheldon Leonard direct *The Danny Thomas Show* (1953–1964), *The Dick Van Dyke Show* (1961–1966), and *The Andy Griffith Show* (1960–1968). I watched and asked lots of questions. Sheldon always had a strong point of view. He would say what he meant and fight with the actors to get his way, but if he saw that an actor could do something better, he'd go along. And so that's the way I thought directors worked."

"What was the first show in which you had full directorial control?"

"*He and She* (1967–1968), produced by Leonard Stern and starring Paula Prentiss and Richard Benjamin. It too was a great learning experience because up until that time I knew cameras but not actors. Benjamin taught me a great deal about working with actors. He'd ask me, 'Why do I say this line?' So I'd say, 'If you say this, then Paula can say the joke.' 'I know that, but why am I, this character, saying the line?' 'Because that's what's written.' And he'd say, 'No, I'm not talking about set-ups for the characters. We need to know *why* this character would say these words.' I learned from that show that camera work was important, but it wasn't as important as what the actors were doing."

"What would you say is the most challenging aspect of the television director's job?"

"It didn't really hit me until I got on *The Mary Tyler Moore Show* that I had to be a buffer between the writer/producers and the actors. It was very difficult for actors to say to the show's writers, James L. Brooks and Allan Burns, 'I don't understand this. It's not working.' So I had to mediate between them. Sometimes the producers would say, 'Just say the line as written.' But the actors didn't feel comfortable with that. I learned that my opinion as a director would sometimes be in total contrast with that of the writers and producers. But I was the one on the set and could see what the actors were capable [of] and comfortable doing. Sometimes when the writing wasn't quite right, I'd make suggestions, which they wouldn't use unless I had a good reason. When writers write lines, they hear them in their heads like music. But the actors don't always hear the same music. I didn't always hear the same music. So I had to stand up and fight for the actors. When you do that, you'd better damn well have a point of view. I was on *The Mary Tyler Moore Show* for eight years, and for eight years Jim Brooks and I fought—on every show. Jim liked bigger performances than I liked, so it was a constant battle. Jim is an unbelievably brilliant writer, but I saw things very differently. I didn't win every battle, but I won some."

"I understand sometimes you also disagreed with the actors. Ed Asner, who won several Emmys for his role as Lou Grant on *The Mary Tyler Moore Show*, said in one of his acceptance speeches that he was thankful to you for never letting him win an argument."

"That's true. We did fight a good deal. Directing comedy is more difficult than directing drama. I don't mean that drama isn't hard, but doing a show in front of an audience and getting laughs is quite difficult. My way of working was to look at each of the scenes as an audience member would, not as a director or a writer or an actor. Is this amusing? Is it interesting? Who do I want to look at? If a scene is working I need to know why it is working or why it isn't. I remember this one episode in which Mary and Lou have a date. She invites him over for dinner. I told Mary what to do so we'd be certain to get a big laugh. When she did it, no one laughed. Mary just kept going on with the scene. Actors realize that you're not always going to be right. But you'd better be right more than you're wrong."

"The relationship between writers and actors is a very delicate one. How did you work both ends so well?"

"You always want the actors to love the writers and the writers to love the actors. I never wanted contention on a set. I always felt it was up to me to keep harmony. Not all actors are comfortable confronting writers when they're unhappy with the lines. I wouldn't tell the writers, 'The actor doesn't like this line'; I'd say, 'I'm having trouble understanding this line.' I didn't mean me personally, but as an audience. So that way I protected and empowered the actors. In the early days when I was an assistant director and the writers would come down to the set, the tension between them and the actors would be terrible. The actors would be upset that they had to do or say things they weren't comfortable with, and you knew the writers were going to take off on them."

"Did you expect *The Mary Tyler Moore Show* to become one of the greatest sitcoms of all time?"

"I don't think any of us thought this show would be such a hit, still talked about and seen on reruns, or that the women's liberation movement would feel it was an important show. It aired on Saturday nights, which was not really considered a good night. But because of the show, women didn't have to feel badly about sitting home on a Saturday night watching television. Mary's doing it. We realized that Mary had a following and that she represented a segment of women in the population. We hadn't seen a character like Mary on TV before, a beautiful and intelligent single woman who was successful in her career."

"How important to you was the message of the shows you directed?"

"I had a certain standard not only about the writing but about a show's message. I'd hold out until I found a script, characters, and writing that appealed to me. Fortunately, I was able to turn down shows and still support my family. I remember being offered a movie of the week, but I didn't like its message so I turned it down. Everybody said I was crazy. But I knew I couldn't do it right because I didn't agree with its point of view."

"*Soap*, your next show after *Mary Tyler Moore*, proved one of the most controversial comedies in television history."

"I read the script for *Soap* and thought, *This will be either really brilliant, if we can cast it right, or it'll be a disaster. Soap* was a gamble on my part. If it didn't work, my reputation would suffer. I knew the show's writers, Susan Harris and Paul Junger Witt, and how talented they were.

They would later write and produce *The Golden Girls*, for which I directed the pilot."

"What made *Soap* such a sensational hit?"

"It worked because it was so well written, had such a great cast, and dealt with subject matter you weren't seeing on prime-time television. And it was very funny. The show was different from anything that had been on television. We'd do a broad slapstick scene followed by a scene with not a single laugh in it, followed by very sophisticated comedy writing. In the pilot episode, the husband is cheating on his wife, who has been lied to continuously and is very lonely. There was a reality to the show because there are lots of real people out there in similar circumstances, and they related to it. The show also caused some controversy because this white family had a black butler, Robert Guillaume's character. We started getting a lot of pressure from the black community, but I assured Guillaume that it was going to be okay, and it was. His character was so accepted he even got his own show, *Benson* (1979–1986)."

"Sounds like your actors really looked to you for guidance and trusted you."

"Every actor wants a director he can respect, who can give him feedback and has his best interest at heart. When I worked on *The Odd Couple* (1970–1975) with Jack Klugman and Tony Randall, Randall and I fought for the first two shows. He said to me, 'Why do you want that? Why do you think this doesn't work?' But he knew whatever I asked for had a reason. By the end we adored working together. When I worked on *The Cosby Show*, I never told Bill Cosby how to do comedy. I would make suggestions, guide and try to explain my point of view, but I never demanded anything."

"What is it that so engages us about fictional characters on television?"

"If you're a fan of a particular show and you see the same characters every week, you get to know them. Hopefully during the course of the show you see them grow and change. I remember the scene we did on *Soap* when the wife, played by Katherine Helmond, finds out that her husband is cheating on her. The next night he gives her some phony story that he's going out. She says fine and informs him that she's going out too. She doesn't come home that night, and he goes crazy. What she did was spend the night at an all-night movie theater. She couldn't go back to accepting his infidelity. Her character was growing and developing. That's what engages the audience."

"What is the underlying thread that connects all your shows?"

"Actually, they were very different from each other—just look at *Mary*

Tyler Moore and *Soap.* But all of them had excellent writing and casting. I can't make a bad script work even with a good cast, and I can't make a bad cast work even with a good script. It needs both."

"Has television humor changed in tone since you started working in television more than fifty years ago?"

"Yes, humor has changed. Just look at our culture. I don't think *The Mary Tyler Moore Show* would last today. *Soap* maybe, but we'd have to get much dirtier. Cosby might last because it's about family. Sitcoms today are all about sex. That's great for young people, but I don't see any adult comedies on TV with really good material. I don't watch any television comedies today because I don't find them funny. In my shows we would make references to literature and plays no matter that half the audience might not know them. It didn't matter. Enough of them would get it. We never talked down to an audience. Children were never treated as idiots, but rather as young people."

"Looking back on your career, are you satisfied with what you've achieved?"

"Yes. I wanted to entertain people and never wanted to waste their time, and I think we did that. If people were going to spend a half hour with us, then we should have something to say. We always had a fairly moralistic point of view in the shows, one that parents could talk to their kids about it. I never felt that we were dramatically changing our culture except for *The Cosby Show,* about an upper-middle-class black family that treated their kids with respect. *The Cosby Show* was saying to America, not all black families are lower class. I am proud to have been a part of that."

"Why did you decide to step away from television directing?"

"I no longer understood what the writers were saying, or their point of view. So I no longer wanted to do it. And I was not happy with network interference. I remember Grant Tinker, producer of *The Mary Tyler Moore Show,* telling the network, 'No, that's not what we're going to do.' I'd seen Carl Reiner and Sheldon Leonard do that on *The Dick Van Dyke Show.* Today the networks own half the show, so the creators have less freedom. They tell people what to make and how to make it. I had earned enough money that I didn't have to work again, and it was just the right time. Life was good. I was in my second marriage and really happy. I am still working in small summer theater, still directing, only not in television."

# James L. Brooks

James L. Brooks, one of Hollywood's most respected writer-producer-directors, has created some of television's popular shows, among them The Mary Tyler Moore Show *(1970–1977),* Rhoda *(1974–1978),* Lou Grant *(1977–1982),* Taxi *(1978–1983), and* The Simpsons *(1989–2013). His films* Terms of Endearment *(1983),* Broadcast News *(1987),* As Good as It Gets *(1997), and* Spanglish *(2004) earned multiple Academy Award nominations and wins, including one for Brooks for best direction on* Terms of Endearment. *I began our interview by asking if he knew from an early age that he would become a storyteller.*

"My only ambition as a young person was survival. I came from a highly dysfunctional family. My father was an alcoholic, and my hard-working guilt-ridden mother went hungry so we could eat. To cope, I read plays. I read for escape, and I read for enjoyment. What I had going for me in school was that I was the class clown and got laughs, but I still got beat up. I don't know if my hard time at school was a result of a learning disability, dyslexia. In college I screwed up because it was the first time I had a good social life. I just stopped going to classes."

"I understand your first big break came when you were hired by CBS News."

"My sister's best friend was the secretary to the person who hired pages for CBS News, so I was able to get a job that routinely went to people who were more educated than I. Later I was promoted to copyboy, a big break. That job normally went to an Ivy League graduate. I always think about that big break, writing news for CBS, and what would have happened to me had I not gotten it. It's always been hard for me to get used to the idea that luck had so much to do with it."

"I read that your ambition was to be a writer."

"Writing was something I always wanted to do. I had been writing short stories ever since I was in high school and sent them out hoping to have them published. I think some of my stories were quite good. I never expected that I'd be successful at it, considering it a great day when someone sent me back a rejection and had nice things to say to me. I took writing courses at City College with Arnold Weinstein, who was a prominent Off Broadway playwright, and with one of the Bernstein brothers from the *New York Times*. I also took playwriting workshops that were an offshoot of the Actor's Studio. On my way home from CBS, I would 'second act,' which means I would mix in with the people who were standing around during intermission outside Broadway shows and go back into the theater with them to see the second half of the show."

"So how did you go from being a copyboy at CBS to one of television's most successful screenwriters?"

"I left the newsroom to come out to Los Angeles to do documentaries. It was not typical of me to take such a chance, giving up a secure union job with decent pay and a real future—news writing. The woman I was married to at the time was very supportive of my move; otherwise I might not have done it. One night I met Allan Burns, who helped me break into television. We formed a writing team and together created *The Mary Tyler Moore Show* for Grant Tinker at CBS. Allan and I were just these two young guys having a great time. We were working with great actors from different disciplines and learning so much. This was my real education. The whole thing was intoxicating."

"You were at CBS News at the end of the Edward R. Murrow era, a time when news reporting was considered one of the most noble of professions. Do you think having spent time in that environment influenced your work as a television writer, producer, and feature-film director?"

"Probably. The newsroom was famously filled with integrity and served a higher purpose. That was what was instilled in me, in all of us. The FCC required us to put on public-affairs shows. William S. Paley gave autonomy to the fact-seeking pure-news division, and Edward R. Murrow's presence raised everything up. Reporting was arguably the highest calling, and reporters were considered priests of truth. I was in awe, slack jawed, working with these people who were serving this higher purpose. The work was more important than anything else."

"How did your experience on television compare?"

"Early on I had worked with director Gene Reynolds on a television show called *Room 222* (1969–1974). Reynolds was a man of immense integrity. He was passionate about doing what was right and had that same sort of standards I encountered at CBS News. He gave me my work ethic. Television executive Grant Tinker, who hired Allan and me to create *The Mary Tyler Moore Show*, also was a man of immense moral character. He protected us from the network so that we could write our scripts without interference. Allan too was an extremely ethical person, pillar-of-the-community type. I'm sure being around all that influenced the work."

"Was it your intention to attract audiences by creating stories that reflected what was going on in society at that time?"

"We wanted the characters to be real, have them evolve and reflect what was going on in our culture. We got some of our best stories from real life. On Mary's show we were doing a character comedy about a single woman who was starting a career. We used the term 'sitcom derisive' to describe the show. Suddenly we had a flurry of people who wanted us to say certain things because they thought we were sharing their cause. For us what mattered most was the writing: 'Does the story work and is it getting laughs?'"

"I found in virtually all of the characters that you've created a need for personal integrity—it's one of the major themes that run through your work. Why do you think you're drawn to that particular human aspiration?"

Jim paused for a moment. "I'm trying to think if that describes anything ever written—*Pirates of Penzance, Robin Hood, Hamlet*? You either want to save who you are, or you want to change who you are. Isn't that true of almost anything?"

"Yes, that's probably true, but when I examined *your* characters, I saw that above all, it was integrity that they're after—not love, justice, power, or wealth. Take Flor's character from *Spanglish*. She's the Hispanic maid who comes to work in an affluent American household. She is nothing if not motivated by her desire to preserve her traditions and values and protect her daughter from being corrupted. Cloris Leachman's character, the mother/grandmother in the story, was once a popular singer, but now years after her success she's become an alcoholic. She has this great line, 'You think your life is embarrassing and then someone finds you encouraging.'"

"If there is a common thread in my work, it's that the characters reflect what's happening in society based on my observations. I want it to be funny, but I hope that it's not just funny and that it has something to do with real life. A big part of what I do is observation. It's reporting. In *Broadcast News*, I captured a new kind of heroine in Holly Hunter's character, June. She was unlike any other woman I ever wrote, perhaps for maybe Valerie Harper's character in *Rhoda*. In the film every key line Jane says about herself in the film came from my research. Her words resonated with a lot of women in a really extraordinary way. In *Span-*

glish, I wanted to present a father as a nurturing parent. I thought a revolution was happening because I had observed a new generation of men, fathers who cared about their kids and took on some of the responsibility of raising them."

"So your characters are based on real people who you observe and report on?"

"Not all, but many of my characters are based on real people. This was the case with Aurora Greenway, Shirley MacLaine's character in *Terms of Endearment*. I had interviewed fifty-year-old women who were empty-nesters to learn what that was like. I remember one woman who didn't want me to leave after our interview. It was around 5:30 p.m., and she had already begun her early evening drinking. Her loneliness was palpable. I don't know whether that is represented anyplace in that screenplay, but that helped me with Aurora's character."

"Tell me about your research process?"

"It typically involves talking to lots and lots of people and recording what they say on a tape recorder. When you record what people say, it sort of enters you through osmosis. In addition to the specifics you hear from the people you interview, you become aware of how people in similar circumstances live and think. It also makes you feel more responsible for how you portray them, because in your mind you have a jury that knows the truth."

"Is that how Carol, Helen Hunt's character, came to life in *As Good as It Gets*?"

"Carol was based on someone I knew who had a sick child, and how that circumstance can come to dominate your life. I feel you have to earn the right to write about someone in that situation. You earn it by living it or by trying to get right something that you've observed. The scene in *Terms of Endearment* when Emma dies in the hospital room is based on a real story I heard from a Texas girl who had lost her brother. She helped me with my research by telling me what she had experienced and that, I felt, gave me the right to write that scene."

"What was your impetus for making *Terms of Endearment*?"

"Reading Larry McMurtry's novel, on which the film is based, was the first time in my life I'd ever cried while reading a book. That emotional reaction set me on the path. But then came the intellectual part: *This has to be a comedy—to be going for the laughs and still maintain the values in the story*."

"For a comedy, it requires a whole box of tissues. It's devastatingly sad when Emma dies of cancer."

"When we made *Terms of Endearment* people didn't talk about cancer. It's hard to imagine this now, when so many people are wearing pink ribbons, but in 1984 you didn't say the word out loud. Emma's friend in the story asks her, 'What should we do?' Emma replies 'Tell them it's okay to talk about cancer. I want you to tell them it's not that tragic.' I thought, *I have to get a laugh on that word, cancer.* And so in the next scene someone talks about cancer very openly and what she says is absurd. So I had a spit-take on that line, where her friend spits out a cocktail frank across the room. That was my way of disarming the C-word because it was so armed at the time. And of course the film's tagline was 'Come to laugh. Come to cry. Come to terms.'"

"Why do you think *Terms of Endearment* was such a popular and critical success, winning five Academy Awards?"

"People gave themselves emotionally to that movie. It sought to be real, and at the same time it was a comedy. People came out of the theater having been affected by it emotionally. I once saw a mother and daughter hugging outside the theater. It was honoring that mother-daughter relationship, but the picture wasn't trading on it. Having it real and funny, it was like life."

"Your films and television shows are always a finely tuned mixture of comedic and dramatic moments. We see that even on *The Simpsons.*"

"In some episodes we want to address something human, and in others we're just having fun. I like working on both. After having the characters be funny, the next big achievement is having them resonate, stay with you. Having characters, even animated ones, that are part of your lives is just an amazing thing."

"How do you know what's going to resonate with audiences?"

"You're really not thinking that when you're creating a work. You're thinking about what makes it come alive."

"How important is it to get the right actor for a role?"

"Every director's work rises and falls with whatever actor is in the room. It's true for everyone, without exception. I spend more months casting than probably anybody, and I do lots of callbacks. Casting is huge to me."

"Where do you feel you need improvement?"

"I do have some perversities in my movies that I'm trying to correct, like on *Spanglish* there was no way to satisfactorily end the movie. That was also true of *Broadcast News* and *As Good as It Gets.* So you paint yourself in a corner, and you see what happens. I've been lucky enough not to have to seek the audience pleasing happy ending. But you've still got to please them."

"Jack Nicholson has appeared in most of your films and won two best actor Academy Awards for films you directed, *Terms of Endearment* and *As Good as It Gets*. What was it like working with him to create the complex role of Melvin Udall?"

"*As Good as It Gets* almost broke us in two because it was so damn hard to thread the needle and be funny. All I knew how to do was say, 'We're not there yet,' which became very frustrating for Jack, as you can imagine. Jack tells the story, and I'm sure there's some truth in it, that I kept saying, 'Too angry, too angry, too angry.' It was so frustrating we would have given anything not to have to do this movie, to just quit. And then he tore a room apart, and I said, 'That's it.' I did something that you don't do: I sent the crew home with still a half a day left for shooting. Jack and I remained alone on this huge sound stage for a couple of hours. I'm not even sure what we said to each other, but the next day everything was better."

"What's it like directing a film you've also written?"

"When you're both the writer and the director, the writer never leaves the room. On the first movie I worked on as a writer, I was barred from the set by its director. He really liked me, but I'd be there noticeably expressing when I liked something and when I didn't. So he said to me, 'Jim, when you're the director, you don't need to know all the answers, but you need the illusion that you do.' I think that was really smart. When you're directing a film and you're also its writer, you can't be barred from the set. In *As Good as It Gets*, when Simon is in the hospital, I originally wrote [that] as a dramatic scene. But later I had an idea for making it funny, and I changed it because I could."

"Is writing still your great passion?"

"I can't imagine existing without writing. Writing makes sense to me like nothing else does. There is something right and eternal about it. If I couldn't be a writer, I'd be a different person and I don't want to be a different person. On the days when writing feels futile, I feel bad. I bump up against my own limitations. It's awful. On the days when the faucet is turned on and I feel like I have the upper hand, life's good. Even on the days when the faucet is on and it's not good water, it's still better because the faucet is turned on."

"What do you do when the faucet won't turn on, when the words won't come?"

"That happened to me once when I was really blocked, and so I asked the venerated comedy writer Jerry Belson what to do and he told me, 'Lay down shit.' It's the greatest advice I ever got. Be bad and it will turn into something. You prod yourself once you're pushing words out. What happens is you're pushing and pushing and pushing, and then at a certain point you get where you're being pulled and you go with it. Something mystical happens just by your showing up."

Mira Nair

Saalam Bombay *(1988),* Mississippi Masala *(1991),* Monsoon Wedding *(2001), and* The Namesake *(2006) are but a few of the films that have brought Indian-born director Mira Nair international recognition and acclaim. Trained as a documentary filmmaker at Harvard, Nair's passion for truth and illumination of the human spirit is evident in every story she tells. Despite her hectic schedule, Nair found an hour to meet with me on an early Saturday morning in Glendale, California.*

"To what do you attribute the global appeal of your films?"

"My films often deal with immigrants who leave their homeland to make a new life somewhere else, so I guess that kind of experience resonates with people. I live that kind of life, having homes in Africa, India, and the United States. So I feel at home in both the East and the West, which expands my worldview. I suppose my work reflects that expansion. For me, it's never a shutting of doors but an opening of them, and that makes a big world."

"Many of the characters in your stories are often on the edge, either struggling to survive in a difficult environment or dealing with some emotional turmoil—like young Krishna in *Saalam Bombay* or Maya in *Kama Sutra* (1996). In *Mississippi Masala* you tell the story of a racially mixed couple that is confronted with prejudice."

"I'm interested in the study of character and drawn to those who are considered marginal to society. My films and documentaries are often about people who don't give up. I find them incredibly inspiring. Even from my earliest documentaries on the strippers of Bombay, I loved exploring the foibles and the multiplicity of behaviors, which I find the most affecting thing about people. The combination of visual storytelling and the human condition is conducive to cinema."

"I imagine that following your characters through the arc of their personal journeys is among the most compelling aspects of filmmaking."

"When you work on a film, you're in the company of those characters and their stories for as long as two years. They become your world. And so when I'm telling their story, I want to enjoy every scene, every frame, in the making of the film; otherwise, I'm just joining the dots. There are several stages in the film process—the shooting to capture it, the editing to distill it, and the music to sweeten it. But it's essential never to lose the story's core. Without its core, its essence, there is just emptiness."

"I've found that the characters in your films are always very well drawn and fleshed out. How do you go about showing the soul of a character?"

"A director's task is to make every character bloom. That requires having a psychological understanding of the characters' heritage—where they come from and why they are the way they are. What they believe and how they view the world is what defines them. It's not that this has to be broadcast on the screen, but you must know what they listen to, what inspires them, how they think. Most importantly, how you come to your character is in the casting. You manifest that character by having the right actor. If you cast the wrong actor, you may end up striving to capture the character's essence and never achieve it. Once I've chosen the actors properly, my task is simply to be as communicative and helpful as possible, so they demonstrate what I want. And it's not only what I want, but what they bring to it. I always try to provide a safe environment, but I steer it. I want the actors to take me deeper, further into the characters. And that's what actors do that is so beautiful—they become transparent."

"You were initially trained as a documentary filmmaker in the style of cinema verité—truthful cinema—being authentic in your storytelling. How is this achieved when telling fictional stories?"

"Real life is infinitely more powerful than fiction, but fiction comes from real life. I am a student of life, and so the stories I like to tell are from life. I don't think I'm trying to *define* truth in my films, but rather recognize it. The challenge comes with having to show and express a story from conception—the writing, photographing, and editing, etc. Does it capture something real? Or is it fake or empty? Does it say enough? We have to be ruthless in the analysis of what we are making."

"How do you know which film projects are worth pursuing?"

"I've realized in these years of making movies the privilege of inspiration. When something comes your way that grabs you, you must follow it. That happened to me with *The Namesake*, which was actually inspired by personal grief. I was completing work on *Vanity Fair* (2004) at the time and preparing to make *Homebody/Kabul*—a Tony Kushner play. I had been working on the development of it for two years, and it was all ready to go when my mother-in-law died suddenly. I had never before experienced the finality of loss. The shock of never being able to see her again was devastating. It was in that state of bewilderment and melancholia that I read Jhumpa Lahiri's book *The Namesake*, and it just captured me. I found solace in the story. I knew I had to make it into a film. Nine months later the film was done. It was like giving birth. I call *The Namesake* one of my most experiential films because I experienced the emotions expressed in the story. Making the film was a way of showing appreciation for what our parents mean to us."

"*Kama Sutra: A Tale of Love* was beautifully and sensuously photographed. What was your process like in creating these lovemaking scenes?"

"Love and sex scenes in general are very delicate to film, so I always have a fair amount of rehearsal. I had the actors come to my hotel room the evening before shooting, and the three of us figured it out. I say what I would like, and they share with me what they'd like to do. Then I invite in my director of cinematography, and we discuss shots. Then on the day of the shooting, which is a closed set, we start with a wide shot and then we come in and slowly film up her body. In *Mississippi Masala*, we worked on creating and maintaining a particular mood. I had a track laid down next to Denzel Washington and Sarita Choudhury's bed. The camera photographed them while moving along the track. It's different with every film."

"Your films are as compelling visually as they are thought-provoking. How do you maintain the right balance between the visual and the narrative?"

"In cinema you have to be attuned to rhythm. If the rhythm is not fully in the flow, you have to recognize what is hindering it. If a particular scene, even with your biggest stars, impedes the story's rhythmic flow, you must cut it out. One must be rigorous in the telling of a story. That means not letting anything get in the way of the story's clarity and forward movement. As the storyteller that's what you listen to. Sometimes I don't want to cut out things that I've shot, but if it doesn't need to be there I'm forced to. My motto is 'When in doubt cut it out.'

"You also have to find a way that best plumbs the essence of what the story's about. *The Namesake* is about the immigration experience, and cinema allows us very beautifully and even more powerfully than the written word to show how we can live between two worlds. Here you are in one place and then suddenly in another. In visual storytelling a woman can look outside her window on Riverside Drive, and instead of seeing the Hudson River, she sees a garden in Kampala, Uganda. It's a cinematic motif I sometimes use. In *The Namesake* I wanted to create a scene in which the audience and sometimes even the characters don't know which city they're in. Are we in Brooklyn or Calcutta? Ashima gives birth to her son in the Roosevelt Hospital in New York and stares out her window. We expect to see the Queensboro Bridge, but instead we see Calcutta's How-rah Bridge. Immediately we go to thoughts: *If I were home, my mother would be here with me, as would my relatives. Instead I only have this nurse who comes once a day and doesn't even know how to fold a sari.*"

"Isn't your use of bridges also a way to show the bridging of two cultures and continents?"

"Yes, in this case it worked very well because New York and Calcutta are remarkably similar in spirit, and in the way they manifest themselves politically and artistically. Their bridges even looked alike. I refer to this motif as the temples of the traveler—the neutral spaces, like escalators or bridges, that allow me to figure out the poetic language of a film."

"Do you think women tell stories differently from men?"

"I don't believe that women have a more gooey bone in their bodies then men when it comes to storytelling. There are some wonderful women filmmakers, like Lynne Ramsay and Jane Campion, who have a particular way of seeing, feeling, and expressing themselves boldly and delicately. But I just see them as great filmmakers. Male directors can be enormously empathetic, as evidenced by such films as *The Killing Fields* (2001) and *Missing* (1982). The one advantage I might have as a woman director is that at times I have greater access to women actors who I can communicate with deeply in a girl-to-girl way. Working with Uma Thurman and the performance she gave in *Hysterical Blindness* (2004) came from her desire to be brave with someone she trusted. I'm not saying that couldn't happen with a male director, but she and I had a hotline into each other. Same thing is true of my work with Hilary Swank in *Amelia* (2009). I've just had that experience with Kate Hudson in *The Reluctant Fundamentalist* (2013)."

"Your film *Saalam Bombay* made a real difference in the lives of its young actors and gave birth to an organization to protect children, demonstrating the power of cinema to raise consciousness and bring about social change."

"I came to cinema with an ideological question: Can art change the world? I know of course that it can't change things in a monumental way, but it can make some degree of difference. *Saalam Bombay* is a case in point. Twenty-two years ago, with the profits from that film we created the Salaam Baalak Trust [*baalack* means child], through which we founded centers in Bombay and Delhi to protect and educate homeless children. Now we have seventeen centers serving about five thousand kids, a great staff of social workers, and it's chaired by my mother. We've been at it for the past twenty-two years. I've also created a film school in East Africa that trains young Africans from Uganda, Kenya, Tanzania, and Rwanda who would ordinarily not have such opportunities in the art of cinematic storytelling. There are now five hundred and fifty alumni from our film school, and they're all working as filmmakers."

"Has filmmaking given you a better understanding of life and human nature?"

"It's not that before I made films I didn't know and now I do. Rather, I believe that being increasingly open to life as you live it helps you become wiser about how the world ticks and how people are. The depth of your understanding and assumption of truth should be reflected in your work. But just because you know something doesn't mean you have to broadcast it. My films seem to reflect the stage of life that I happen to be in. In India we believe there are four stages of life, and I think my work in a way corresponds to those stages—youth, work, spiritual, and wandering. When I made *Salaam Bombay*, I was young, single, unfettered, and could jump into eight months of working on the streets. After I was married, I learned about the marriage between cultures and that came through in *Mississippi Masala*. *Monsoon Wedding* came out of my becoming a mother and having a family. And as I had mentioned earlier, *The Namesake* came out of losing a parent. My current film, *The Reluctant Fundamentalist*, is about what is going on in the world—crime, terror, the economy, etc. I like to think of my films as reflecting the ongoing wave of life."

"Does filmmaking enable you to better understand the artist within you?"

"It's taken me decades to even utter those words, 'I'm an artist.' Being an artist is a sacred, almost holy thing. It's not for us who make work to say that about ourselves. I don't ever think about what it means to be an artist. I find that a distraction. If you think it's art when you're doing it, you're sunk. But after so many years of making films, I do recognize that there is artistry in some of my films. What's important to me is reaching someone else's heart and mind when I shoot an arrow through the air."

Michael Apted

British-born director Michael Apted began his career in television with one of England's most respected documentary series, 7 Up, *which followed fourteen children of various economic backgrounds from the age of seven every seven years, beginning in 1964. Decades later, he's still at it. I met with him right after completing his eighth film in the ongoing study,* 56 Up. *Apted's movie career has also brought him international recognition with such renowned motion pictures as* Coal Miner's Daughter *(1980),* Gorillas in the Mist *(1988),* Nell *(1994),* The World Is Not Enough *(1999), and* The Chronicles of Narnia: The Voyage of the Dawn Treader *(2010). Over coffee at his West Los Angeles office, Apted explained how his seemingly diverse films are really not that diverse at all, but share an underlying message.*

"What sparked your interest in filmmaking?"

"At sixteen I discovered movies and I had my epiphany with Ingmar Bergman's *Wild Strawberries* (1957), which I saw at the Academy on Oxford Street in London, a little theater that has since disappeared. The film was emotional, existed on a dream- as well as a reality-level, and it was clearly drawn from a piece of complex writing. Before I saw *Wild Strawberries*, I regarded films as nothing more than popular Saturday-night entertainment. Now I saw that cinema could be a very creative place to play with ideas, great writing, and good acting. I began thinking about becoming a filmmaker and, while a student at Cambridge University, did a lot of acting and started directing. My peers were Stephen Frears, Mike Newell, and the Monty Python people. But not knowing how to get into the entertainment business, I followed my parents' advice, and in my third year studied law. But in 1963, the year I left Cambridge, Granada Television and ITV, which had been in business for six or seven years and survived by poaching from the BBC, opened a course to train people for the first generation of English television. I applied and was one of the six chosen. This was very exciting as it promised a new and innovative approach to television broadcasting, and we were hired to help push the envelope in terms of current affairs and dramas. I was assigned to work on a weekly affairs program called *World in Action*, which was

doing a special on the future of England. They came up with the idea for a series called *7 Up*, which followed the lives of seven-year-old children from a variety of backgrounds, revisiting them every seven years to examine how well they fared. As you know I've just completed *56 Up*."

"I understand that you also made a name for yourself with the BBC."

"In 1969 I joined what was then perceived as the real jungle of British television—the British Broadcasting Corporation. After nine years in television I was thinking about moving on, when I heard that some people were looking for a director who could work fast, like you do in television, and complete a film in only six weeks. It stared Glenda Jackson. I got the job based on my experience of working in fast-paced television. This was a turning point."

"This started your filmmaking career."

"Yes. In the seventies I made four American-financed movies, worked in television at a very high level, and engaged in a bit of theater. Then I met with a young executive at Universal Studios who had seen some of my British films and hired me to direct *Coal Miner's Daughter*."

"That film was a huge commercial success. Sissy Spacek won an Academy Award for her portrayal of Loretta Lynn."

"Yes, the success of *Coal Miner's Daughter* made it possible to fulfill my dream of moving to America. And it came at a particularly good time—the early 1980s, when there were great films being made in America. The English film industry had no serious infrastructure at the time, so to create a serious body of work I understood that I needed to relocate here."

"You must have had a lot riding on *Coal Miner's Daughter*. If the film did well, you were assured to remain in America and build your filmmaking career."

"Yes, that's true. After arriving on location in Kentucky, I realized rather quickly that neither the New York nor the Los Angeles crew knew what they were doing. They were uncomfortable in that environment. But there is a huge English heritage in that part of the state that I very much responded to. I also understood that most American films about this subject were prejudiced. Take for example the patronizing tone of Robert Altman's *Nashville* (1975), which disparaged the people of Appalachia as 'white trash.' My approach was more in line with what I had learned from watching the Italian neorealists and the English films of Ken Loach and Jack Gold in the 1960s. I've always taken a more documentary approach, particularly from the *Up* series and what I had learned from English television, and I brought all that to *Coal Miner's Daughter*.

Much of the success of the film really had to do with the casting. Ken Loach had made movie stars out of people he had gotten off the street. He saw that he could get wonderful performances out of them because there was a reality to what they did. So I used that too. My instinct was to use local people, because if you're going to film a community, it's not just the geography but the people you shoot, giving them a real voice. And there was something else. Singers become alive when they're performing, so I insisted that Sissy Spacek and Beverly D'Angelo not lip-sync but sing their performances live. If Gary Busey could sing Buddy Holly, then Spacek and D'Angelo could sing Loretta Lynn and Patsy Cline. I had made that decision instinctively, angering Universal Studios executives, but it paid off."

"How did you pull off *Gorillas in the Mist*?"

"The first thing I thought was, *We're never going to be able to cast wild gorillas for this film!* But I took it on, and looking back, maybe I was a little bit crazy. But we achieved it."

"Sounds like you were actually very courageous."

"Casting real gorillas to work closely with actors was courageous. But actually the gorillas we put in this film had been used in research and had previous contact with humans. They were as curious about us as we were about them. When we first encountered them on the mountain in Uganda, we were advised to stay very still and quiet. As one of the gorillas approached Sigourney Weaver, who was playing Dian Fossey in the film, we all held our breath. The gorilla began stroking her. It quickly became clear that we were dealing with one of the gorillas who knew Dian Fossey and thought Sigourney was her. Sigourney resembled Dian, and so the gorilla thought that she had come back."

"I'm noticing the posters here on your office walls: *Gorillas in the Mist*, *Nell*, *The World Is Not Enough*, *Enigma* (2001), *Amazing Grace* (2006), *The Chronicles of Narnia*, your documentaries—the *Up* series (1964–), *Inspirations* (1997), *Me and Isaac Newton* (1999). It's a very diverse body of work. What draws you to particular material?"

"I'm drawn to many different kinds of material and genres, and then I figure out what I can bring to [them]. I'm not a screenwriter and don't originate the material. Sometimes the material comes to me in a primitive form and sometimes in quiet a finished form. What I enjoy is interpreting it through the filmmaking process. I think people can look at my films and not know that I did them, and that's because I don't necessarily work toward creating a signature look. My friend Steven Soderbergh says, 'There are two sorts of filmmakers: Those who have a style and find material to fit that style, and those who bring a style to the material.' I would be the latter."

"It's my impression that you're a sociologist at heart and that you care about how people get by in society. I detect an underlying message in most of your films about the unique power and perseverance of the human spirit."

"Yes, I suppose that's true that I have a kind of socio-curiosity. Many of my films—*Amazing Grace*, *Thunderheart* (1992), *Gorillas in the Mist*, and *Enigma*—are based on real people and on true stories. The *Up* films for me were originally about the lack of opportunity and unfairness of a class system that wastes people's potential. I brought a strong political hammer to the series, which lasted through three of the films, and then it began to soften as the politics became less significant and the people in it became more significant."

"Why did the people suddenly become more significant?"

"You can't predict what's going to happen to people. Look at Neal: at age seven you wanted to take him home and cuddle him. He would later become a smelly, homeless person. When we interviewed him at twenty-eight, I imagine most viewers thought they'd never see him again. But even at his low points, there was still that little twinkle, that little piece of life that he had at seven. When I interviewed Tony at twenty-one, he was hanging around the dog track, placing bets. He was completely convinced that he was going to end up badly, that he'd be in prison by twenty-eight. So I made him take this taxi ride around the East End of London to show him all the places of villainy. I warned him that if he continued to do what he was doing, he would end up in prison. I imposed myself on his life in that instance and more or less played God. I tried to set up his next seven years. After that, I made a conscious decision that I was going to concentrate on the close-ups, on the individuals. I've always been nervous about trying to elbow my way into their lives, so I essentially invited the children, now adults, to own the material. I felt if I empowered them and gave them much more freedom about what they wanted to do in the film, where they wanted to do it, and accepted what they wouldn't do, then the series would be more interesting and less formulaic. It wouldn't just be a catch-up each time—*This is where they are seven years later*. There is a lot of interplay between us now. The ones who are good about it *own* the series, and the ones who moan about it and say, 'Okay, we'll do the interview but you can't ask this, this and this,' come across as dull people. The whole tone of the series, as you may have noticed, changed when in *49*

Up Jackie turned on me, becoming confrontational. As the series and the people in it mature, I've given them a greater voice and become just the messenger."

"How much longer do you think you can go on documenting these people?"

"In England the *Up* films have a huge audience, all through these generations people have embraced it and want to see it. So far, there is no feeling that it's run out of steam. So I'll keep on going until too many of the subjects drop out or no one wants to watch the series. So far, neither of those things has happened."

"How has the *Up* series affected you on a personal level?"

"It has taught me to try and not be judgmental and to let people really express who they are. It has also made me look at my own parenting—the care that it requires to raise a child and knowing the damage you can do as a parent by imposing your own set of beliefs on them. It doesn't get you anywhere. It just affirms what you believe in, not what they believe in."

"Your fiction-based films also reflect social consciousness and focus on the human spirit—discovering oneself, self-actualizing, overcoming the darkness. *Nell* and *The Chronicles of Narnia* come to mind."

"I've always been drawn to heroic stories. I don't see the point in doing nihilistic films that dwell on depression or despair. You watch them and think, *Why did I have to sit through that?* Some may be well done, but they're miserable. I've even sometimes distorted history to present a more uplifting ending, as with *Gorillas in the Mist*. Dian Fossey was much crazier in life than we allowed her to be in the film. She was mad as a hatter. She was actually going around shooting at tourists in order to protect the gorillas. But my intention was to honor her courage. She spent eighteen years in this hellhole and saved this whole breed of animals from extinction. She threw her body in front of it. What attracted me to her was that she was not by nature a recluse. She loved men and liked to wear nice clothes. I didn't want the film to portray the demise of a mad woman who had taken on too much. I wanted to show a woman who had lived a heroic life, even though it took an ugly turn toward the end. So I always look for stories like Dian Fossey's, even if it makes the film too soft. I want people to come out of my films feeling some sense of uplift, with a sense of having seen something worth remembering. Life is hard, so I want to flash a bit of encouragement by highlighting the strengths people find, whether the character is real or fictional. That's always been a guiding light of my work."

"Even though you convey a very strong message in your films, you're rarely present in them"

"Why does the storyteller have to be in the story—or the interviewer in the documentary? I don't want to impose my own personal views onto the work. I don't take my personal baggage into the interview. It should be more like a blank page that you want to fill. But to a great extent it is unavoidable that I am in all of my work. My soul and heart is in it. My instincts are in it. My attitude toward the people and politics are in it. I don't think you can ever really separate yourself from your work or totally abstract your fears and emotions. Nor should you try. In fact, the more passion you bring into a project the better it's going to be."

"Do you view yourself as an artist who expresses himself through the medium of filmmaking?"

"I feel that I have the instincts of an artist. I feel a creative urge to make films and documentaries, to tell stories and to express myself. I live in fear of not being able to do that. I live in fear of doing mediocre work that doesn't express anything, that just sits there for two hours."

"What's your greatest challenge as a filmmaker?"

"Holding on to my central vision, the spine of the film, and allowing it to grow and improve because of what other people bring to it. That's torture and hellishly difficult, especially when you're first starting out because many people—not always with malicious intent—want to impose themselves on the work. In this collaborative medium there's always things you have to give up: an idea, a line of dialogue, a location. The real key is knowing what you can and cannot give up."

"Have the demands of filmmaking forced you at times to sacrifice your personal life for your professional life?"

"I have always been ambitious and paid dearly for subordinating my home life to career. I've had two failed marriages, and as a parent of young children I wasn't around very much. When I left England, I transported the family here, and it was difficult for them. I've never been able to keep the ordinariness of a responsible family life. Making a film is very intense and difficult work. On any given day you might have to answer anywhere from one thousand to five thousand questions. It's so all consuming that everything else becomes of secondary importance."

"The filmmaking business seems a world unto itself."

"Yes. It is a very odd and disturbing profession because it's very fragmented. You're often on location for long periods of time. You get very close with people when you're working together, but when the project's over everyone moves on to their next project and you lose contact with them. I've always gone from job to job, but now I'm getting older and see how much this is an ageist business. It's also highly unstable. Money is tight, and people are taking fewer risks, and fewer films are being made. All this affects you emotionally. I don't think you ever retire. You get retired. I'm surprised more of us aren't balmy, stark-raving mad."

Joseph Cedar

Joseph Cedar's finely nuanced films have received high honors not only in his country, Israel, but on the international film-festival circuit in Cannes, Dublin, Asia Pacific, Berlin, and elsewhere. Beaufort *(2007) and* Footnote *(2011) earned Academy Award nominations for best foreign film. Capturing the human spirit with clarity and simplicity, his films have won the praise of audiences and critics alike. I met with Cedar in New York City, where he was doing research for his next film and posed for me on a chilly morning in Central Park.*

"Why do you think you're drawn to filmmaking, storytelling?"

"I don't know why. The most honest answer I can give is that everything I am comes from my parents. I think I inherited from them the desire to organize the world in the shape of a story and to express myself that way. My father, a biologist and professor at Hebrew University, has done work on how information is delivered from one generation to another. My mother, who raised six children, taught drama and now works as a psychodrama therapist. I think who you become and your interests find their way into you without your actively knowing it."

"You've made four films—*Time of Favor* (2000), *Campfire* (2004), *Beaufort*, and *Footnote*—all of which received prestigious honors. Does your success make you feel confident as a filmmaker?"

"No. I don't have confidence in myself. Most of the time when I begin a project, I feel that what I'm doing is unworthy of anyone's attention. It's only when the internal logic of a story reveals itself to me and gives me a clear sense of purpose that I gain confidence. It usually happens somewhere between the first draft and the second draft of the script, when it becomes so perfect in my head that I understand what the story's about, what it should look like, what it should sound like and what it will take to deliver it. Only then do I feel it's worth the energy to continue, and its becoming a film is inevitable. After I complete a film, that confidence disappears and I feel a tremendous void."

"How difficult is it to bring to the screen something that you create from your imagination?"

"When you're directing a film that represents a reality, you have to answer many questions about what that reality is made up of. They're not abstract questions; they're actual. What make of watch is that character wearing? Why does he do this thing and not that thing? Everything is in question because once you've suggested it, you have to justify and argue for why it's one way and not other. The only films I'll commit to are those for which I have all the answers."

"Do you usually understand the full depth of a story's message before it reaches the filmmaking stage?"

"Sometimes you're already in the project before you have that complete understanding. That happened to me with *Beaufort*. It was probably the easiest film for me to sell to financiers because it had a big theme, was based on a historical event—the war with Lebanon—and [promised to] be of interest at least in Israel. I wrote the screenplay with Ron Leshem, a professional journalist rooted in practical storytelling—reporting. It took us two years to turn it into a script that I thought would become a decent movie. Once we were on set and I was talking with the actors, designers, and the cinematographer, I suddenly was overcome with a kind of blindness about the film, and it was not until the third of fourth day of shooting that I understood its meaning and everything fell into place."

"That sounds pretty frightening and risky."

"Let me explain it this way. I have a friend that was just diagnosed with cancer, given a twenty percent chance of survival. When something like that happens, all you can think of is how to turn that twenty percent into eighty percent survival. Directing feels like that. Many times you hear, 'It's just a movie. It's just a job.' It's not. For the person who's putting his life, his destiny, in this work, it's just as frightening as a fatal disease. A start date is established, sets are built, cast and crew arrive, and they're all waiting for the director to tell them what to do. At that moment you have to understand the story better than anyone else. It's terrifying when you don't know if or when that moment will come. It feels like a life-and-death situation. Fortunately, so far, those understandings have come to me when I needed them. Still, I can't always rely on that happening."

"Are you on a particular path of inquiry through the medium of filmmaking?"

"No, no path, just the decision not to repeat myself, do something new each time. If what I'm doing is not much different from what I've already done, it's because I've hit my limitations."

"How much of yourself do you consciously infuse into your films?"

"I try not to make movies that are about me. They end up being a little bit about me because that's unavoidable—everything you do is a reflection of something in you—but it's never on purpose. I've come to resent films that have a main character that is about the person who is making the film. I think it's inappropriate to engage so many people so long in something that is just your little thing. I know that artists are self-indulgent. I don't think they can pretend that they're not, and they need to be, but they disguise it. The work that I do is not intentionally autobiographical. I don't see myself in any of my characters. I try to look for settings for my stories that are unlike the setting I live in. If there are things in my film that are closely related to my own life, I only recognize them after the fact."

"What draws you to examine profoundly moral and ethical themes in your films?"

"I don't want to talk about any of these things. I'm sorry. Talking about concepts is too messy. It's like trying to hold liquid. You can't. You can feel it and touch it, but you can't hold it for more than a second. So all these things about themes I just don't discuss. Stories alone capture something better than trying to articulate that which is contained within them. A good story can't really be taken apart once it's constructed. My job is to create and condense a story to something that's dramatically loaded and entertaining from beginning to end. It's not about the big themes and finding the philosophical core of the story. It's about making sure that it's not boring. It's about sweeping the audience into its world and not letting go until it reaches the credits. That's my job."

"Why is storytelling so important in our culture?"

"There's a reason why so much of our human communication is in story form. It's a way for us to organize the world around us so we can better understand it. I once had this conversation with my father about the similarities and differences of human behavior. He explained how every scientist looks at a problem that at the beginning seems chaotic—like an organism that you don't understand. Inquiry leads to how or why something works. In a way this is what storytellers do too. They examine something like a human experience that at the beginning is confusing and doesn't make sense. They know intuitively that there is something important and vital about it, so they try to figure out what it means. The story represents the results of that inquiry and is comprised of a very complex blend of emotions, truths, lies, and facts. Through story we are better able to understand and contain that human experience at least for a little while."

"Should the director steer the story he's telling, or should he allow it to reveal itself with its own voice and intention?"

"When a story is good, what has to happen happens, and everything falls into place. Many unintentional things happen during the making of a film that turn out to be very significant, but they are not accidents. They reflect a story's inner logic. You know when a story isn't good enough because too many things are hard to grasp or explain."

"Have you had the experience of working on a film in which the story or a section of the film wasn't good enough and started to fall apart?"

"Yes, on the set of my first film, *Time of Favor*. Some directors do their best work on their first film. Because of their inexperience they're free to make mistakes, and no one has any expectations of them. For other first-time directors, they're so nervous and trying to please every one that they do things with the wrong intentions. I was the second kind. I knew going in that there was something wrong with a scene in the third act. I didn't want the movie to be so serious and wanted it to have a playful wink, like so many American action movies do, particularly films from the early nineties. For example, Bruce Willis in *Die Hard with a Vengeance* (1995) is never really in danger. The audience likes to believe that he is and goes along. I thought I could do that with Israel reality, but I found out that I wasn't speaking the same language at all and didn't have the right tone to produce that. Because I used a real political situation, the wink and playfulness was lost on the Israeli audience. They were not going to go there with me. The movie ended up working, but I really hate it for that reason. I made a promise to myself that I'll never again look at a scene that isn't working and go forward with it. I have enough experience now so that I know never to lie to myself. It's so tempting to say that something is good when it isn't. And it can happen in preproduction, when you're shooting, or in the editing."

"The characters in your films are so carefully drawn it seems you don't miss a detail in your understanding of what makes them tick, particularly for the dueling father and son in *Footnote*.'"

"For the filmmaker there is no choice but to treat every detail, including the character's personality, as if the entire project relies on that one detail. While working on *Footnote* I became aware of how philologists study the Talmud at the Hebrew University in Jerusalem. This is the scholarly pursuit of the main characters, Eliezer and Uriel Shkolnik, in the story. Philologists refrain from analyzing content; instead they focus on whether or not the text is accurate. In other words, they don't care what the letters or words mean. They just want to know that what they're looking at is not a mistake so that maybe five hundred years from now, if they do their job right, there will be someone who will have a text that is accurate enough to understand. In a way, filmmaking is very similar. On every film there are those who have to be aware of content—the director, producer, screenwriter, actors, cinematographer, editor—but most of the time while working on a film, we're not focused on content. We're doing exactly what a philologist does: examining the most specific details. The focus puller, for example, doesn't care what's in front of the lens. His job is to make sure that the lens is in focus. The director tells the cinematographer to tell the focus puller, 'I want the focus on the left eye and not the right eye or the tip of the nose and not the rim of the nose.' The focus puller has to measure the distance between the tip of the actor's nose to the lens, making sure he's got the proper lighting and the correct area in focus. Why is that important? If what we're shooting is not focused correctly, the storyteller's intention and meaning are lost. Every good film is larger than its parts, but that doesn't mean that while you're working on it you're preoccupied with the big picture. You drown yourself in the tiniest of details because if you don't, there is no big picture."

"The Arab-Israeli conflict is a great part of the fabric of Israeli life, and yet there are no major talking points about that in any of your films. Even in *Beaufort*, which is about a platoon of Israeli soldiers positioned in an occupied fort just before their withdrawal from Lebanon in 2000, the dialogue among the soldiers does not address the reasons for this war or their attitudes toward the enemy."

"In *Beaufort* these soldiers are put into a situation that has a political meaning because they're fighting in the name of a political idea. But for each of the soldiers the experience is personal, not political. It's about survival, not being physically uncomfortable and deprived of basic needs. These soldiers were so isolated that conversations from outside the fort never leaked in. They don't see their enemies. They don't see their leaders. They don't hear the debate. They're in their own world and that world is not about why they're fighting, but rather how are they going to get through this."

"Your films are seen by audiences all over the world and typically feature Israeli life. Do you feel any sort of responsibility to enlighten the world about what Israeli life is like?"

"My only responsibility is to get the story right. A good story is about individuals dealing with something extremely specific to them. Putting it into a national context is to ignore that. 'Universal themes' have a negative connotation for me. I believe that there are cultural differences among peoples. Not everything is universal, and not everything can be understood by everyone. I'm more curious about a story that is described as unique than one that is described as universal."

Emily Mann

Award-winning playwright and director Emily Mann has interpreted an extraordinary body of classic work that includes Chekhov's Uncle Vanya, *Ibsen's* A Doll's House, *Edward Albee's* All Over, *and Tennessee Williams's* A Streetcar Named Desire, *as well as contemporary works such as Danai Gurira's* The Convert *(2012) and* Greensboro Requiem *(1999), which was written by Mann. I visited Emily at the McCarter Theatre in Princeton, New Jersey, where she has directed for the past twenty-two years. After our conversation I photographed her on the stage, backlit by a single exposed light bulb. Emily called it the ghost light.*

"It's unusual for playwrights to direct their own plays. How did you come to do both?"

"I was writing short stories and poems from the time I could hold a pencil, so I always knew that I would write. When my family moved to Chicago in my high school years, I found myself searching for new modes of expression. I loved so many things—psychology, painting, music, sculpture. I took a theater class in my junior year, and after I participated in a show, the director said to me, 'You should think about directing. You're capable of seeing the whole, not just the parts.' I thought to myself *Yes, that's true. I do.* So he offered to let me direct a play—something fluffy and light—*No Exit*, by Jean-Paul Sartre. I knew immediately what to say to the actors, where the music should come in, how to stage the scenes, and how to close the play. I found myself in a zone that I would sometimes get into when I was writing, when everything is just flowing out of me and I'm soaring, flying. You know the moment when you've hit gold. That's when I found out what I wanted to do in my life."

"It's interesting that your teacher recognized your aptitude for directing at such a young age."

"Well, I was probably not a very good actress. But I was a very thoughtful kid. I felt that I needed to know more about my character in order to play her, so I asked a lot of questions—big questions. It must have been clear to him that I had a broader sense of things, and a deeper vision. I looked at the play thematically, analytically, and tried to understand how all the components added up to the whole. I also had a very tender-hearted nature."

"Do you think that the plays you've written and directed have been motivated by a deeper purpose beyond entertainment—a way for you to express personal, political, or philosophical ideas?"

"Absolutely. If you examine my body of work you'll find that it's autobiographical. You can tell what I'm about just by looking at the titles of the plays I've directed and the way I've directed them. I'm drawn to work concerning women and people of color. My work is often considered radical, especially by the Broadway community, which is why I work mostly outside Broadway. I'm very fortunate to run a theater here in Princeton where I can do what I want and have an audience who wants to see the work. I don't have to depend on outside people to hire me to do the plays that I'm interested in."

"This is a magnificent theater in a beautiful setting here on the Princeton University campus. Is it also an inspiring environment?"

"This is a place where pure artistry can be made—art backed by passion and rigor. It's a place that's not afraid of a strong woman's voice or of a socially active vision. We have a great mixture of work here, and all of it is artist-driven, whether it comes from the writer or the director. What I have found over the years is that there is a real split between commercial theater and art theater. People today are not looking for thoughtful plays in the numbers they once did—during the golden age of theater. Commercial theater in New York and other big cities is plagued with a real malaise, a rotten core. Tennessee Williams had it right when he said, 'There is a real lust for mediocrity and a celebration of the anti-intellectual and anti-emotional.' There are so many fantastic playwrights writing today, but their work is not considered commercial enough and therefore not being produced. Where you choose to make your art says a lot about you as an artist. My play *The Convert* received standing ovations here in Princeton, at the Goodman Theatre in Chicago, and at the Kirk Douglas Theater in Los Angeles. But we cannot get a New York producer to take it, commercial or otherwise. Too often, plays that have great integrity, import, and impact don't get to Broadway. And that's why I've decided to run a theater outside of New York."

"Many of your plays document historical events. Has your work been effective in raising consciousness about the issues that are important to you?"

"Yes, very much so. I often refer to my plays as theater of testimony or documentary dramas. I can answer that best by giving you two anecdotes of how documentary theater can affect lives. *Having Our Say* (2009) is a play I wrote and directed based on the book *Having Our Say: The Delany Sisters' First One Hundred Years* by Amy Hill Hearth. It's the oral histories of two African-American sisters, both over a hundred years old. The production was an enormous success here at the McCarter Theatre, on Broadway, and around the country. After it premiered, I got a note from a Princeton matron whose name will go unmentioned. She wrote, 'Thank you so much for introducing me to Sadie and Bessie Delany. I have never known a black person who didn't work for us. It's the first time that I realized that I could have a friend that is African American or even be part of my family.' Her seeing our play was so profound she had to admit these things. She had never met an African-American person of her own class, education, and someone whose emotional life she could relate to. Her entire perception about African-American people changed after seeing our play.

"Another play that I wrote was *Greensboro Requiem*. It tells of a massacre that happened in 1979 in Greensboro, North Carolina, where the KKK attacked an anti-Klan rally, murdering five, wound[ing] countless others, and destroying their neighborhood. The men responsible were all acquitted. One would expect something like that to happen in the 1930s or '40s, but because it happened in 1979, I had to write about it. We premiered the play in 1999. A whole group of survivors from the actual massacre attended the performance along with the new mayor or Greensboro. She was so moved by what she learned from the play that she helped form the first Truth and Reconciliation Committee in this country. Desmond Tutu helped found it. It was revealed that the perpetrators of the Greensboro massacre were members of the Greensboro police department and also of the KKK. *Greensboro Requiem* had a huge political impact and affected audiences intellectually, emotionally, and spiritually. I want a play to give the audience something that they may not have felt or known before. I want our plays to matter. That's one of the reasons I wanted to bring *A Streetcar Named Desire* to Broadway with a cast of color."

"I just saw the play on Broadway a couple of nights ago."

"How did you feel about it?"

"I thoroughly enjoyed it and thought that the performances were extraordinary. The story and the dialogue is pure Tennessee Williams, and the fact that the cast was all African American didn't necessarily alter or enhance the power of the play. *A Streetcar Named Desire* is not a play about race. It's a play about four complex characters and their interrelationships, and that's what I responded to."

"That's exactly what I would have hoped you would say. What we're finding is that white audiences who exit the theater after the performance are not talking about race. They're talking about the story and the performances. The added benefit for black people is that suddenly the great American playwright's masterpiece is a play that African American's can share in. They're no longer kept off the Broadway stage to play these roles. It's about inclusion in the theatrical, artistic community. One African-American playwright said to me, 'I knew I was indebted to August Wilson, but now I also want to live up to Tennessee Williams because of his understanding of the human heart.'"

"Tennessee Williams's plays have been performed continuously around the country for decades. Are you saying that they were not accessible to the African-American community?"

"Yes. They haven't been. I say that because of what it took for producers, Stephen Byrd and Alia Jones, to bring this production of *Streetcar* to Broadway."

"Byrd said something in *Playbill* about bringing in African-American audiences that you might find interesting. 'Tyler Perry became a billionaire catering to the audience ignored by Broadway. There is an audience between Perry and August Wilson that hasn't been addressed. That's the sweet spot.' Byrd has produced *Cat on a Hot Tin Roof* with an all–African-American cast and is next looking to do the same with *Who's Afraid of Virginia Wolf*. Is this really serving the African-American community or has he stumbled on a formula to make himself a billionaire?"

"I think we've made a work of art with *A Streetcar Named Desire*, regardless of Byrd's attitude projected in that article. Much of the work that I do is quietly radical, and I'm often bashed by the Broadway press. But Stephen Byrd and Alia Jones don't care about the press. They can fill theater seats without the *New York Times*. They've supported me all the way through and treat me with great respect. They know that they're making real art here and that I'm a director with a vision. I've wanted to do *Streetcar* for twenty years and would not have been able to without their backing."

"What does an audience need to bring with them when they go to see a dramatic play?"

"An open heart and a clear mind . . . that's all. But that's big. The theater asks you to do a little work—to receive it and have it live inside you. It asks you to concentrate. It's not delivered to you like a TV show or movie. Theater is not about sitting back. Theater is about leaning forward. Athol Fugard, the great South African playwright, put it very well when he said, 'To me great entertainment is the interplay between heart and mind.' That's what I'm all about."

"Directors and playwrights often work collaboratively in the early stages of putting on a play. What's it like for a director when the playwright in no longer living?"

"That's such a great question. It's so helpful when a playwright is there with you to clarify his or her intention—*She shouldn't kiss him there* or *Here is where she breaks down*. Those notes in my ear from the playwright are invaluable in finishing a work. So when the playwright is not there, it's much more difficult. I was pining for Tennessee while working on *Streetcar*. I had to dig back into his journals and letters to know what he would have wanted me to do. Tennessee used to say, 'I want humor in my plays even though there's tragedy going on.' He liked to stand in the back of the house cackling during a performance while no one else was laughing. I learned that he thought that the line 'I've always depended on the kindness of strangers' was going to be a laugh line. He wrote it thinking that is was funny. And so I directed it like that."

"Do you think that Tennessee would have been proud of this production of yours?"

"I do. I don't want to be too self-aggrandizing, but I think he would have loved it.

"I was a young woman when I met him in the last years of his life. We did get close, and he had a very important effect on my life. Remember earlier I told you that I was a very sensitive child? Tennessee was very much like that too, and he recognized that in me—and I in him. I think that's one of the reasons we connected."

"Tennessee Williams's last years were desperately wretched. What do you know of that time in his life?"

"I remember this one night when he was sobbing in my arms, and these three awful young men with blue eyes and blond hair and mean little faces came in to take him out to feed off and exploit him. And he let them. He always needed the company of men and paid for it. Despite his having achieved greatness in his own lifetime, it was very difficult for a gay man in those years. I don't think he squandered his talent, but he did lose his gift a little too soon. What I learned from him was not to become an alcoholic and not to do your work in a way that makes you crazy, because, if you do, people will prey on you.

"Tennessee wanted me to direct one of his plays. It would be his last, although I didn't know that at the time. I worshipped him as a writer, but this play was a total wreck. He asked me to come live with him in Key West—'We can work on it together Miss Emily.' Those drunken orgies down there were legendary. I freaked out and didn't do it. For a long time I really regretted that decision, but the truth was that his writing was pretty much gone by then."

"How did knowing Tennessee Williams influence your life and your work?"

"Tennessee showed me the meaning of fragility. He taught me that you have to protect yourself, if you're sensitive and fragile. I've had to work very hard my whole life to build protective walls all around me. I need an institution around me, like this one; loyal and supportive people in my life, like my husband; and lots of trees and flowers and green lawns. I need people between me and *them*—the bullies out there. Tennessee taught me about bullies. His whole life was about having been bullied, first by his father and then by the Stanley Kowalskis of the world. He said that in order to move forward as an artist you have to protect yourself and your sensitive nature. That's what *A Streetcar Named Desire* is all about—not letting the brutes destroy you."

Michael Mayer

Tony Award winner Michael Mayer is one of Broadway's most innovative and original stage directors. Through his untraditional creative process and highly conceptual approach, his shows such as the revival of Thoroughly Modern Millie *(2002),* Spring Awakening *(2006), and* American Idiot *(2010) have helped reenergize New York's theater district. Additionally, his shows have found audiences all around the country. I met with the busy director at his Manhattan apartment on a Sunday afternoon. With* On a Clear Day You Can See Forever *(2011) in the works, and having just directed the pilot for television's* Smash *(2012–), he sat down with me to talk about what drives his love of storytelling and the challenges and risks he's willing to take to exercise that love.*

"How did you become interested in entertainment?"

"I can track that back to when I was a kid and my mother called me into my grandparents' bedroom in Alexandria, Virginia, to watch the dancing Scarecrow in *The Wizard of Oz* (1939). I was memorizing watching Ray Bolger on that little TV set. Watching the annual telecast of *The Wizard of Oz* became for me more important than my birthday, Halloween, Christmas, or Chanukah. I even owned a record from the film and would act out scenes from the movie. I performed it in the backyard or the basement, anywhere, and I'd recruit my brother and sister, cousins and my friends to help me reenact the film. I was *directing* without realizing that I was setting up my future. It wasn't until I was in the sixth grade that I understood that one could do this sort of thing as a profession."

"When did your directing career actually take off?"

"The year was 1993. I was working at NYU in their graduate acting program as a guest director on a production of *Hay Fever*. It was also around the time that *Angels in America: Millennium Approaches*, which would go on to win a Pulitzer Prize, was coming to the Broadway stage. Its playwright, Tony Kushner, was a friend of mine and asked me if I wanted to help him develop part 2 of *Angels in America*, *Perestroika*, and workshop it to make it ready for the stage. I said yes and began working on it with many of my *Hay Fever* cast members. I imagined it as an actor-driven piece with a scene-to-scene flow that incorporated a live musician. I was very comfortable with the material, confident in my craft, and inspired by our cast and design team. This little workshop would become the second hottest ticket in town. The preview had a line clear around the block. We literally jammed people into the theater. Everyone wanted to know about this amazing show. Our production was fanned by 'angel fever' that was sweeping New York at that time. I found myself directing a really important and highly visible show just as *Millennium Approaches* was opening. And so I became a director to be taken seriously."

"How do you describe your creative process?"

"I'm highly intuitive and work very much in the moment. I tend not to plan things out so that I'm unhampered by decisions made ahead of time. I prefer to just be in the space with my actors, a copy of the play, and the design team, and together we create a world that feels right. My designers and I will come up with a concept that supports the way I like to work. I always prefer to begin with an empty space. Sometimes it's a big messy room with a ton of crap in it, as was the case with *American Idiot*, or it can be a room that's practically empty, only eight chairs like with *Spring Awakening*. My process is to have absolute flexibility so that I don't need walls. I can define the space through the actions and dynamics of the characters in order to tell the story. With *Spring Awakening* I put two chairs down on the floor and said to the actors, 'Okay, you're in the forest, and that is a giant log and you're going to lean up against it.' Does the audience actually need to see a real log there? No. What matters is what's happening between those people. There is another scene in the show that takes place in a hayloft. I had this image of the boy floating on a square on the floor with ropes hanging from above. [The female character] says to him, 'What are you doing in a hayloft?' So it's a hayloft. It's how Shakespeare worked. It's how Brecht worked. This is how I love to work; when the text tells you where you are and what you need to know."

"By working this way you engage the audience to use their imagination."

"That's right. When I did *A View from the Bridge* (1998), which is a kitchen sink drama where every production traditionally has had walls decorated with wallpaper, furniture, and staircases, and it's all very literalized, I did my own version as though it was in a Greek amphitheater. I used a single table and a few chairs—that's it! The actors moved around on the stage, and the scenes were clearly delineated by the lighting, behavior and staging. The play was unrestrained and allowed to breathe in an almost operatic way. With *American Idiot* you look at the set and think, *This is some kind of warehouse space.* The characters are living in a warehouse in Bush's post-9/11 America. Later these three guys leave the warehouse, get on a bus, and go on a psychic journey. The scaffolding became a bus. We slide the bed over there and pretended it's a car. We can do whatever we imagine. At the end of the day, the limits of the stage are really only the limits of the building we're in. That's a really exciting way to work."

"How do you direct your actors?"

"I don't direct the actors. I direct the audience. I tell them where to look, what to feel, who to root for. I want them to invest themselves emotionally in the characters and encourage them to *hear* the music and *see* what's happening on the stage. I want them to take a very particular journey with me and my team through the tools I have at my disposal: the acting, spoken word, stage design, music, and dance. My job is to say, 'Come with me, this way and that way; look here; go there. Get it?' I enjoy the interaction between my actors in scene work, but what I really love are the transitions from scene to scene—where the characters are and where they're going. These have the potential to enlighten, seduce, and intoxicate us with anticipation for what's coming next. I specifically look for projects with interesting juxtapositions, like a story set in one time period with the cultural expression of another, as was the case with *Spring Awakening*. It's based on a controversial German play by Frank Wedekind set in nineteenth-century Germany about teenagers discovering their sexuality. We set it to a twenty-first-century sensibility, using alternative rock music and contemporary choreography."

"How does storytelling against a musical score enhance the experience?"

"I'm fascinated by a narrative that is delivered not only through lyrics but through melody. A melody can be highly seductive and is in fact also telling us the story. The audience is receiving information sonically, melodically, rhythmically as well as visually. So when you have this crackle between the lyric and the music, there is a powerful tension that is like a metaphor for what the character is experiencing. I found this to really work with *American Idiot*, which was inspired by the American punk rock band Green Day and their album of the same name. Audiences discovered that their music contained a lush melodic element, which helped deliver the story."

"How can you tell when you're on the right path and creating something that will resonate with audiences?"

"The beautiful thing about being a director, unlike the actor, is that you're really on the outside looking in. While working on a show I'll sit where the audience sits. I try to become them through a kind of shape-shifting transformation. I might become my mother or father or some housewife from New Jersey. I try to imagine being them to make an assessment of what I'm actually seeing. Then I put my director's hat back on and decide, *That's not good enough or this is what I want*."

"The content of your shows tend to deal with socially driven issues. Is that because you are personally concerned with the issues that face us as a society?"

"Yes. Let's look at my revival of *Thoroughly Modern Millie*, which has traditionally been such a conventional, crowd-pleasing show, a tap-dancing extravaganza. But the way we presented it was fairly subversive, talking about social issues in a fairly sly way—feminism, racism, and the value of having money over not having money. I was trying to keep one eye on the history of this show, while creating something entirely new that would be relevant to what people are thinking about today. It requires knowing the original source material and how best to adapt it. If you're paying attention to the show's subtext, you can get much more from it than just a wildly entertaining evening. That's actually been my goal. I'd like to touch people, connect with every individual who comes to one of my shows, and have them walk out knowing a little bit more about how and what they think. What we do in the theater is tell stories. Stories are often reenactments of real and imagined events. Those reenactments in time become legends and those legends become a massive reservoir of our culture's collective consciousness."

"Are most of your productions motivated by themes that have deeply personal meaning for you?"

"Usually they do. It's the reason I wanted to do *On a Clear Day You Can See Forever*. I'd been working on reviving it for the past fifteen years. The story spoke to me. It's about letting go of someone you love and moving on to the possibility of loving someone new, but also letting go of an idea of who you are, and allowing yourself to become the person you were meant to be. This production is based on my own personal vision with the concept of reincarnation that seemed like a useful metaphor. I hoped that by bringing to it a new concept, a more soulful and serious context along with its glorious score, it could be rediscovered."

"Owning a show's vision means having to protect it from veering off track as well as from the influences of your collaborators who might consciously or unconsciously try to change it?"

"There's a famous line in the theater that goes, 'The musical is an organism hell-bent on self-destruction.' Musicals are delicate, and often I feel like I'm only there to keep it alive, like I'm the chief surgeon in the OR. Sometimes I have to make sure that I'm not forcing a procedure on the patient because of my ego or because I'm so hell-bent on fulfilling my idea of what it is. Even though I may have my own agenda and want to control it, I have to listen to what *it* wants; otherwise I might force things and end up killing it. When I can keep things in balance and work closely with my actors, dancers, choreographer, designer, stage manager, writer, producers, musical director, orchestrator, and sound designer, I do better."

"You recently ventured into television, directing the pilot for the show *Smash* on NBC. How does it compare with the theatrical stage?"

"TV is more of a writer/producer's medium. The kind of influence a director has on a television show is mostly limited to the series pilot, which establishes the look, the feel, the cast, the theory behind all the production decisions, including the way it's going to be shot. It's not exclusively my voice just because I'm the director. *Smash* is about the making of a Broadway show. It's a drama with musical numbers written by Theresa Rebeck and is very much Rebeck's vision. But the show's producers, Steven Spielberg and Bob Greenblatt, also have a good deal of input as does NBC and DreamWorks."

"You've devoted the better part of your life to theatrical storytelling. Today there are so many options for audiences due to new digital and electronic advances, do you feel any sort of responsible to help keep the theater alive?"

"I believe in the power of the American musical to change lives, not just the lives of the people making it, but those seeing it. I feel that many of the musicals I've done—*Spring Awakening*, *10 Million Miles*, *American Idiot*, and this revival of *On a Clear Day*, have the potential to move this art form forward while honoring its fabulous tradition. I love that decades after Carol Channing walked down her long staircase in *Hello, Dolly!* at the St. James Theater, St. Jimmy makes his entrance in *American Idiot* down a big rickety scaffolding staircase in the same theater."

"How do you handle disappointment when a show doesn't find its audience?"

"I tend not to give that too much thought. If I did, I probably wouldn't be able to get out of bed in the morning. I've had shows that failed and my work trashed and dismissed. It's a heartbreaker when that happens. You want what you do to matter and at the same time push the envelope. I don't care so much what the *New York Times* says, or even if people will buy tickets. What I don't want is the work to go away so fast. It's tragic when something doesn't have a long run. You want it to live long enough to reach people and grow the way a show does when it has legs. You want it to become much more than what you've imagined. I don't need something to run for thirty years like a *Phantom of the Opera*, but I'm always afraid of not accessing the truest part of myself and the most honest and deepest part of my humanity as a storyteller/director. At the end of the day, I'm willing to risk the terrible possibility of failure to do what I love."

Susan Stroman

I first interviewed director-choreographer Susan Stroman in 2000 for my book Masters of Movement: Portraits of America's Great Choreographers. *At the time, her shows* Contact *and the revival of* The Music Man *had just opened.* The Producers *(2001) was still in the works and would go on to win more Tony Awards than any other musical in Broadway history. Stroman continues to direct critically acclaimed shows like* The Scottsboro Boys *(2010), which garnered twelve Tony nominations. We had a warm reunion at her Midtown office, where we picked up where we'd left off twelve years earlier.*

"*The Producers* turned out to be a huge hit. To what do you attribute its success?"

"It hit at a good time, in fact, just at the right time. I worked on *Thou Shall Not* (2001) that same year. It was a musical based on Emile Zola's very dark novel, *Therese Raquin*. We were about to go into previews when the Twin Towers fell. Suddenly it was very difficult for me to rally the cast and crew to go on. I tried pointing out to them that this is what we do for a living—the show must go on. It closed after eighty-five performances. Audiences were in a somber mood and weren't interested in seeing a story about a murder. But people flocked to see *The Producers*. They came for relief and to be uplifted in the same way that people went to see Fred Astaire and Ginger Rogers on the big screen during the Depression. *Thou Shall Not* could not break through because everyone in New York was grieving. So the timing of a show is vital to its success. It needs to connect with where people are in their thinking and in their lives."

"Why do live theatrical shows affect audiences so deeply?"

"What makes a play or a musical unique is that every performance is done specifically for that particular audience. The next night will be different and the night before that was different; therefore, each time is a rare and personal experience. What happens is a one-time connection between the performers and the audience who are seeing real people on the stage tell a story, portray characters, sing and dance and are committed to doing this eight times a week. Whether it's a straight play or a

musical, the theater has its own way of storytelling. It's very much about the use of spoken language. Everyone who works in the theater has command of the language, and for some audience members, words and dialogue could be something that's missing in their lives. It's quite different from films, which are more visual with much less dialogue, a back-and-forth of action and reaction shots. Because of these things and its unique look and feel, you remember every play or musical you've ever seen. I'm sure you can't remember what movie you saw last week. Can you?"

"Hmmm . . ."

"See? You're struggling to remember. But when you go to see a play or a musical you remember where you had dinner that night and who you went with. There is something deeply human, and that gets inside of you as an audience member."

"What do you think we can learn about ourselves as a culture by the way we respond to theater?"

"I think a show like *The Scottsboro Boys*, which didn't run long on Broadway but is now on a regional run, affected audiences very much. It's based on a story that took place in 1931 about nine African-American teen boys unjustly accused of raping two white girls. It's a story about race, which is something we're still talking about today. You go out to dinner after seeing the show, and you have to talk about it and how it relates to your own life. This show provokes conversation. It makes us think about this country's history. It brings up our feelings of guilt and makes us wonder about how we react to the color of someone's skin."

"What's your process for preparing a book for the stage?"

"One of the important things you do as a director is reference the decade and geographical location in which the story you're telling takes place. With a show like *Oklahoma!*, you base the look and choreography on what was going on at the turn of the century — people fighting for territory and the lives of pioneering women. With a show like *Contact*, you recreate the sensual, sexual underworld of the 1990s nightclub scene. If you're doing a show like *The Producers*, you have to immerse yourself in the world of Mel Brooks! All of his screenplays take a nod to musical theater. In his film *Blazing Saddles* (1974), the railroad workers break out into Cole Porter's 'I Get a Kick Out of You.' In *To Be or Not to Be* (1983), he and Anne Bancroft sing 'Sweet Georgia Brown.' And, of course, we all know the musical number 'Springtime for Hitler' in *The Producers*. Mel loves musical theater. For this show, however, the comedy was first and foremost in the staging, lyrics, orchestration, and choreography. *The Producers* is really a comedy-musical more than a musical-comedy. Not only was the show successful because of its timing, but because it was so well written and performed by its lead actors, Nathan Lane and Matthew Broderick."

"How did you go about adapting it from a film to the Broadway stage?"

"When Mel approached me to work with him on *The Producers*, he didn't know how to structure it for musical theater. He had written the screenplay and a few songs that would ultimately be in the show. But in the theater everyone involved is swimming together in this big pool. We're either going to win a medal together or we're all going to drown. We continue swimming together past opening night. In the movies the cast and crew never see each other after the last day of shooting. The director works with the editor and then the marketing people, and no one's ever in the same room together. But in the theater there is a desperate need to make a show work, and that desperate passion is shared continuously with everyone involved. That's very different from filmmaking, and I think Mel loved that so much he wanted to do it again with [the 2007 stage version of] *Young Frankenstein*."

"You once told me that your rehearsal process is vital to the success of the show. How does it work?"

"I go into rehearsals with a vision of what I would like the show to be. I don't necessarily share that vision with the performers, because I'd like for them to feel that they've been a great part of its creation. With *The Producers*, we began by talking about each of the characters and how they would move physically on the stage. Max Bialystok moves very differently from Leo Bloom. He is very comfortable in his skin and uses his body and gesture with great abandon. Leo is shy and nervous, and so his movement is quite small and close to the body. Every character has his own body language, and it's this language that helps [communicate] their character to the audience."

"Filmmakers often do storyboarding. Do you have a similar process to convey to cast and crew what you have in mind?"

"By the time you get to rehearsing with your cast, you've worked it through with your set, costume, and lighting designers, first individually and then together as a team. By the first day of rehearsal, it's pretty well all sorted out. Because I visualize music, it's very natural for me to work through an entire show in my mind, even before I get together with the designers. Often I work on something for two, three, or four years before bringing it to a producer."

"Though you may have invested years developing a show, backers' auditions determine if it makes it to Broadway or an Off Broadway stage."

"That's absolutely right. We used to call them backers' auditions. Now they're called readings. What we do is present it to a bunch of producers to see if they're interested in putting money behind it. I'll never forget the reading we had for *The Producers*. I was nervous and thought to myself, *There will only be a handful of people who will go with this*. I couldn't imagine producers wanting to back a show with songs that had lyrics like, 'I was a cheat. I was a lousy person, but I was a Broadway producer.' To my utter surprise, backers were throwing money at it."

"You went from being a choreographer to director-choreographer. Why was it important for you to also direct?"

"In musicals it's common for dance numbers to look added on and break the flow of the scenes, as if the director stops rehearsals and says, 'Okay, call in the choreographer and have her put some steps in here.' When you're telling a story, you don't want a lot of stops and starts and inconsistencies. Owning the overall storytelling journey makes the show much more cohesive. The director's job is to make sure that there are smooth transitions from scene to dance to scene again. When you have the total vision, the show becomes more seamless. Audiences today have a more refined cinematic eye, so as the director you want even the transitions to smoothly move the story forward."

"How can choreography be helpful in developing the arc of your characters?"

"Well, let's look at *The Music Man*. When Harold Hill first comes to River City, Iowa, the people are very stiff, erect, and move their bodies very little. But as he infuses the town with music and song, people start loosening up and pretty soon everyone is doing the 'Shipoopi.' Every character on the stage is evolving and changing, and that is realized not only through the book and the lyrics but through the music and dance, with its emphasis on forward motion. Even the scenes are constructed that way."

"You've had a great many successful Broadway shows. Is it ever really possible to predict if a show will be a hit or a flop?"

"If there was a formula for success, we'd all be doing it. In the theater you're a gypsy. You go from show to show to show, and you never know how things will turn out. In the words of Mel Brooks, 'You hope for the best, but expect the worst.' Every new work involves a new creative team, a new family that you're involved with until you give birth on opening night. There are always going to be stories to tell, and we're all trying to find new innovative ways of telling them. With *The Scottsboro Boys*, which was staged in the form of a minstrel show in a semicircle, we flipped it on its ear and had black men playing white parts. So there were no cliché black roles. They played the parts of a white sheriff, white judge and lawyer, white girls [that] actors would never have expected to play. It's all about finding interesting and new devices for storytelling."

"It must be extraordinarily upsetting when a show doesn't find its audience and have its intended theatrical life."

"When a show doesn't work, it's a great disappointment and very hard to recover from. I always feel bad when there's money lost from a show, but I never feel that it's a failure artistically. Never! I remember saying to Bernie Gersten, one of the Lincoln Center Theater producers after *That Shall Not*, that I was sorry about the money that had been lost. And he said to me, 'We don't lose money. We spend money on artists.' He truly understands what we're about, and this is a real comfort. As I go from show to show, I think of each of them as stepping stones of what I have learned and can apply to the next."

"What if you're not fortunate enough to have a next show?"

"One of the most famous directors of the Broadway stage, George Abbott, once said, 'When you open a show, you have to have a meeting the next day to start another one.' And I've always done that, whether my previous show was a hit or not. You can't get caught up in the mindset of successes or failures. You have to just keeping moving on. The truth of the matter is that great art is often not recognized in its own time. When I worked on *The Frogs* (2004) with Nathan Lane and Stephen Sondheim, the day after the reviews came out, and they were very mixed, I said to Sondheim, 'I'm really sorry.' And he said, 'Oh, it doesn't matter. I've never gotten a good review in my life.' 'What?' I said. 'Excuse me?' To which he replied, 'I only get good reviews when the shows come back ten years later.'"

"So what's next for you?"

"I'll be co-directing the Hal Prince retrospective, *Prince of Broadway*, with Hal. After that, a show called *Big Fish*, adapted from the film about a man who tells his son big fish stories and his son's quest to find out if the stories are true. I am also working on a musical theater piece based on Degas' famous statue of the little dancer. In researching this statute, we found out that when it was exhibited, Degas received the worst reviews of his career. It upset him so much, he hid it away in his closet and it was not discovered until forty years after his death. Now it's hailed as one of the ten greatest statues ever made. Like I said earlier, often one's work is not appreciated in its own time."

"The Broadway scene—all of these old historic theaters around Times

Square seem to give off a kind of nostalgic, magical vibe. Whether I enter a theater through the main entrance or backstage door, I always feel something in the air. It's almost like the place is haunted."

"We who work in the theater believe in ghosts and the spirits of the performers who have played there. If you walk through Shubert Alley, the corridor between Eighth Avenue and Broadway linking West Forty-fourth and Forty-fifth, you can feel the electricity in the air. There is something going on there. I feel it every time I walk by. We in the theater are very superstitious. You can't whistle onstage. You can't ever say 'good luck' before a performance; you have to say 'break a leg.' When you're on the stage, you never mention the name of the Shakespearean play with the three witches. I'm talking about *Macbeth*," she whispered.

"You've garnered numerous Tony, Drama Desk, and Laurence Olivier awards. Has success affected your creativity, your artist within?"

"There is no such thing as success in the heart of the artist. And that's because artists move immediately on to their next work of art, which requires one hundred percent of them each time. If you really believe that you have something to contribute, you just follow your heart and your instincts. In the theater, you're telling a story with blocking, choreography, design, and music. You are doing it for yourself, but the very last thing that's added is the breath of an audience. They bring it to life."

This was show business! So that was the beginning and, God bless him, Don Appell was the means. He thought I had promise. I remember he said to me one day, 'Look, you'll never be a leading man. I can tell you that now. But you can always be a second or third banana. I know you'll make it in this business.'"

"Not only did you make it in this business and make it big, you eventually did become a leading man."

"Well, yes. No one was going to give me the part of a romantic lead, so I decided to make myself the lead in two of my own films: *High Anxiety* (1977) and *Life Stinks* (1991)."

"How did you come to write comedy for the television hit *Your Show of Shows* (1950–1954)?"

"Don Appell was also the social director of the Avon Lodge, where he gave me a job playing drums. That's where I met a tenor saxophone player named Sid Caesar. Sid was not only a musician, but very funny, and Don used him as a utility comic when he needed another funny man. Since I was a drummer, Sid and I would get together for jam sessions, and we became friends. But then came the war, and I went off to an army-specialized training program, and Sid went into the Coast Guard. Then one day Don took me to see a movie that was raising money for the Coast Guard called *TARS and SPARS* (1946) starring Alfred Drake and Janet Blair. Sid Caesar was in the film as the comedy relief. This was the era of all those war pictures, and Sid did these hilarious impressions of the Germans and the Japanese. He was amazing! Max Liebman, who had discovered Danny Kaye, saw the movie and liked Sid, and that's how it all began. Max put together a television show called *The Admiral Broadway Revue* (1949), starring Sid and Imogene Coca. It was a variety show with comedy acts and musical numbers. I'd often have Sid in stitches, laughing so hard he'd be rolling on the floor. So he said to me, 'I'll give you forty bucks a week if you'll be my personal writer.' I said, 'Wow! Boy! Sure!' So I began writing for *The Admiral Broadway Revue* but got no screen credit. I created the popular airport interview sketch 'Here We Are at Idyllwild Airport.' Sid would always arrive from some far-off place and be interviewed by cast member Tom Avera."

"How did you know how to write comedy?"

"I didn't know how. But I had this gift to put ideas and pictures into words. It took a long time for me to get good at it. I was mentored by Mel Tolkin, who I had met on *The Admiral Broadway Revue*. He later became the head writer on *Your Show of Shows*. He was Russian and a big fan of the Russian writers, so he suggested that I read *Dead Souls* by

Nikolai Gogol and the works of Dostoyevsky, Tolstoy, and Isaac Babel. I learned to write from reading the Russian writers and also from being in the company of Mel Tolkin and Lucille Kallen, the show's sketch writers. I studied the way they put words together to describe scenes and how to be clear. Neil Simon, Larry Gelbart, and Woody Allen were also on the team. Gradually I learned my craft. And I had revelations, big, beautiful, brilliant revelations. I discovered that the actual writing wasn't as important as the ideas for the sketches. We were creating a revolution. What we were doing with comedy was different from a guy standing in front of an audience with a microphone and telling twenty-two bad jokes like 'I met a girl she was so thin. I brought her to a restaurant. The waiter said, 'May I check your umbrella?' We were creating sketches with characters drawn from life, but larger than life. We were doing playlets with a beginning, middle, and end. 'A married couple can't sleep because they moved into a new apartment. The builder made the walls so thin that the glow from the television in the next apartment shone through the walls and disturbed their sleep.' Sid's character broke his lease by walking through the walls of six apartments. I came up with that one. The concepts were critical. What we were doing with our sketches was commenting on issues of the day, like cheap building construction. We went way beyond what was happening in comedy at that time, moving from reality to beautiful comic absurdity. While others were painting with primary colors, on *Your Show of Shows* we were painting in pastels. We were Braque and Picasso and Mondrian!"

"And the shows were live!"

"That's right. Videotape didn't yet exist. Back then, live meant live, not like what you see today on *Saturday Night Live*. What you saw on your set was happening in real time. If your fly was open, everybody saw it. If you had to cough while you were speaking, so you coughed. You miss a line, that's it, no going back. You accidentally dressed for the wrong sketch and walked out wearing a Roman soldier's costume for a scene set in a modern office, it was televised like that."

"Sounds like you really were making it big."

"Well, I got no credit at all on *The Admiral Broadway Revue*, even though I wrote a lot of the material. On the first season of *Your Show of Shows*, I only got 'additional dialogue' credit. I was always worried about being let go because I wasn't *really* a staff writer. I was Sid's personal writer, and he was still paying me privately forty bucks a week. I was beginning to get really sick about it, not sleeping at night, throwing up, anxiety attacks. So Mel Tolkin said to me, 'There is this new thing called psychoanalysis. Why don't you try it?' 'How can I do that? I said. 'I can't even pronounce it.' But I decided to do it and went to an analyst named Clement Staff. I saw him for two years. Staff filled me with enough confidence to finally stand up to Max Liebman. 'Max,' I said, 'I'm not coming back next year unless I get writer's credit and officially paid by the show.' So Max says, 'That's fine with me. Don't come back.' When Sid heard about it he got crazy and offered to pay me anything so I wouldn't leave. But I said, 'No, it's over. I'm not going to do this undercover writing anymore. I'm going to be Mel Brooks! I can make a living writing on other shows. I have an agent now at William Morris, and I'll be fine.' So Sid went to Max, and after a good deal of yelling, Max said, 'Okay, you've got billing and $150 bucks a week.' Sid Caesar went to bat for me.

"But let me tell you what happened two years later. Sid was then at the top of his game, so brilliant and so funny. He was making $5,000 dollars a show in 1951. That was really big money then, incredible. He had finished the season and was about to sign a new three-year contract when I proposed, 'Sid, let's be brave. You're going to quit and come with me. We're going to go make movies. Max Liebman discovered you and Danny Kaye, but look what Danny Kaye is doing. He's making movies. Movies will live forever. TV is here and gone. Nobody really appreciates television. It was around that time that a producer from Columbia Pictures had brought me in to write screenplays for them. They thought I was talented and were ready to do movies with me and Sid. So Sid said, 'You know, I agree one hundred percent. The art we create should be more permanent.' So Sid went to Max and told him, 'I'm not coming back. I'm going to California to make movies.' I called Carl Reiner, and he said, 'If you guys go to California, I'll go.' It was thrilling. I was twenty-three years old; Sid, twenty-seven. We were just kids. I was so excited, I started packing. It took me a few minutes—a couple of t-shirts and some socks, and I was ready to go. In the meantime, Max called Pat Weaver, the genius at NBC who organized the network's schedules. When [Pat] informed him that we wanted to leave, he went crazy. They had meetings all week, and finally Sid called me around two in the morning and said, 'I can't do it. I just got off the phone with Pat Weaver and they're offering me $25,000 a show.' 'What?' 'That's right, $25,000 a show! I've signed for three more years. If we're still alive after that, we'll go make movies.' So I said, 'Okay.' What could I say? One couldn't say no to that kind of money. We continued on television until 1959. Six years went by, but by then things had changed. I still had my mind set on making movies, and so I went on to make movies. Sid appeared in a couple of them."

"Did you learn how to direct from observing how things were done on *Your Show of Shows*?"

"Yes. We had a wonderful director/cameraman on that show, Bill Hobin. I learned from him how to cut from one camera to another. 'You're on camera one, go to two, go back to one, go to three.' But Hobin learned a lot from me in terms of staging and timing. I understood how to stage Jewish Russian comedy, like how long do you wait for someone to respond to someone else for comic affect? I knew things like that. If your character was a stutterer, I knew how long he should stutter before breaking it off because I remembered Mr. Katz from Brooklyn."

"Your comedy maintains a strong Jewish philosophical view of life. You deliberately use Jews and the Jewish experience as source material. In *Blazing Saddles* you even cast yourself as a Yiddish-speaking Indian chief!"

"That's right. I wasn't ducking it. I was a flat-out Jew. I was proud of it and blessed with it, and so I used it."

"You took some heat from the Jewish community after *The Producers* came out."

"Yeah, I did. I got something like two hundred letters from rabbis and people of authority protesting *Springtime for Hitler*. 'How dare you? This is shocking. People died in concentration camps and you're using Nazis for comedy.' I wrote back to each and every Jew who wrote to me and explained that you can't bring down despots, dictators, and murders like Hitler by getting on the same soap box with them. The only way to win is to humiliate them, to heap comedy on them and make them ridiculous. That's how you win."

"One of your most hilarious scenes in *The Producers* is the audition for the singing and dancing Hitlers."

"Hitler is such an easy character to make fun of, with that little mustache and that 'heil' salute. As time went by, audiences got what I was trying to do. Bad taste turns out to be good instructive comedy."

"You use racial humor again in *Blazing Saddles*. Cleavon Little's character, Bart, rides into town as the newly appointed sheriff. The town's welcoming committee is appalled when they see that he's black and call him by the N-word. You were showing us how bigoted and stupid these white people were."

"That's exactly right. What drives that story is hatred for the sheriff because he's black. The best defense is to make them the joke. A lot of people thought I was just making fun of westerns, but there's a really big message there."

do it!' And so he sent me out on the road in 1963 to direct my first play, *She Loves Me*."

"What was Broadway like when you started out?"

"First of all, the producers were artists, and they created plays that mirrored their tastes. You could walk into a Broadway theater and without seeing the program know immediately who had produced that play because that was *his* kind of play. But that's changed. Now it's just a big commercial craps game. Everybody today is trying to recreate what we had from the thirties, forties, fifties, and sixties, but can't. The people who call themselves producers—more or less rich people who put up the money—are really backers, and if they get a Tony Award, they bought it with an investment. My backers knew they were backers, and they made money. My backers were proud of their investment, so proud and the return so good that when I wanted to do *Follies* (1971), they didn't care if it returned their investment. They were just proud to have been part of it, like they were with *Damn Yankees* (1955), which actually made them a fortune. And the same thing applies to *Pacific Overtures* (1976). Only a crazy person would do *Pacific Overtures* as an investment. They were willing to back a work of art—a historic Japanese piece, Kabuki, no women, but we wanted to make it. I never thought I'd get rich. But I got rich. But it was not what I thought would happen. I thought I would live my life in the company of artists whom I respected."

"Are you as driven now as you were when you started out? Is the passion the same?"

"Yes! The passion's the same. As long as I've got my energy, I'm going to work just the same as I've always worked. I don't feel a day over forty, but I'm eighty-three. The only thing that's different now is that no one can take it away from me. If they slam me in the papers the day after a show opens, I still bleed. I still have enough of an ego to feel that, but you can't erase my career. I got what I wanted, and I'm terribly grateful for it, but I do believe that luck had a hell of role in it."

"How so?"

"I recently told Sondheim, in reference to a new autobiographical show I'm working on, that I owe much of my career to luck. He thinks I'm nuts. He was eighteen and I was twenty when we met, and he says, 'It's not luck! Are you kidding? You were the most driven, ambitious, and focused person I ever knew.' But he's wrong. I could have been all those things, but I ran into George Abbott when I had to—that was luck. I was twenty when I was drafted during the Korean War at a point when my ambition was dangerous—that was luck. I was sent to Germany, not

Korea, and when I came back I was twenty-four, calmer and more ready to rein in a little bit. That's luck!"

"You thought you could make it big on Broadway at twenty?"

"Yes, I did. I had seen that success at a young age was possible. I went to the same private school as Truman Capote, who had been a year ahead of me. He became a huge star at twenty-one. And so when I was a senior I thought, *I've got to do that too by the time I'm twenty-one*. But I had to wait. And so I was twenty-six when it all happened for me when I produced *Pajama Game*. But what if my first show had been a failure? I would have been resilient, yes, but how quickly would things have happened for me? Bad luck in my case was good luck. Going into the army was something I deplored. It was a disaster for me to have been drafted. Would I have a job when I came back? Well, I did because Abbott promised me one. And I was lucky to have hung out at Maxim's, a bar in the basement of a bombed-out church in Stuttgart after the war where I observed this little guy, an entertainer in that bar. That memory lingered, and in 1965 when *Cabaret* wasn't working out the way I thought it should, I used that fellow as a metaphor for a Germany that was on its heels in the depression. I saw that entertainer as a pathetic, self-deluded little guy who turns into a fascist. That trajectory became the bones of the show.

"It was luck that brought me to Moscow where I observed first-hand the nuts and bolts of the Russian theater and got to know the parameters of working within a black box and empty space. I understood from that experience that you could stage things that hadn't been seen before. It gave me fortitude and conviction. It was luck that I was exposed to the abstract theater in Germany, including the influences of [Erwin] Piscator's techniques, which emphasized the sociopolitical content of drama. And it was luck that I experienced Noh and Kabuki theaters of Japan that inspired *Pacific Overtures*. All of this has gone into producing shows that are diverse and [have] great range."

"How do we know what we're really capable of and when we're on the right path?"

"In the theater you know one thing. Your first show better be a hit! I was desperate not to be a one-trick pony. Fortunately, my first five musicals were hits, though one of them was not initially. When *West Side Story* opened, we had hundreds of walkouts night after night after night. It didn't matter. People kept coming, and the rest is history."

"How do you feel about theater critics and reviews?"

"Theater critics are necessary. You have to have them because they spread the word. The best thing a critic can do is make the show controversial. Any review that takes people to the theater to make up their own minds is good. I did a show a few years ago called *LoveMusik*. It got mixed to bad reviews, which is very usual in my career. One reviewer said it's the best musical he's ever seen in his life, and another said it didn't work. That's the nature of this business, but I'm extremely proud of that show and learned things from directing it. So that show is a success, even though it only ran for ten weeks at Manhattan Theater Club Broadway Theater. You've got to take chances each time and aspire to creating something new for audiences. But you also have to be pragmatic. I would never have attempted *Pacific Overtures* when I was only twenty-five years and hadn't yet proved myself in the theater. You do those things when you can afford to take big risks and when a show like that doesn't have to be a hit.

"I've had more bad reviews than good ones over the years. No one remembers what the initial reception of critics was, as long as the show keeps running. When I did *Fiddler on the Roof*, the reviews were not good. So in its ninth year when it became the longest-running show on Broadway, I printed the show's early reviews and handed them out to the audience. That was fun."

"Another one of your greatest hits is *Phantom of the Opera*, which has been running for twenty-four years. What drew you to that story?"

"I was thinking about how the mechanism in the brain reacts when we encounter someone who by sheer ill fortune is grotesque, someone who may have been trapped in a fire for example. Our natural response is to recoil. But our intelligence says, *Stop that! Stop that right now—engage.* So that was the key to my wanting to tell that story. I was also very interested in the fact that this was a big Victorian melodrama with all these ladies wearing multiple layers of clothes before they take them off. Girls of that period had been brainwashed not to react sexually, so it's highly erotic to see them responding to inclinations awakening within them. Interestingly, my wife saw the show again a few years ago and said, 'You know, I didn't realize all these years how erotic this show is. You dirty old man!' And I said, 'Yeah.' I knew it from the get-go. And I knew that's why it would work. I don't know if *Phantom* is great art, but it surely is great popular art."

"Whenever I'm in Manhattan's theater district and I walk past such historic venues as the St. James, the Majestic, the Shubert, I feel a rush of emotion. How do they make you feel?"

"I love these venerated and venerable theaters even though they are much less comfortable then the newer ones, which are more pleasant backstage for the artists and roomier for the audience. I remember the old Empire Theater on Thirty-ninth Street. I had to walk down these long rails to get to my seat in the second balcony. The theater had no sound system, entirely acoustical. The actors like Julie Harris in *Member of the Wedding* (1952) would have to project their voices to the back of the house. You could hardly hear what they were saying. So you'd have to lean forward and really pay attention. You were essentially collaborating with her, becoming complicitus in the experience. And that's the theater."

"You are both artist and businessman. Do you ever know in advance that your show will make money?"

"I have gone headlong into shows that I knew would not pay back their investment. But I also knew that the show that preceded it did make money and that we'd made a profit. I remember saying to Sondheim, 'We'd better do a money-maker next time. So the next year was *A Little Night Music*, and we made some money."

"Have you had periods when your shows just didn't make it?"

"There was an eight-year period where I did one flop after another. Eight years! Eight years of going to opening nights with my wife and children and reading the worst reviews in the world. Then closing the show and starting over again. I had put my heart into those shows, delved into subjects or ideas that interested me, but the critics or the public did not discern what I was reaching for and rejected them."

"But this is the artist's life, is it not?"

"Yes, it is, and it begins with that lucky moment when you realize something profound and say, 'I'm going to express something on the stage that I haven't quite seen expressed before.' Scripture says there is nothing new under the sun, but there is. The idea is to raise the level of art. When you have the confidence to take the chance to truly express what's inside of you—your own vision—it's the most important thing that you can do."

Walter Hill

I expected Walter Hill, the director of so many popular male-dominated action films like Hard Times *(1975),* The Warriors *(1979),* The Long Riders *(1980),* 48 Hours *(1982),* Geronimo: An American Legend *(1993),* Wild Bill *(1995), and others to be as tough and hard-edged as many of his protagonists. What I found was a warm, sensitive, and generous man with sage-like wisdom about the power of cinematic storytelling.*

"When did you first become interested in dramatic storytelling?"

"Hard to say. My best guess is that, for me, it probably stems from my childhood and that fact that I was terribly asthmatic. For quite a while, my parents and my grandparents were convinced I wasn't going to make it.

"And, of course, I picked up on that. I'm still cognizant of the notion that, as a child, I thought I might die, and fairly soon. Kind of alters the way you look at things. I didn't go to school much and spent most of my time at home or at my grandparents' house. My mother and grandmother taught me to read at a very early age. I became a voracious reader and was immediately drawn to stories about adventure and survival. I remember I first read Jack London when I was about nine or ten years old. I think I was also a good listener. This was the heyday of radio dramas and serials. And I loved movies. Just loved them. My brother and I used to see three or four films a week. We grew up in the north part of Long Beach [California]. On Saturdays we'd see the first-run films at the better movie house, and on Sundays the B-westerns at the Old Circle Theater. I liked comedies and musicals, but I really loved westerns and mysteries. I was always interested in cheap heroics and adventure stories, but what kid isn't? I guess, in my case, I never got past it. As a filmmaker, I believe in staying in touch with what pleased you, emotionally, when you were twelve, fourteen, fifteen years old. This is a real pet theory for me. Stay with your first compulsions and inclinations. Use them in your work. They're much more valuable, aesthetically, than the sensibility you acquire when you're in your early twenties—that's when you get influenced by others, things you read. Often you can start to develop a kind of elitist sophistication that takes you away from your basic instincts. Americans tend to be enormously indulgent about the purity of childish impulses, and I, for better or worse, tend to share that view. In my movies I try to valorize those foundation impulses and make them primal in the storytelling and the approach to character. I don't mean dumb. I mean basic."

"Can you recall a particular movie from childhood that really moved and inspired you?"

"There were so many. When I was eleven or twelve, *Shane* (1953) made an enormous impression on me. I cried at the end. Every once in a while I'll see it again and I still cry. When I was young, I thought of it as a perfect western. Now I see faults. Not many, and they're irrelevant. *Shane* is almost otherworldly. The Alan Ladd character is so deeply mysterious, so deeply withdrawn that he's like a visitor from another planet. It's almost as much a science fiction story as a western. There are many westerns that strike me as science fiction, the films of [Sergio] Leone, are kind of sci-fi opera. Through the exaggeration of characters, he brings us into a landscape that is very different from any kind of social reality. The later westerns of Howard Hawks, particularly *Rio Bravo* (1959), almost seem to take place on some space station out in the middle of nowhere."

"Is that because such films are worlds unto themselves?"

"Yes, exactly. Each is an interior landscape. Interesting directors occasionally make what I call an essay movie—basically a long musing about life and the conduct of life within an entertainment form. For example, one of the best essay movies is Hawks's *Only Angels Have Wings* (1939)."

"How is cinematic storytelling useful to us as a society?"

"Movie stories make things neater, clearer, and cleaner than reality. Life is messy, complicated, vastly more detailed and nuanced than movie storytelling. The most mysterious questions that bedevil all of us—*Who are we? Why are we the way we are, and how the hell did we get here?*—aren't solved by films, but good storytelling gives you a sense of completion. Gives you a momentary relief from the external anxieties. Despite the audience being perfectly aware of the fragmentary nature of things. Life is a kind of mysterious journey isn't it? Nobody really knows where they're going or how they're going to end up—except dead. That's the one sure thing. But that's why we all respond to good stories. Stories help us make sense of our lives."

"Is filmmaking mostly an art or a craft?"

"Telling stories cinematically is a craft, and if you develop your craft well enough, it turns into an art. I don't think the principles of the craft as it pertains to film are terribly difficult to learn, but they are terribly difficult to master. I'm still trying."

"Any advice?"

"If you want to be a screenwriter or film director, I still think the best preparation is to study literature, try to learn the history of our civilization, be familiar as best you can [be] with the background of our culture."

"How is cinematic storytelling different from literary storytelling?"

"Well . . . obviously there's the photography and editing and performance. All worlds of their own, in a way, but they have to come together, complement each other or you have nothing. Less than nothing. Beyond that, you have to come to grips with the fact that telling stories through movies is a shorthand experience. With your protagonist, you are, generally, restricted or condemned to an exterior visualization, and you usually don't have the ability to really get inside a character's head. Novels do that a lot better. With a film, the ultimate definition of character is behavior.

"In cinema you have to balance character with the narrative, and hopefully some kind of thematic concern, but you don't have a lot of room or time in which to do it. If you take a lot of time to tell your story, you do so at your peril, especially, and this applies to me, if you're working on a limited canvas. I don't tend to tell stories with many different characters and a lot of different things going on. So if you have a limited canvas, even if purposefully self-imposed, then, as always, the form should follow the content. For me and what I'm trying to do, I think a brisk style is better than the epic. I remember having lunch with Jacques Demy after we had both seen *Raging Bull* (1980) and talking about various aspects of the film, including its running time. He was a friend, wonderful guy. He said something to me that really struck home: 'You Americans are forgetting one of the great gifts that you discovered and gave to the world, that the perfect length for a movie is ninety minutes.' I think he was essentially correct. Ninety to a hundred minutes is, usually, plenty of time to tell a story and develop characters. In that time frame audiences don't get too twitchy, feel biological urges, get hungry or sleepy. My movies tend to be pretty short, and I think part of the reason is from that conversation with Jacques."

"I think your first film *Hard Times*, the story about a drifter, a boxer during the Depression, and his relationship with his gambling promoter, is probably your greatest film. It revealed a brand of storytelling that would become your signature style."

"I don't want to be immodest, but I think you're probably right. I waited a number of years to become a director and didn't know if I was ever going to get a real shot at it. So I felt an enormous tension when I was making the movie. Very unlike me. I had this story pent up inside probably my whole life. It stems from the kind of stories I heard from my father and my grandfather, who were very interested in boxing. The story is emblematic of their values, the kind of men they admired and others they were wary of, and the kind of cultural world they understood. If we have some luck in our careers, we get to make movies about attitudes we respect."

"What was it like directing a first film?"

"I was determined to show that I could tell stories in a professional manner, to be an equal to other established storytellers and not be viewed as just some new kid on the block. I had the usual anxiety, I suppose, about being a first-time director, but the real tension came from my wanting to tell this short story with an economy of style and with rigorous discipline. As usual, the hardest thing is directing yourself."

"Did *Hard Times* usher you into the Hollywood mainstream?"

"Not really. The film was a modest hit and made some noise in Europe, but I remained a Hollywood outsider. There's probably some self-deception in that remark. During the first ten years that I was a director, I had a real sense of desperation, a fear that it was not going to last. But the phone kept ringing, and I kept getting offers to do some of the scripts that I'd worked on. Also, the films I did tended to do pretty well—modest hits, I guess you'd say. But this is a business that only loves big hits. Modest hits are like a ballplayer that only hits singles. Anyway, gradually I started to have the feeling that maybe I was going to be around for a while and, frankly, thought I could make a contribution, particularly to action films, a genre I regarded as serious drama."

"You've said, 'Every film I've made has been a western, even the contemporary stories.' Is that because the characters in your stories tend to exist in some uncharted, unfamiliar, and often dangerous landscape?"

"I like to strip things down to where the components are rather stark and bare. But it's not just about the landscape; it's the fact that the characters have very little recourse to normal avenues of survival and civilized behavior. These become stories of coping and prevailing via the intrinsic nature of the character. The essence of a western, a biblical story, or an outer space story, is that the characters are in a place beyond the normal social controls."

"Your characters are usually quite physical."

"I'd say that's fair. My characters are usually athletic, capable of physical feats, but not superheroes. They can be shot dead and feel pain. But as we all know, physical courage and physical grace are no guarantee of moral superiority or even good sense. I try to get that idea in there as well.

"Beneath the plot line, the action sequences, the dialogue, I observed three reoccurring themes in nearly all your films—justice, personal ethics, and survival. *The Warriors* demonstrates all three. A New York gang is falsely accused of killing another gang member and must make their way back to their own turf in Coney Island amidst attacks by rival gangs in order to clear their name."

"That's exactly right. A great injustice has been done. This gang has been wrongfully accused of a terrible thing. Then they have a kind of expiation through courage, and they make it out. Most of them anyway. I tried to do it like a comic book. But the whole thing is about codes, behavior, ethics . . . Directors are famously cheap moralizers, and we use our stories as a kind of pulpit. No apologies. I take the unfashionable and old-fashioned view that one's ethical stance is of deep importance to one's audience. As a storyteller, my favorite is a kind of Old Testament morality: The way you live is the way you will be treated and, ultimately, how you will end up. And that fits right in with being an action director. Fits right down to the ground. Let me tell you a true story. While I was a high school and college student, I worked during the summers in the oil fields in Signal Hill—my grandfather was an oil man—wildcat driller, ended up with a couple of stripper wells. He got me some jobs, and I was out there digging pipeline trenches with work crews made up mostly of white Southerners and Midwesterners, guys who did this kind of roustabout work for a living. Our crew leader was a quiet guy, but the strongest and most physically adept. One day while we were all sitting around at lunch, one of the guys, a funny, noisy Texan says, 'I don't believe in God, and I don't think there's heaven or hell or any need of going to church. And when you die, that's it.' Then he looks at our natural alpha leader and says, 'What do you think, Bill?' And Bill turns to him and says, 'You really think you're going to get off that easy?' Best philosophical conversation I ever heard. The Texan said, 'Yeah, I guess you're right.' At the risk of being pedantic, what Bill meant was, it's kind of hard not to believe that some form of elemental justice applies to all of us. Such a belief is not based on logic. It's based on intuition. That's kind of where I am."

"You're often been compared to Sam Peckinpah. Was he a big influence on you?"

"There's no filmmaker who hasn't been influenced by other filmmakers or writers. Has my work been influenced by Sam Peckinpah? Of course. Why not? I worked with Sam. He was a great talent. I admired his films. Peckinpah himself was influenced by [Akira] Kurosawa, who in turn, was influenced by John Ford, who was influenced by D. W. Griffith, who was influenced by Charles Dickens. In one way or another we all stand on each other's shoulders. At the same time, Griffith had a unique artistic personality, as did Ford, as did Kurosawa, as did Peckinpah."

"The men in your films are proud, stubborn, and have violent tendencies. They're men who can't easily be had—like Geronimo in *Geronimo: An American Legend* (1993), portrayed by Wes Studi; Wild Bill Hickok played by Jeff Bridges in *Wild Bill* (1995); and Jack Cates, in *48 Hrs.*, played by Nick Nolte. Are you like the men in your stories?"

"I think that's for other people to say. I can say that I believe there is some truth to the central tenet of the old French film criticism: 'Know the film, know the man.'"

"So if that's the case, you are revealed in your films."

"Rose, we all make movies about ourselves or some aspect of ourselves. I don't think there is really any doubt about that. Very simply, the contribution of storytellers has more to do with the personality of the storyteller than anything else. It's the storyteller's unique perspective, vision, and understanding that makes a film."

"Do you feel different directing a film you've written as opposed to one written by someone else?"

"I'd be less than honest if I told you that I had completely equal passion for everything that I've ever done. If I've written something, I have a different attitude toward it, and I'm probably more protective of it. But since I've never told a story that I didn't want to tell, once I'm shooting it, I try to do the best that I can. You give it what you got. At that point it doesn't matter if I wrote it or someone else wrote it."

"Has experience given you greater insight into the gestalt of filmmaking?"

"I knew what I was doing much better when I was thirty-five years old than I do now. You don't really survive as a filmmaker if you're not intrigued by the process as well as [by] the stories you're telling and the questions that the process raises. You're always left with deeper questions, and frankly, you never work out the answers. I'm smarter now than when I started, but I don't know as much. You never know more. And by the time you get to be a veteran like me, you only have questions."

"You've worked with an extraordinary number of great actors. Do you have a particular way of dealing with them?"

"Cast the right person and stay out of the way. You direct best when you direct the least. If you've given them the right things to do and you stage it reasonably well, you don't have to get into the actor's process. Most people confuse being a film director with being an acting coach. That's not our job. However, if an actor has a problem, you have to be adept and sensitive enough to address the situation and hopefully be of some help. Actors need to feel that they're in good hands. Before I became a director, many of the directors I admired and observed were people of quiet confidence who seemed to instinctively know their way with actors. That's the way I wanted to work."

"It seems to me that directors don't retire but rather get retired by the industry."

"Very true. Directors tend not to have graceful ends. If they're old and make a film that flops, they generally can't get work again, even though they keep trying. We're like ballplayers who keep playing until someone takes their uniform away. A lot of the time it's a cruel business with a lot of disappointment, discouragement, and failure. It's difficult to stay positive and do good work. Many years ago, a very well-known filmmaker warned me about getting into all this: 'You have to be prepared to see lesser men do better. You have to live with that feeling, and it can be very tough.' Obviously, he was talking about himself, but I don't think there is anyone in this business who, deep down, doesn't feel that way. What's the old line? 'The world breaks everyone . . .' But permit me a smile, and let's not end on that note. A much better one is: No complaints."

John Landis

John Landis fell in love with movies after seeing The 7th Voyage of Sinbad *(1958) at the age of eight at the Crest Theater in Los Angeles. "It was for me a transformative cinematic experience," he told me. "I was illuminated, transported, and knew then that I wanted to make movies." Landis would go on to forge a filmmaking career out of sheer will with his low-budget features* Schlock *(1973) and* The Kentucky Fried Movie *(1977). Shortly thereafter he blew the lid off Hollywood with* Animal House *(1978),* The Blues Brothers *(1980), and* An American Werewolf in London *(1981). His videos* Thriller *and* Black or White *for Michael Jackson revolutionized the music video genre. I visited the filmmaker at his Beverly Hills home and learned that a filmmaker's life can be one of many unforeseen challenges.*

"You've written and directed some of Hollywood's most commercially successful films of the late 1970s and 1980s, and yet you never finished high school or went to college or film school. How did you break into the industry?"

"I started out as a mail boy at Twentieth Century Fox when I was seventeen. I've been a production assistant, a stuntman, and an actor. I've written screenplays and produced films. I've worked on over a hundred feature films and can't even tell you how many I've directed. I've done everything you can think of in this business with the exception of hair styling. I had a good fifteen years when I could go from movie after movie. If I could do that now, I would."

"Why can't you? Has the industry changed that much?"

"Yes, it's a very different business now. The miracle of Hollywood was that the studios were great factories designed to make a product called movies. William Wyler used to say, 'We're in the tin goods business—canned goods.' What was extraordinary about the Hollywood studio system was how much quality they managed to produce. Hollywood was solid for about seventy years. I was there for the death of the motion picture studios. I worked in the mailroom at Twentieth Century-Fox when they tore down their backlot to build Century City. That signaled an end of an era. Fox, Paramount, Sony, MGM, Warner Brothers, and Universal are essentially all alike—gigantic multi-corporate distribution and marketing companies. That's it."

"So getting a movie made today is extremely difficult."

"That's right. People ask me, 'Why aren't you making movies?' They have no comprehension of how expensive it is, how complicated it is, how infrequent the opportunity, and what's expected of you today. Back in the days of *Animal House* or *The Blues Brothers* you had some time to build an audience for your film, and it spread by word of mouth. There is no longer such a thing as word of mouth. Today, if you don't make sixty or seventy percent of your money in your first three days of release, you're a failure."

"Measuring artistic success can be difficult in the film industry."

"I've had that schizophrenic experience of being shit on by American movie critics, but when I go to Europe, Japan, or Mexico, I'm lionized as a great artist. I don't think I'm a great artist, but I also don't think I should be dismissed. When Mark Twain received an honorary doctorate from Oxford, he said, 'In Europe an artist is regarded for his greatest work. In America an artist is regarded for his latest work.'"

"And only if it is commercially successfully and makes money."

"That's right. But while comedies and horror films make money, they get no respect. In the entire history of the Academy Awards, only one comedy has won the best picture—Woody Allen's *Annie Hall* (1977)."

"Why are comedy and horror so easily dismissed?"

"A comedy is either funny or it's not. Horror is either scary or it's not. Both of those genres are designed to evoke a visceral, physical response from the audience—a scream, a gasp, a laugh, and if they do that they're successful. It's far more difficult to get an audience to suspend disbelief and get emotionally involved with the characters than to horrify them with a character like Boris Karloff playing the Frankenstein monster or Christopher Lee playing Dracula."

"How do you make a really funny movie?"

"There is no formula. Filmmaking, regardless of genre, is completely collaborative and a lot like staging a circus. You rely on many people, using a lot of equipment, working toward the same objective. It's also why I've never taken what's called a possessory credit—'a film by John Landis' or 'a John Landis film.' Personally, I think it's obnoxious. 'Directed by' is the appropriate credit for a collaborative art form."

"Can you predict if a film you're working on will be a hit or a flop?"

"No. I've worked on films in which everyone hated each other, the experience was a nightmare, and the movie turns out great. I've also worked on films that were like love-ins—a real pleasure, all of us thinking we're geniuses, and the end result is that it stinks. So the actual experience of making a film is not necessarily a good indicator of quality."

"Is film considered a director's medium because it presumes to reflect the director's artistic vision, interpretation, and/or world view?"

"Yes. Film is probably the easiest medium with which to influence people through manipulation. As Jean-Luc Goddard famously said, 'All films are political.' The camera is not objective. Just consider a courtroom trial being filmed. The height of a camera, the angle of a camera, the lens on it, everything impacts the perception of what the viewer is seeing. I've often heard filmmakers say, 'I have no influence.' Well, they're either lying or they're stupid. The filmmaker has a responsibility to understand the impact of what he's doing, regardless of the intention. If you pointed out to Robert Altman that *Mash* (1969) was misogynistic and racist, he'd get pissed off. But look at that movie. I don't think that Altman set out to be misogynistic or racist, but *Mash*, while very funny and very much of the moment, sent these messages as well."

"What was the political intention of *Animal House*?"

"*Animal House* is obviously a political picture. It takes place in 1963, just before President Kennedy's assassination. Who is Dean Wormer? He's Richard Nixon, and the Omegas are ROTC Republicans. How does the movie end? It ends in civil insurrection. It's not subtle. Making it a period piece enabled me to be more outrageous. *Animal House* also plays on and exaggerates racist stereotypes. There were racist overtones in it, but that was the point. These white college kids who go to the black bar near the university are sheltered and naïve. The key moment is when Peter Riegert's character walks in and says to his friends, 'Wait till Otis sees us. Otis, my man.' Otis looks at them thinking, *What the fuck are these white kids doing here?*"

"John Belushi's character, Bludo, is beyond outrageous—especially the way he treats women."

"Belushi's character, as initially written, is all appetite, destructive, a rapist. I realized that he had to be sweet, because if he's not sweet, he's a pig. I told John, 'This character is a combination of Cookie Monster and Harpo Marx.' Cookie Monster is totally destructive—'I just want cookie!'—but he's sweet. And Harpo is always chasing those blonds and destroying everything he touches. He's complete anarchy, and yet so sweet. Wanting the audience to be sympathetic to Belushi's character, I softened it in the script. Of course the strength of that character was John."

"What was the intention of *The Blues Brothers*?"

"Music was the impetus for the film. Dan Akroyd and John Belushi used their own fame to focus attention on legendary blues and rock-and-roll artists. People forget that when we made *The Blue Brothers* in 1980 the disco scene was popular. By that time black music had fallen away. People would ask me, 'How did you get those incredible artists from Motown and Stax Records to be in your film?' Are you kidding? They were desperate except for Ray Charles, who was performing a lot of country music. *The Blues Brothers*, for all its craziness, brought back a style of music that had gone out of fashion."

"You often blend genres in your films, which makes them difficult to classify. Is this a comedy, a musical, a horror film? How would you label *An American Werewolf in London*?"

"*American Werewolf* is always referred to as a horror-comedy or comedy-horror film. I don't consider it a comedy at all. It's funny and is meant to be funny, but it's a seriously tragic story. Those two boys played by David Naughton and Griffin Dunne are basically dead from the first frame. It's a fairly linear, straightforward, tragic version of the 1941 film *The Wolf Man* written by Curt Siodmak. In his version Siodmak made the wolf man a victim. Larry Talbot, played by Lon Chaney Jr., wakes up in the morning and asks, 'What did I do last night?' Talbot did nothing, but the wolf man he turned into at the full moon killed all these people. Now he's got all these horrible things happening to him. I took that as the film's theme."

"What inspired you to write your own version of the wolf man?"

"I wrote the screenplay in 1969 when I was eighteen and working as a schlepper on *Kelly's Heroes* (1970) in Yugoslavia. In witnessing a funeral among the gypsies, I was impressed by the seriousness of their burial ritual, conducted by a Greek Orthodox priest. The corpse was in a canvas shroud, covered with garlands of garlic and rosaries. We had just landed a man on the moon, and these gypsies thought that this dead guy could climb out of his grave and cause trouble. The premise of my story was the question, 'How does a thinking, educated, sophisticated person deal with the fantastic, with something that you know is untrue when you're confronted, and still affected by it?' It comes down to faith and religion. In *American Werewolf in London*, David's faith is his reality, but he learns that reality is not what he thought it was. He ends up murdered by reality. The film is about how one deals with powers beyond their control, powers of the universe, mysteries, and belief systems."

"*Animal House*, *The Blues Brothers*, and *An American Werewolf in Lon-*

don are considered by many to be classics. And of course, your Michael Jackson videos *Thriller* and *Black or White* remain iconic. They've endured."

"Peter Bogdanovich, a wonderful film critic, once said, 'The only true test of a movie is time.' What's amazing to me is how many films I've made that still resonate. People still watch them, and I find that flattering, gratifying, and mysterious. Even films like *Trading Places* (1983) and *Three Amigos* (1986), which were not big hits, still play. Most people think that my most commercially successful film was *Animal House*; in fact, it's *Coming to America* (1988). I'm most proud of it because it accomplished what I had set out to do. Eddie Murphy was a huge star when he came to me with this story about an African prince who comes to New York to find an African-American bride. It was like a Cinderella story with a predominantly African-American cast, but their skin color had nothing to do with the plot line. As silly as that sounds, to make a movie with a mostly African-American cast and not have it perceived as a 'black movie' was revolutionary for Hollywood at that time. Today you have Tyler Perry's chitlin' circuit movies, in which the character's color isn't necessarily the plot point, but that wasn't the case when *Coming to America* came out."

"The accident that occurred during the making of *Twilight Zone: The Movie* (1983) which killed actor Vic Morrow and two young children was a terrible tragedy followed by a grueling court case. Looking back, how did you cope with those events?"

"*The Twilight Zone* incident was horrific for me and everyone involved. It's been difficult to not let something like that make you completely cynical. How it was represented in the media, and continues to be, is just awful. The trial lasted eleven months, and the whole thing went on for eight years. The misinformation and disinformation was amazing. I was characterized as an egomaniacal, arrogant asshole and portrayed in court as an evil-genius manipulator of people. This was an accident. What is an accident? It's an incident with unforeseen results. Human nature cannot accept accidents. Our legal system is set up in a way that an accident must be someone's fault. The way our belief systems are set up is that there must be a reason. And what's interesting is that none of this is necessarily true. I don't think most people know that the skid of the helicopter crash was less than a foot from where I was standing. It crashed right in front of me. The helicopter pilot who had lost control during the explosion was really a hero because of the way he ditched the helicopter. He saved lives. But instead he was vilified."

"You were on trial for your life and could have gone to prison."

"That's right. Throughout the trial I assumed only the worst and just zoned out.

"What I learned from the experience is that people will exploit anything for personal gain. I was horrified to learn that in this legal system you can buy experts in any field—doctors, scientists, and politicians to say whatever you want them to say. What also amazed me was that everyone doesn't tell the truth. The whole thing was horrifying. People actually came to the courtroom to watch the trial with bags of popcorn."

"After you were acquitted, you went on to make several popular films: *Trading Places*, *Coming to America*, and Michael Jackson's landmark music video *Thriller*, which was inspired by your film *An American Werewolf in London*."

"That's true but the media still likes to write that my career never recovered."

"Hollywood is very different these days due to the astronomical cost of filmmaking and the technological advances, but isn't storytelling still just storytelling?"

"Yes. The basic principles of cinematic storytelling and montage are exactly the same as they were a hundred years ago. If you look at a production still from 1912, you'll see a camera on sticks, actors in front of it, and a crew behind it. If you look at a production still from 2012, you'll see an elevated recording device on a crane, actors in front, and the crew behind it. It's still piecework: cutting together footage that's been recorded. What we're doing in both instances: telling a story. The only difference is that movies are now called motion pictures because 'film' as we once knew it will be obsolete within the decade."

"And the director-storyteller, is he or she still as vital to the process?"

"Movies get made sometimes in spite of the director. I've worked on movies where the star was actually directing it, or the cameraman or the producer was directing it. I've seen mediocre scripts made into really good films, and I've seen really good scripts made into terrible movies. There are filmmakers who are highly irresponsible. Some are responsible. Some are really nice people and some are jerks. A picture is like a juggernaut. It leaves the station, goes down the track, and arrives. Whether it's good or not is an entirely separate issue."

Barry Levinson

Barry Levinson's first feature, Diner *(1982), earned him an Academy Award nomination for best original screenplay and quickly tagged him a filmmaker with a bankable future.* Diner, *now a classic, also set in motion the careers of Mickey Rourke, Kevin Bacon, Steve Guttenberg, Ellen Barkin, and Daniel Stern. Levinson went on to write, produce, and/ or direct some of America's most popular films, among them* The Natural *(1984),* Good Morning, Vietnam *(1987),* Rain Man *(1988),* Avalon *(1990),* Bugsy *(1991), and* You Don't Know Jack *(2010). During our interview at his beautiful Connecticut estate, Levinson shared some thoughts on the art of screenwriting and revealed a rare understanding of human nature.*

"Your acclaimed 'Baltimore Trilogy'—*Diner, Avalon*, and *Tin Men*—were autobiographical. What led you to create these stories?"

"I was exploring what a particular time in my life was all about, looking at what I did or what others did, and how I responded to things. Why didn't I do this or that? *Oh, God almighty, what was I thinking?* I would tell Mel Brooks about the diner guys of my youth, and it was he who encouraged me to write *Diner* and turn it into a film. But it wasn't until I started to write the script that I understood what those years were really about—male and female relationships or lack thereof. I followed up with *Avalon*, the story of an extended immigrant family like my own, but it wouldn't have intrigued me to write only about immigration to America. I told the story by exploring how the advent of television became the new storyteller and changed the family. *Tin Men* looked at the end of an era in terms of how guys behaved toward women as a result of the rise of feminism. I used the characters—amazingly irresponsible aluminum-siding salesmen. I needed these tin men to propel the story. I needed something like that to propel me. With each one of those films it was a subject that launched it rather than 'recollections of.'"

"What's your writing process like?"

"I basically rely on my instincts. Once the brain starts to figure out where it's going, it begins gathering stuff, sort of Googling information on its own. If the writing is working well, my imagination transports me off

into another place. I write quickly because I'm so in there I don't want to put it down. For a very concentrated period of time, I'm eager to find out what's going to happen. I don't know. When I'm writing, I'm responding to the story as if I'm the audience. I might think, *Oh this is boring. I'm saying too much. This is more than I want to know right now.* Screenwriting is a trick anyway. You try to write naturalistically, at least I did in those Baltimore pieces, but you know it's not naturalistic because the conversations end in three and a half minutes. A real conversation in the diner could take hours, so you have to create a sense of time that seems like real time, but only show it taking place in three and a half minutes."

"How do you bring characters to life so that they appear real and believable?"

"By having your story driven more by character than by plot. You can't rely just on the plot. Plot is never enough. It's the journey of the characters through that plot that you're going to remember. We can talk about *Casablanca* all we want, but it was the characters. Humphrey Bogart and the other characters fascinate us. What is going to happen between him and Ingrid Bergman? If he didn't care about her and if she wasn't such strong a character, the piece would have died no matter how well it was plotted. So I always look to the character. The character is going to take me on the journey."

"Isn't a character-driven story with a lot of dialogue more difficult to pull off than one full of busy action sequences?"

"Yes. Sometimes it's a scary proposition. When you do character-driven pieces and there's no car chase or big explosion, something to prop you up, it's like you're working without a safety net."

"What makes a great cinematic character?"

"I'm not sure I know the answer to that. When you see a great cinematic character, you know it. John Wayne achieved this in many of his films like *Red River* (1948) and *The Searchers* (1956). But how he did it is hard to say."

"You've invented some great characters, like Boogie Sheftell in *Diner*, played by Mickey Rourke."

"Boogie is supposedly a tough guy, but you can sense that underneath he's trying to mask his vulnerabilities, and that's what makes him so compelling. In and of itself a tough guy is not necessarily interesting. What made Marilyn Monroe's characters work? That a woman is beautiful is not particularly interesting; however, that she's flawed draws us to her. Another flawed character is Terry Malloy played by Marlon Brando in *On the Waterfront* (1954). He wants to be a fighter, but things go wrong and he doesn't achieve his dream. Because of his inability to express himself in an articulate manner, you have to pay closer attention to him. An articulate character is not as interesting because we simply have to listen and we know what he's saying. The slightly inarticulate character, on the other hand, makes us sit up in our seats because we're trying to understand him. And that's what engages us."

"Another of your fascinating characters is Sam Krichinsky in *Avalon*, played by Armin Mueller-Stahl."

"What makes him fascinating is the small things he does. He shows his grandson how to hang wallpaper but then tells him, 'This is something you should never do.' All great characters have to surprise us. They do certain things and you think, *Oh my God!*"

"Many of the characters that populate your films have a very strong moral compass. Why is that?"

"I don't think I do that intentionally. When I'm trying to form a character that has credibility, morality is one of the aspects of a character's credibility. A full-blooded character must have a number of specific qualities, including imperfections. This is what makes him interesting and draws us in."

"In so many of your films men and women often misunderstand one another. For example, there's a very poignant scene in *Diner* when Beth (Ellen Barkin) files Shrevie's (Daniel Stern) record album out of order, and he blows up at her. Stunned that she's overstepped some unspoken boundary, she cries in frustration, not knowing who he really is."

"Part of the success of *Diner* is that women like it. And that's because they get an inside view into why men do what they do in their relationships with women. But with characters like Ellen Barkin in *Diner* and Barbara Hershey in *Tin Men*, women's points of view are revealed as well."

"To what extent are your stories/films politically motivated or meant to have a social impact on society?"

"I don't think of that. I did *Good Morning, Vietnam* for no other reason other than to tell a story about the Vietnamese who go to school, go to the movies, eat, laugh, and to see people going on with their lives before the war that came to town. In the script I thought, *These people have real lives and not just from the standpoint of war.* I wasn't trying to make a political statement."

"What drew you to tell Jack Kevorkian's story, *You Don't Know Jack* (2010)?"

"I wouldn't want to just do a film about an issue—assisted suicide. I found Kevorkian's character interesting and surprising. He's a man who is beyond intimidation, determined to do what he feels is correct. Kevorkian believed that the terminally ill individual had the right to end his or her own life—as opposed to convention, which holds that you're supposed to lie there and suffer until you die. What I found fascinating about Jack Kevorkian was how he navigated through the system, his way of thinking, and his relationship with his sister."

"You got to know him personally while working on the film?"

"Yes, and he would say things that would surprise me so much I put them in the film. One day we were sitting together, and I asked him, 'Would you like some coffee?' and he said, 'Yeah, coffee would be good.' 'Decaf?' 'No,' he said, 'decaf is for cowards.' That was such a funny line I used it in the film. I thought it humanized him in a way. Working on this film I had to decide how far I could go, what to show and what not to show. I realized I couldn't back away. I had to take us to the edge, to that moment when we become really uncomfortable, like the scene when he puts this device on the patient's head and things go awry. Sometimes you have to make tough decisions: *What should I show and what isn't necessary? Should that line be said while the character is walking away? Would that conversation work better said in a dark scene where you don't see their faces that well?* You're always trying to sort out those things."

"It sounds like directing movies is a lot like putting together a puzzle without knowing in advance what the picture looks like."

"Yes. You're always asking, *How do you do this?* You thought it was this way, and then it doesn't feel right. How do you fix that? How do you improve it? There is no definitive answer to how things are done. Sometimes, things just happen. Wow, what a great moment that is. You can try to bring all the elements to the table. You've got the right actor, you've got all this and that, but there is that one unknown ingredient of how things actually come together. There is a certain degree of magic to filmmaking."

"How did you come to direct *Rain Man*?"

"Tom Cruise and Dustin Hoffman were already attached to the film by the time I came in. There were three other directors on it before me. They couldn't develop the script enough to get it to work, so they all bowed out, one after the other. I changed the script and evolved it by removing the plot mechanics, which took away from the characters. I just made it a journey of two guys going across country. The simplicity of that ultimately cleared the way for the behavioral stuff to come front and center."

"You made it character driven, which turned it into a touching human story about two brothers, one of whom has autism and has inherited their father's wealth."

"Yes. My job was to get the script to go that way, but I also felt in order to make it credible and honest I had to allow humor to be part of it. When there is humor, it becomes more human. There will be times in the film when we ask, *Should we laugh? He really has this affliction.* But we come to terms with it, and we're drawn into the lives of these two brothers."

"There is always some degree of humor in the stories you tell. Why is humor so important?"

"One can find humor in the most frustrating of circumstances. We may not see it when it's happening to us, but when we observe it in others, we can grasp the absurdity of the situation and think, *This is the craziest conversation. You two make absolutely no sense. What are you talking about?* Our ability or inability to communicate defines who we are as people. We often do not understand one another, which can be comedic one second, dramatic in the next, and then comedic again. It's not like it has to be one or the other—it's both! You often hear the criticism, 'That film doesn't know if it's a comedy or a drama.' Yes, it does. It's both comedic and dramatic because that's what goes on in real life. Life is both and more."

"Does one have to have a good sense of humor to see the humor in life?"

"If we can't see the humor that exists around us, then something is wrong with us; we have somehow shut down one of the big components of our existence."

"In *Liberty Heights* (1999), you blend drama and humor in the scene when the son of this Jewish family wants to dress up as Adolf Hitler on Halloween."

"That came from my cousin Eddie, who actually dressed up like Hitler when he was fifteen. My grandmother was beside herself, but it was nevertheless funny. In *Liberty Heights* the mother is saying, 'You can't go out like Adolf Hitler!' The kid is saying, 'Why? What's the big deal?' This is a generational issue, and the kid can't understand why his choice of costume is so offensive. 'You're not going out of the house!' 'Okay, I'm not going out of the house.' And so what happens? He sits down and now he's watching Sid Caesar on TV who's playing a character in a uniform talking in German gibberish, and everyone is laughing."

"The irony of life . . ."

"Yes. And that's what's so funny."

"The line 'You cut the turkey without me, we leave!' from *Avalon*, when the eldest brother of the Krichinsky family arrives late for Thanksgiving dinner and everyone has started eating without him. At first it's funny, yet [it] becomes an important turning point in the movie. You realize it's literally the final act, a really big deal. The scene goes from comedic to dramatic."

"Do you consciously look for material that examines the complexity of human behavior?"

"I don't know if that's the motivation or not. It's hard to say. I'm curious about many different things. For example, I did *What Just Happened* (2008) because I liked the idea of doing a film about the life of a producer. The public's perception of a producer is that he's always in charge and knows what he's doing, when in fact producers are constantly under the gun and live in constant fear. Ben, played by Robert De Niro, is under siege. In a very short timeframe he's beset with problems with his actors, his wives, his kids, and he's thinking, *I'm just trying to stay afloat. I'm trying to keep my head above water. I've got one movie in previews, another about to begin. I've got problems! I've got problems!* To see how he deals with everybody was fascinating to me. And this by the way is fairly accurate portrayal of a producer's life. And that was enough for me."

"I understand that most directors feel 'under siege' when working on a film. Has that been your experience too?"

"It is a marathon, mentally and physically exhausting. Sometimes you're standing on your feet for fifteen or sixteen hours, working at high speed. It's hard for me to go out to dinner and see friends while I'm on a film because everything else feels like it's slow motion. My brain has been working quickly all day and suddenly you're talking and it's . . . all . . . too . . . slow. *Speed it up, speed it up, get to the point, get to the point!* Then there's that long process in the editing room—*What do you do? What do you do? What do you do?* You've got to keep pushing it and pushing it forward along with a lot of other people until you finish it. It's like you've been working on this little invention in your garage, and finally you take it out for the world to see."

"What's that part like for you—the world seeing it?"

"I always feel a certain amount of self-doubt because you're never really sure of what you have. And you can expect no support from the studio executives because they are fraught with doubt too. Time becomes the ultimate judge, but you can't wait for time. You just do what you do as long as you have the energy. Some people will always love your work, others will hate it, and many will be indifferent. You just have to understand that this is the reality. I don't do this because I want to be loved. What motives me is that I want to share a particular story and that's all there is. My career is ultimately about the work I've done while I'm on my own personal journey. Nothing can be more fulfilling."

John Carpenter

*I met John Carpenter, the legendary screenwriter, director, and composer of nearly thirty horror and science fiction films in the office of his vintage California bungalow in the heart of Hollywood. Surrounded by movie posters from some of his films—*Halloween *(1978),* The Fog *(1980),* Escape from New York *(1981),* Starman *(1984),* Village of the Damned *(1995)—I was curious to learn why he had made a career of telling scary stories. The tall, silver-haired filmmaker obliged, holding nothing back.*

"Are you still as passionate about directing as you were when you began your career more than thirty years ago?"

"My drive to become a movie director goes back to when I was eight years old, after I first saw *Forbidden Planet* (1956). I didn't really know what it meant to make movies or how hard it would be, but that's when I fell in love with cinema. It was only later, in film school, that I realized that in order to become a Hollywood director you have to be utterly driven. You have to be so single-minded about it that you put the rest of life on hold. Your normal life becomes clutter that gets in your way. When you're directing a movie, you don't care about what's going on all around you. All you care about is what you're staging and seeing through the lens. When I was trying to get my foot in the door, I couldn't think about anything else. After thirty years of doing that, I got burned out, just couldn't do it anymore."

"How did you recognize the signs of burnout?"

"I viewed the behind the scenes special features on the DVD for a movie I did called *Ghosts of Mars* (2001). The footage that was shot at the beginning of the film showed me looking fresh, well rested, and ready to go. The footage at the end of the special features had me doing the music. What I saw behind the console was a dead man. I had been the writer, director, and composer on that film, and it was killing me. I looked at myself and said, *I can't do this for a while. I don't have anymore to give.* Stopping gave me a chance to reflect on my work and gain some perspective about my life."

"What did you learn about yourself?"

"That a great deal of my work comes from a deeply instinctual place.

I got my training at USC's film school and learned the plumbing of how to make movies, but beyond that, everything else has been inspired by my childhood experiences. What I took in as a kid, what happened to me growing up, and how that shaped my view of the world. It's very hard for me to articulate the kind of life I had, but I could do it in a story. I could do it in a scene."

"So is your work essentially autobiographical?"

"Yes, at least emotionally. I respond to movies in which the characters are trapped and pursued by the antagonist, whether it be the darkness, the evil, the other—or whether they are coming in on themselves. I'm very attracted to those kinds of stories."

"Why? Have you had times in your life when you felt trapped?"

"Yes! Yes, yes! Very much so," he laughed. "The particulars of my formative years put me in that situation and not until I matured did I get out. When I was a kid, my dad moved our family from New York to Bowling Green, Kentucky, where he took a teaching position at Western Kentucky University. He was a very accomplished violinist with a PhD in music. I had no idea where I was. Who are these people in this small Bible Belt southern town? We lived in a log cabin on campus behind the museum with no TV. My mom was an ambulatory schizophrenic, which means a functioning schizophrenic. She had an enormous fantasy life that was passed on to me. A lot of that was very confusing at the time— *What's going on here? Where am I? Who am I?*

"I played alone on the beautiful grounds of the museum and lived out my fantasies and daydreams. Everything beyond those grounds was an alien world that made no sense to me. Everything I learned about evil, not fictionalized evil that you read in novels but real evil, I learned in that little town in Kentucky. This was the Jim Crow South where a lot of awful things were happening, awful things. I'm talking about brutality and inhumanity. I learned very early about how unfair and cruel the world was. And because I was so different from the other kids, I was constantly bullied. My dad made me play the violin, so imagine this boy carrying a violin case to school among these hillbillies, these country boys. It was horrible. It was the beginning of my interest in stories that deal with evil and malevolence."

"Going to the movies must have been a good escape?"

"I was happiest in a theater watching movies. Scary movies and westerns, in particular, transported me, but I didn't want to just sit there and watch them, I wanted to create them. When I was very young I asked my dad what I should do with my life. And he told me, 'Just create something. It doesn't matter what it is. Create!' That was his big push, his big drive: 'Write something. Paint something. Perfect playing an instrument, whatever it is. Create!' So that's where I was guided."

"Why do you think so many young people have been drawn to your films?"

"Horror films generally work best for younger audiences because they don't yet fear death. When you're young, you're brave and stupid. You're just going on a ride. Let's go on a rollercoaster. Let's take a dare. Let's break the rules. Let's go to a horror movie that's really going to scare us."

"I think all human beings, regardless of age, are terrified of evil. You've created a body of work based on just that."

"Very good, Rose! You've just stated the two stories that make up the horror film genre—fear and evil. Human beings may be tuned a little differently, but essentially we are all the same. And therefore we are frightened of the same things. Maybe our need to understand and cope with evil stems from our primordial past. The big question is always where does evil come from? To answer that, we have to imagine ourselves back to a time when we lived in tribes of hunters/gatherers, a time when we turned to witchdoctors and wise men, who gave explanations so that things made sense of the world. Imagine two scenarios: We are sitting around a campfire at night and the elder begins to speak: 'I'm going to tell you where evil comes from.' Pointing out beyond the firelight, he says, 'It comes from out there. It's the other tribe. The other tribe is upstream urinating in our water and stealing our women. They crawl through the underbrush and drag away our children. They are ferocious beasts. They are not like us. *Evil* is out there and we have to protect ourselves from it.' Scenario two: The same scene, but a different elder gets up and says, 'I'm going to tell you about evil and where it's located.' Pointing to his own heart, he says, 'It's within us. *We* are the beasts. *We* are capable of evil. *We* are capable of murder and mayhem and rape.' So the two themes you're dealing with when telling a scary story are *Where is the evil?* and *How do you overcome it?*"

"How does watching a scary movie help us cope with our fears of evil?"

"It's cathartic. Scary movies are a kind of coping mechanism. It's an attempt to explain things that can't be explained. Why are people murdered, raped, disfigured, tortured? How could Adolf Hitler do what he did? We all have within us the capacity for evil, but some of us have been able to overcome it and wrestle it down. The majority of us stop ourselves from committing brutal acts. We have feelings. We have empathy. And that's why we celebrate, worship, and try to emulate those in our society who can embrace goodness and nonviolence. But the truth is that no one is immune. Each and every one of us has within us a spark of evil."

"Do you try to use horror and suspense as social commentary?"

"I don't think about it in that way. Cinema is not a polemic. It's not an announcement to the world, *You should do this! This is the way you need to be! This is what you need to correct.* You can't do it that way. It can't just be stated. It has to come out of dreams and poetry."

"So how do you convey the subtext or deeper meaning of a story?"

"Stories are never just stories. Yes, you have to have a narrative structure, but within that there are a lot of other ideas and themes you're investigating. And sometimes you can't articulate at the beginning of a journey exactly what you want to do or where you want to go. So you say to yourself, *Let me find my way through this.* I might be different than other directors who feel that everything has to be laid out in advance. I tend to be looser and say, 'Let's see how this scene works when we stage it.' I tend to be fairly open about it, especially when the actors walk in the door. Actors are magical folk who bring a whole other voice to the work and part of what you're trying to do gets shaped by them."

"Most of the characters in your films are loners, outcasts, people on the fringe of society, or they're psychopaths, ghosts, aliens, etc. There's even a haunted car in one of your films—*Christine* (1983). Are your characters in some way an exploration of yourself?"

"Oh, every single one of them! Every single character is me—including a lot of the women. A lot of the female characters are parts of me or parts of the gender that I understand. You have to be everyone when you're the writer and/or director, or at least understand them and what's motivating them. What's *he* doing in this scene? What's *she's* reacting to? How is *he* feeling? Why is *she* afraid?"

"You mean there's a little John Carpenter in Michael Myers, the slasher-killer from *Halloween*?"

"Yes, some. He came from my imagination. Michael Myers is pure evil. He is everywhere and nowhere in the darkness behind you. He is literally nobody and has no personality. He's almost a supernatural type, a force like the weather, like the wind. And *we* don't know his motivation. He wears a mask and featureless outfit throughout the film so we really don't even know what he looks like. And then you meet the Donald Pleasence character, the psychiatrist, at the mental hospital from where Myers has just escaped. As soon as he says his lines—'Don't underestimate him! You don't know what you're dealing with'—you're totally spooked. So the teenage girls are talking nonsense about their boyfriends and babysitting and making stupid jokes to each other, and meanwhile you're caught up in this whirlwind of evil, but it's very quiet. And Pleasence is saying, 'He's the evil. You don't understand . . .'"

"Are you also Snake Plissken, the character played by Kurt Russell in *Escape from New York* (1997)?"

"Yes, of course. We all want to be cool like him. But the real secret of his character is that he doesn't care; he doesn't care about you or me. He just wants to move on. He doesn't do what he does for love of country, but because he has to. He's a tricky character, a wish-fulfillment. I'd love to be able to feel the way he does. I'd love to not care. Life would be so much easier."

"When you make a really dark movie, do you get sucked into the darkness?"

"No. I'm not a 'method' director who experiences all these things. I have to stay in control to tell the story. It's all illusion in a rectangle. It's not real; it's entertainment."

"*Halloween* inspired the genre of so-called slasher films. How did its success affect you artistically?"

"The release of *Halloween* was met with terrible reviews, vicious reviews. I remember the producer calling me up and saying, 'This didn't work.' But later, it was re-reviewed and word of mouth began to build. My first reaction at the time was *Ah, failure*. That experience taught me a very important lesson: don't chase what *they* want; please yourself first. So every time I finish a movie, I ask myself, *How do I feel about this? Is this as good as it's going to get?* Then I send it out and see what happens. I'm usually harder on myself than anybody else. But I'm also much gentler when things don't go well. I think, *Ah, they're probably not seeing this. Ah, that's really too bad.*"

"Was it your intention to push the envelope by ratcheting up violence in your early films?"

"I didn't really know what I was doing when I started out in the movie business. I was just raw. I look back at some of my work now, after having had children, and feel completely differently about it. The murder of the little girl in *Assault on Precinct 13* (1976) was done as a cinematic trick to get the story cooking. I didn't realize then how powerfully it would affect the audience. I stepped way over the line. I'd never kill a child or an animal now, but back then I was dumb and young. I wanted to hit you in the face so that you paid attention to everything that was coming."

"Does composing the music for your films give you an added dimension of creativity to enhance your storytelling?"

"It does. But it was a case of necessity being the mother of invention. When you're making a low-budget movie and lack the money for composers and orchestras, you have to do it yourself. My job is to ask, 'What kind of music or sound does this scene need? Or does it need any at all? Is silence better here?' I improvise ninety percent of my scores while I'm watching the footage and playing the synthesizer. Over the years synthesizers have become so advanced that I can use them to produce all kinds of amazing sounds. I rely on what feels right to me instinctively, influenced by the music I heard as a child being around my father, listening, and having it seep into me."

"There is no mistaking a 'John Carpenter film.' Your name always appears above the title. How did you know to brand your movies this way?"

"If you know the history of cinema, you know that all the great directors did that—*Howard Hawks's Rio Bravo, Alfred Hitchcock's The Birds, John Ford's Stagecoach*. And so I thought of it for myself. You see it from my very first movie, *John Carpenter's Halloween*. I can put my name on the title to establish myself as this stylist storyteller, as if to say, If you give me complete control over this I'll make the best movie I can. That was all planned out in my head. And it worked. I've had a great career. Wow, I've been lucky. The most talented people in film school never got a shot. I don't know what it was for me—the right place, the right time, the drive, the series of events, refusing to let failure destroy me, and constantly having a very simple goal—'professional Hollywood director.' It was really no more complicated than that."

"It's widely known that one of your cinematic heroes was Howard Hawks. What did you most admire about him?"

"Hawks didn't want the viewer to be aware of the camera or of the editing and the cuts. He just wanted you to watch the people on the screen. He did draw moral points with his characters, but he didn't want to hit you over the head with them. There's a simple scene in *Rio Bravo* (1959) when Dean Martin regains his self-respect. All he does is pour a drink back into a bottle, and his hands don't shake. Hawks is drawing a moral point here about competence, self-respect, and self-worth with only demonstrating a close-up of Dean Martin. This is a brilliant cinematic moment and so very simple."

"Looking back do you understand the intensity of your drive as a filmmaker?"

"No, I really don't. It was just something that I had to do. I'm not as driven now, more at peace with my life. I don't generate the scripts anymore, but if the project is right, if I like the story, I'll do it. Making a film takes a lot out of you. Part of the director's life also means that you sacrifice a normal home life. You're constantly preoccupied. A movie lives with you before you shoot it, during, and after. It becomes this huge part of you, and sometimes it can go on inside of you for years. And some films you can never get over. You can't just walk away and say, 'I'm done.'"

"It's been a while since you've made your last film."

"This hiatus has given me the ability to appreciate what I had done in the industry. No one can ever take my movies away from me. I'm taking things a little easier and having a lot more fun. I've actually started living life again."

Lesli Linka Glatter

Meeting Lesli Linka Glatter was like befriending a long-lost cousin—instant rapport. We had both come from dance and experienced a similar passion for the art form. Glatter has become one of television's foremost directors, having worked on such hit shows as Law and Order *(1999–2001),* The West Wing *(2002–2006),* ER *(1995–2008),* Mad Men *(2007–2010), and* Homeland *(2011–). Visiting her at her Pacific Palisades home for our interview, I learned that her personal journey to become one of the industry's most respected female directors was as compelling as many of the dramas she tells on screen.*

"How did you first become a director?"

"I started out as a dancer and choreographer. While teaching and performing modern dance throughout the Far East on a grant, I had an experience there that changed everything for me. In 1978 I met Yutaka Tsuji in a Tokyo coffee shop. The man who would become my mentor was in his seventies and I [was] in my twenties, but when we looked at each other the connection was immediate. We spent the rest of that day together, just talking. I learned that he had been Japan's top foreign war correspondent during World War II, and at the time of our meeting [was] head of the country's Cultural Affairs Office. The first thing he said to me was, 'Meeting is the beginning of parting.' 'Oh, this is so sad,' I replied. 'When you know this is not sad,' he said, 'you will know something very great.' He then went on to tell me a number of stories about his life. I knew right then that I would want to retell his stories and pass them on because of how they illuminated the human condition. But I also knew that I couldn't tell them choreographically. They needed a more literal telling, more than dance movement could convey. And that started me on the path that I'm still on—telling stories. My first film told two of Tsuji's stories. The first was about his experiences as an officer and translator in charge of a Japanese POW camp in Hong Kong during World War II. The second story was about how later he became a prisoner in the very same camp he once ran. I called my film *Tales of Meeting and Parting* (1985)."

"It's stunning how a chance encounter can so dramatically change the course of your life."

"I've often wondered, What if I had chosen one of the other two coffee shops on that street? If I had been into myself that day and come in with a book, I never would have noticed Yutaka."

"What did you find especially compelling about this stranger's stories?"

"They had to do with human beings finding themselves in unimaginable circumstances and how, as a result, they discovered who they really are and what they're made of. I want to believe that if I were in a very difficult circumstance that the best part of me, my humanity, would come out. I'm very curious about how we as human beings face unexpected challenges and how we cope with them. This is a theme that I find myself coming back to over and over again, and Yutaka Tsuji's stories had that."

"So how did you go about figuring out how to tell his stories?"

"At first I thought I could tell them as theater pieces, but that didn't feel quite right. Then I met an Australian filmmaker, George Miller, who had directed *Mad Max 2: The Road Warrior* (1981). I told him a few of Tsuji's stories, and he said, 'I think that's a film.' I knew nothing about film at that time, had never even been on a movie set. But Miller was incredibly generous and allowed me to shadow him so I could learn about directing. In 1985, despite having little experience, I was accepted into the American Film Institute's directing workshop for women. To learn about the filmmaking process, I assisted other women on their films. Then I co-wrote *Tales of Meeting and Parting* with a friend and storyboarded it. The short film was comprised of two of Tsuji's world war stories and the characters spoke mostly Japanese. Because I was new to the language of filmmaking, I needed to visualize every scene before shooting and plan out everything in advance. At the same time, I wanted to be completely open to the unexpected spontaneous moments. I work that way to this day."

"How did your first film do?"

"It was nominated for an Academy Award—best live action short. Practically overnight I got an agent and started getting phone calls, including one from Steven Spielberg who said, 'I saw your film and loved it. Will you come in for a meeting?' At the time he was doing a TV anthology called *Amazing Stories* (1985–1987). It would become my film school. I shadowed him and Clint Eastwood. I was on the set all the time, asking questions, watching how they were shooting things, spent time with the actors and in the editing room. It was an incredible education. I ended up directing three episodes of *Amazing Stories* which were very well received."

"What was one of the most important lessons you learned from being around Steven Spielberg?"

"When I was about to begin shooting one of the episodes, 'No Day at the Beach' (1986), a World War II story involving two hundred men storming a beach, I started having panic dreams—*I get to the location and I don't know what I'm supposed to do*. I told this to Steven and he said, 'Oh, I always have dreams like that.' It made me feel better to know that someone of his stature and experience also had panic dreams. But there was something very important that he told me. He said, 'If you're watching a scene and something is not working, and your instincts tell you that— listen to your instincts, pay attention to what they're saying. Because if you tell your instincts to shut up, they will, and they won't talk to you anymore.' To be told to respect and listen to my instincts was invaluable when I was first starting out."

"Just a few years later you worked with David Lynch on another very successful television series, *Twin Peaks* (1990–1991)."

"Yes, I directed several episodes of *Twin Peaks*. Working with David Lynch was an amazing experience and unique in a completely different way. One of the training points for me happened during the show's pilot. Actors Michael Ontkean and Kyle MacLachlan are having a conversation sitting on either side of a table, and on top of the table sat a moose head. I asked David Lynch how he got the idea of putting a moose head on the table. He looked at me strangely and said, 'It was there.' 'What do you mean it was there?' 'The set dresser was going to hang it on the wall, but I told him to just leave it there.' When he said that, something just cracked wide open for me. Yes, plan everything, but be sure that you're open to the moose head on the table—open yourself to unexpected, lucky accidents that you don't plan."

"How is directing satisfying the artist within you?"

"It's like when you dance on the stage and everything comes together perfectly—the movement, the music, the lighting. In that moment you feel totally alive. That's what it feels like when you direct with a good piece of material and the right cast and crew. Does it happen every day? No. But when it does, it's thrilling because you're engaging with and mobilizing as many as a hundred and fifty human beings to tell a story. And I love that every project takes me into a new world that I get to explore and research. Working on ER, I experienced the inside of a hospital emergency room and on *The West Wing*, the inside of the White House."

"Do most television directors have control over their work in the way film directors have final cut?"

"With television, it's more a writer's medium. If I only direct two of the twelve season episodes of *Mad Men* for example, I'm not there for the full run of the show. The show's creator, Matt Weiner, is with it from beginning to end, so the power lies with him and his writers. But the writers and the directors need each other to tell the stories. A screenplay is just words on a page until the director translates them visually onto the screen. So in television the final cut is usually with the writer and not the director—unless you're a permanent fixture on that show."

"In a show like *Mad Men*, which is about the New York advertising world in the 1960s, you have to maintain the look and mood of that era while moving each week's plot line forward."

"Yes. I have to work in the style of the show, what things were circa 1960, but before I direct my episode, I review what the original pilot looked like, how previous episodes were done, and then I examine my episode. It's part of a broad vision, but each episode is its own specific story. With *Mad Men* we don't use a Steadicam, which is a hand-held camera stabilizer that is fairly standard today. Matt Weiner decided that because the Steadicam hadn't yet been invented when the show takes place, using it could not accurately convey the feeling of what things looked and felt like then. I'm not going to come in and ask to use a Steadicam. That wouldn't be appropriate."

"It must be interesting and challenging to direct television characters whose circumstances and relationships are already set and don't change much week after week. Is it also your job to make sure that your characters maintain continuity and believability?"

"Well, I would never go up to Jon Hamm, who's been playing the role of Don Draper, and say to him, 'This is who your character is.' He knows better who the character is than I do, but he still needs to be directed in terms of behavior."

"How does one direct for behavior?"

"The story informs everything, so you have to really know what story you're telling. Behavior comes out of the subtext of that story and what each scene is about. Often there is a fine line between what an actor says and what he does. So what I have to do is find something in the actor's behavior that will inform and enhance each scene. For example, sometimes there's more power in holding back emotion then showing it, or directing someone not to be sexy in a scene that's romantic. And what I plan in a room by myself as part of my process can change dramatically once the actors come in, because their job is to expose themselves as they tap into their character's behavior. The director's role is to make them feel safe and support them in their process of digging down and finding something within themselves that they didn't know was there."

"How do you do that?"

"The first thing we do before each episode is have a reading and talk about the story. Then we put it on its feet in terms of what that scene is about. Each actor has to have a very clear reason why they're behaving the way they are. Let's say this is the scene about Don Draper, his ex-wife, and their young daughter who has just cut off her own hair. Don is a guy who wants to be a good father, so when he brings his daughter back home he tries to protect her from her mother's rage. Everyone in that scene has a point of view, including their son, who just wants everything to be okay and doesn't want them to fight. As the director, I have to be inside the mother's head, the father's head, the daughter's head, and the son's head."

"What do you look for when deciding whether or not to take on a project?"

"I have to see it visually in my mind. I have to love the writing, love that world, and feel I'm the person to tell that story. It's as simple as that. And, I'm open to different genres. I've done action, drama, and comedy. I never thought I was very much of a vampire gal, but I loved directing HBO's *True Blood* (2008–). In the last five years, some of the best writing and directing has been happening in television, especially cable television, and that's a very exciting development for everyone who's telling stories. Directors that had only worked in features are now crossing over into television primarily because the writing is so good."

"How do you initially approach the material?"

"Most important is the world in which the people in the story exist. I begin by asking, 'How does this story best need to be told?' Where you place the camera, for example, helps define how you tell your story. If I filmed us having this conversation, and I put the camera way over there and shot through the window on a 600mm lens, it would feel one way. If I came inside here, and did a 360 camera move, circling us a different way, it would feel very different. Or I might just show you asking me the questions, and the viewer is only hearing me respond. Another way to go is to have the camera first show my foot and then slowly move up my body to reveal my face. That again would be a very different way to tell the story, even though the words don't change. All of those are big creative choices. The scene of two people having an interview can vary greatly, depending on the perspective taken by the director. For me, it's about faces and spaces, how I want to see the world and how human beings react in that world."

"Is directing a means of self-expression for you in the same way that dance and choreography was?"

"It's not the same. With dance it was more direct and immediate. Directing for me is more of an investigation than overt self-expression. This is an art form that requires hundreds of people. I'm not doing this alone. So it's very different than choreographing a dance or writing a poem. What I love about it is that you have all these other creative artists involved in the process, and you're working together as a team. The actors, production designer, director of photography, prop master, and editor all come in and fit in pieces of the puzzle. Every part of me is engaged in that process, even though I'm not the person operating the camera or acting out the scenes. I'm more like the captain of the ship with an amazing crew who contribute their vision and talent, and my job is to navigate how we get to where we're going."

"Did you ever come to understand what Yutaka Tsuji meant when he told you, 'Meeting is the beginning of parting'?"

"Yes, I did. What he meant was that you can't always know the impact of an encounter when you're in it. You need the element of time to fully understand the power of an experience and how it will affect you. Our meeting changed my life. His words, so steeped in Japanese philosophy, taught me that nothing ever stays the same and that everything in life ebbs and flows. It's unwise to get too attached to one's circumstances because we are continuously faced with choices, dilemmas, and struggles to find balance in our lives."

Jonathan Frakes

Jonathan Frakes, aka Commander William Riker on Star Trek: The Next Generation *(1987–1994), beamed into directing while still an actor on the show. He went on to direct Star Trek spin-offs* Star Trek: Deep Space Nine *(1993) and* Star Trek: Voyager *(1995), and feature films* Star Trek: First Contact *(1996),* Star Trek: Insurrection *(1999), and* Star Trek: Nemesis *(2002). Since 2007 he has directed a number of popular television dramas, including* Burn Notice *(2007–),* Castle *(2009–),* Leverage *(2008–), and* NCIS: LA *(2009–). I photographed Jonathan at Hollywood's Paramount Studios, where he was directing an episode of* NCIS: LA. *In our interview, he shared with me how being a part of the Star Trek legacy has informed his life and his work as a director.*

"How did you land the role of Commander Riker?"

"I auditioned for the part with creator-producer Gene Roddenberry seven times over a period of six weeks. When I was chosen, Gene phoned me himself and congratulated me. It was a tough role to cast because Roddenberry saw the character—some daring-do with a Machiavellian glint—as a combination of himself, Captain Kirk, and Captain Picard. At first he wanted my character to have this mid-westerner, stoic, never-smiling persona, which was very much against my nature. But as the series progressed, he allowed the character to become a little bit more like me. I play the trombone, and therefore so did Riker. I really admired Commander William Riker who was honorable, loyal, articulate, and honest. He set an example for how I've tried to lead my life."

"Why do you think *Star Trek* (1966–1969) and *Star Trek: The Next Generation* were so popular and developed such a cult following?"

"People wanted to believe that the future of mankind was going to be positive. In Roddenberry's vision of the twenty-fourth century, there would be no racism or sexism, and the diversity of people's beliefs would be honored. When Whoopi Goldberg joined *The Next Generation* cast, she told Gene Roddenberry that *Star Trek* had helped her survive. She said that she felt that she could be a woman of power because she saw Nichelle Nichols play Uhura. Here was a black woman working shoulder to shoulder with white men, and all were treated as equals."

"Was it Roddenberry's intention to show us by example that human beings could improve?"

"Yes, but in many of the episodes not all human beings and life forms had embraced a more moral and ethical directive, which led to conflict and served for thought-provoking scripts and dramatic stories."

"You achieved success playing Commander Riker, so what inspired you to go behind the scenes as a director?"

"With eight regulars on *Star Trek*, I was always waiting around for my scenes. I wanted to be more involved. Looking around the set, it became clear to me that the guy who had the ideal job was the director. I expressed to the show's producer, Rick Berman, that I was interested in directing, and eventually he gave me some episodes to direct. We shot *Star Trek* at Paramount Studios, where I had the opportunity to shadow directors and learn about editing. I still refer to it jokingly as Paramount University, because that's where I learned about preproduction, editing, postproduction, and scoring. I already knew how to talk to actors and about staging."

"What most surprised you about directing that you didn't know as an actor?"

"As an actor you worry about your character's arc, selfishly, protectively, with blinders on. But as a director you're responsible for everyone's arc, for each season and for the legacy of the show. In television not only do you have to tell the story, but you have a responsibility to stay on budget. On a network show you have eight days to get it done so it is essential during prep to work closely with a good first assistant director, line director, and show runner to the writer's room to make cuts in the script and shooting locations so that you work within the time and budget allotted."

"Episodic dramas on television are for the most part very formulaic. What's your prescription for maintaining audience interest?"

"It's important to maintain the mood, feel, and production design of a particular show so that they're identifiable. I approach the direction of each show that I direct in the style in which it was created. You know it's *Leverage* because of the moving camera. You know it's *Burn Notice* because of the hot lighting. In *Castle*, you expect those old-fashioned close-ups. These shows are formulaic, but that's actually what makes them successful. The actors in *Burn Notice*—Jeffrey Donovan, Gabrielle Anwar, and Bruce Campbell—say what they're going to do, they do it, and then they talk about how they did it. 'Here's the Columbia drug dealer, here's how we're going to bust him and bring him down.' Then they eat a yogurt and say, 'Yeah, we really kicked his ass.' For some reason viewers have responded to that formula, and the show's in its seventh season.

"On *Castle*, murder-mystery writer Rick Castle, Detective Kate Becket, and their team lay out all the possible murder suspects and, hopefully, by the end you're surprised to know who the guilty one is. Castle and Beckett have this comedic romantic thing going on, which is probably the main reason people follow the show. I think the same is true for the show you visited, *NCIS: LA*. Somebody from the navy has been murdered, and our guys are the only people who can figure out who did it. So you have our heroes, two of whom are played by Chris O'Donnell and LL Cool J, who go about their business to solve the murder. But meanwhile we're enjoying their buddy-cop relationship, the kibitzing about their outside lives, or their quirkiness.

"This formula has worked on television and in movies for years, *Star Trek* included. Gene Roddenberry envisioned the crew of the *Enterprise* as a family with close personal relationships, not just as officers on a spacecraft. Riker was in love with Troy, and she with him. Riker saw Captain Picard as a big-brother/father figure. Riker took it on himself to help Data become more human. Riker and Worf were competitive but friendly. So when I'm directing a scene on *NCIS: LA* and the members of the *NCIS* team come together for a briefing, it's like being on the bridge of the *Enterprise*."

"Are you saying then that a show's premise is not as important as the interaction of the characters?"

"Yes. The plots are secondary to the personal relationships in virtually all of these shows. One of my chief responsibilities as a director is to focus on those relationships. The success of the show depends on it, because this is primarily what audiences respond to. They wait for those moments that come at the beginning and end of the action sequences. A crime fighting show has to come up with anywhere from twenty-two to twenty-six murders in a season. How many people can you murder? How many different locations can they be murdered in? The show can't be just about that."

"Many of the plot lines of popular shows on television today are really far-fetched, yet viewers are willing to suspend disbelief and tune in. Why is that?"

"Yes, we are attracted to shows that are hard to believe, and yet we can't take our eyes off of them. Take *Dexter* (2006–2013), which is about a police forensics expert who moonlights as a serial killer of criminals. *Homeland* (2011–) is about a CIA officer named Carrie Mathison who believes that a former US Marine named Brody has turned against America and joined Al-Qaeda. In trying to prove that he's a security threat, they become engaged in a love relationship. All the heroes and villains in this show are liars. They're all morally corrupt in some way and struggling with the truth. A show about homeland security in an age of terrorism is compelling, but here again, it's really about the relationships of the characters: Brody's relationship to his wife, his love relationship with Carrie, Carrie's relationship to Saul Berenson, Middle East division chief, and his relationship to the director of the CIA's Counterterrorism Center, David Estes."

"Can television dramas help us to live better lives?"

"Dramatic stories can help us because what the characters are going through [is] often relatable to our own lives. The show *Parenthood* (2010–), for example, revolves around three generations of a family—matriarch, patriarch, their children, and grandchildren. I have a wife and two kids, and so I get very emotionally involved in that show because the characters have to make some of the same decisions I have to make, like where to send my kid to college. I observe the choices that the characters in the show make and ask myself if I would do the same thing or something different. Watching shows with characters with whom we can identify helps us examine ourselves and evaluate the decisions we make."

"Crime fighting shows like Dick Wolf's *Law and Order* franchise and *Criminal Minds* (2005–) get high ratings. What's the big attraction of murderers, rapists, arsonists, and other characters who commit ghastly crimes motivated by hate, jealousy, lust, and greed?"

"We like to watch crime-fighting shows because we want to see morally corrupt people get their comeuppance. We're fascinated by these despicable characters, but we do want them to get caught and put away. What really interests us in these crime dramas are characters struggling with their own morality and ethics. Most of us, to a greater or lesser degree, have that same struggle. And that's relatable. These stories ask us to consider, *Are we as morally sound as we'd like to be? Do we behave in an ethical manner and treat others in the way we want to be treated?* Shows like *Breaking Bad* (2008–2013), with characters who commit heinous crimes like murder or torture, are not relatable for most of us, but they have value as a cautionary tale. What I worry about are the disturbed and damaged people who are exposed to villainous characters in movies and television, and they commit copycat crimes. That's dangerous! I think a case can be made that violence in entertainment, including video games, sometimes can lead to violence because they show how easy it is to commit murder and other crimes."

"How do you express yourself artistically through the scripts you direct?"

"I think I bring my own experience and personality to the stories I tell. The part of storytelling that I like best is comedy, so I try to milk the lighter moments, especially in a show that's dry and filled with exposition. I'm good at blowing up shit, doing a lot of green screen, but I prefer delving into the nuanced personal relationship of two actors and their backstories."

"What's next for you?"

"I'm trying to get out of movie jail."

"What's movie jail?"

"I've made four movies. Three of them made money. The fourth was a flop.

"When the movie bombed, suddenly the rug was gone, as was the office space at Universal Studios and the apartment in London. And, once you go to movie jail, it's very hard to get out. I'm lucky that I do television, and I love television, but I would like to return to the big screen. I have a few things percolating that I hope will get me out of jail."

"Observing you on the set of NCIS: LA, I could see that you really love directing. You seemed to enjoy every minute of interacting with the cast and crew."

"My dad once told me, 'Do something that you love.' And I've found it: directing. I can't wait to get to the studio every morning at 6 a.m. When I get home at 8 p.m., I have this great feeling of satisfaction. And I take pride in knowing that I'm creating an environment for cast and crew—around a hundred people—who can express themselves creatively and not be punished for making mistakes. I want everyone I work with to feel good about themselves, to know how much I appreciate what they do. I'm very big on thank yous. 'Thank you for framing that shot so well.' 'Thank you for delivering those lines so well.' 'Those costumes are terrific!' I've seen how much better the work is when people know that they're appreciated and respected. I love being the leader of a creative team and am very comfortable in the role of commander."

is completely different from the first? It happens because the director has lost control over the actors and the medium to tell the story. When that happens, the viewer becomes conscious that they're watching a movie instead of being transported by it."

"The choreographed fighting sequences in all three of the *Rush Hour* movies were dynamic and highly complex. How were those conceived and staged?"

"Jackie Chan choreographed the fight sequences, but we collaborated on how best to shoot them. Jackie can't really direct himself while he's throwing a punch and a kick. Someone else has to be his eyes and ears to tell him if it looked good, if the punch or the kick worked. I was that guy. But I'd set up the scenes: 'You walk into this pool bar and say to the bartender, 'What's up, my [N-word]?' A fight ensues. You can use all the props on hand: the cue stick, the balls, the triangle, the hanging chandelier to beat up those guys. I don't care how you do it, but when you're done, just walk out.' Remember, Jackie has been directing movies longer than I've been alive. If he says, 'Brett, move the camera over there,' I'll usually say, 'Yeah, you're right.'"

"Do you think that the current trend of computer-generated imagery (CGI) and 3D technology has in some way replaced good old-fashioned storytelling?"

"Right now the trend is 'sword and sandal' movies like *300* (2006) and *Clash of the Titans* (2010). My feeling is that ten years from now those films will look like *Back to the Future* (1985) looks to us today, totally dated. But if you look back to a film like *Spartacus* (1960), which is more than fifty years old, it holds up because it's got a great story with great characters. There are no gimmicks, no special effects. When filmmakers get caught up in spectacle—*Look how cool this battle is!*—they make the special effects the foreground and the story and the characters the background. It becomes soulless if it's all about the effects. My thinking is to be aware of the technology because you need it if you're going to build ancient Rome, but that should be the background. The story and the characters should be what it's all about. These are the films that stand the test of time and touch people."

"The cost of making a film in Hollywood continues to spin out of control, doesn't it?"

"I remember when I first saw *Batman* (1989). I couldn't even fathom making a movie like that. How did they construct Gotham City? Was it a painting, a visual effect? That movie cost around fifty million dollars to make, which was a huge amount of money then. Fifteen years later I directed *X-Men: The Last Stand*, which cost two hundred million dollars! The economics of selling a movie is based on how successful your last film was. Successful films breed sequels and franchises. It used to be if you had one hit you could make four bombs. Nowadays, if you have one bomb, no one will give you money to make your next film. This is a business. You can't just be an artist. Well, you can, but no one's going to give you money to make your films."

"Sounds like you've never had a bomb."

"No, but the more successful I become, the more I fear that I'll have one. When I made my first film, I was totally fearless—just dove in. If you've never had a hit or a bomb, you don't know what to expect. You're just in a fun and naïve place. But every film has different problems that require different skills, so I'm continuously gaining experience. I set realistic goals and am always challenging myself. Unlike most filmmakers, I've done films in multiple genres. Most comedy directors would never attempt a thriller like *Red Dragon*. To grow as an artist, I'll do things that I haven't done before."

"Do you think movie theaters will become a thing of the past?"

"When I was a kid I desperately wanted to see *Star Wars*. I waited in line for three hours but didn't get in. I had to come back the next day and wait all over again. Today there are twenty-seven screens showing the same movie at 7:05, 7:15, 7:30. You can even watch it fifteen times in a row on your phone. Eventually what's going to happen is that only the 'big movies' will be shown in the theaters. But Hollywood is still a place where dreams come true. It's a place where stories get told. There's nothing like sitting in a theater and sharing laugher or tears with lots of other human beings. Nothing can replace that, and I hope nothing ever will."

"*Radio Flyer* is message-driven, but it is also a moving and magical story about two boys who believe that they can escape by building a flying machine. In panel discussions during previews, I was amazed how many times people said, 'I've never told anybody, but I was abused as a kid.' I realized the subject's importance. The studio had other ideas. The film wasn't testing that well, so they wanted the film to have a happy ending. I told them, 'I can't.' Having found out that the film's screenwriter, David Mickey Evans, had been an abused child, I refused to change the ending."

"You were an extremely successful television director, so what prompted you to move into feature films?"

"It was just the next step in my career. I was very fortunate not to have been put in a little niche as a TV director. That was not the experience of many other directors; if they directed a half-hour comedy, that's all they did. If they did action, that's all they did. I got my taste of everything, so when the opportunity came to do a feature film and tell stories more fully, I grabbed it."

"What makes a Richard Donner film?"

"In the last thirty years it has been about feeling good. I stopped delivering messages after *Inside Moves* (1980) and *Radio Flyer*. I felt that the world was already very depressing. If you want to be depressed, all you have to do is turn on the news. So I decided to make feel-good movies for escape. With *Inside Moves* I had an argument with screenwriters Valerie Curtin and Barry Levinson, who adapted the story from the Todd Walton novel. I imposed myself on them to write a happier ending. It was going to end with Jerry's old girlfriend reappearing just as the gang from the bar is getting on a bus to see Jerry, David Morse's character, play basketball in the big leagues after his knee surgery. She tells Roary, John Savage's character, 'I don't care about Jerry; he's a cripple and he's always going to be a cripple.' She asks Roary for money, and he gives it to her, to which she says, 'I'm a whore and you're a sucker.' That's the way both the book and the screenplay ended. I didn't want it to end that way. After all these characters have gone through, I wanted to see Jerry playing to cheers on the basketball court, the bad guys get their comeuppance, and that life can be good. *Inside Moves* was a turning point in my moviemaking career. I wanted my films to make people feel good. It's as simple as that."

"How do you determine the look of a movie once you've read the screenplay?"

"An interesting thing happens to me when I read a screenplay. I see the whole thing in my mind. I can shoot it the next day. I don't need three months of preparation. All I need to do is cast it. I think this has to do with the ADD. But interestingly, it never ends up the way I've first seen it in my head. From the first reading it takes on many things—my personality and the personality of the people I'm working with. I like to listen to everybody, including the guy who makes the coffee. If he has an idea about a scene, I want to hear it. If it's a good one, I'll use it and make sure people know where it came from."

"Your film *The Omen* was a huge hit and ushered you into the big time of feature films. How did you come by that script and what attracted you to the story?"

"A dear friend of mine and former agent, Eddie Rosen, informed me that a screenplay called *The Antichrist* had been turned down by every studio in town and would be on the market soon. He said, 'I think it's something that will tickle your fancy' and sent to me. I sat down with it, turned a page, turned another page, turned another page, and before I knew it, I had read the entire script. I knew immediately why it had been rejected by the studios. The writer's heavy-handed devil scenes left nothing to the imagination. So I thought if these terrible events happened in the life of a man, in this case Gregory Peck; if they existed only in his mind and we have him asking what's real and what's not—that's a good story. It was that simple. So we had it rewritten. I saw the potential for great entertainment, a scary edge-of-your seat-story, and while we're at it, let's outdo Billy Friedkin!"

"Friedkin's *The Exorcist*, which had come out a few years earlier, had revitalized the horror genre."

"Exactly."

"*The Omen* had some really scary scenes, like the one in the graveyard when the Rottweilers attack Gregory Peck and David Warner's character. That scene played on our fears. How did you execute it?"

"It's a basic use of objectivity and subjectivity. The actor is very subjective, down there in the graveyard reacting to what he's seeing. The audience is up here watching objectively, but they too become subjective when they think they sense a dog stalking at the top of the ridge, but it's just the eye of the camera. I had the camera move ever so slightly, which brought a little life to it and then added the sound of a dog's breathing. It's just enough to force you into what I would like you to think and feel—fear."

"The dogs do attack."

"Well, you manipulate things in the shooting and in the editing to make it look real. You ask yourself how will I cut this and not let the audience see the piece of ham in the shoe of the stunt man [standing] in for

Gregory Peck. How can I hide the rubber bands that are holding the dog's jaw open so they look ferocious? These are all just tricks of the trade."

"I believe you are the first to make a feature film based on a comic-book hero. How did *Superman* (1978) come about, and what drew you to it?"

"When the original script for *Superman* arrived at my house, it was so heavy you could get a hernia from just carrying it. It was written by Mario Puzo, Robert Benton, and Leslie and David Newman. When I read it, I realized that these writers, although very accomplished, had not been brought up on comic books and especially not the character created in 1939 by Jerry Siegel and Joe Shuster. Their version of *Superman* was written as a farce. I said, 'Superman is apple pie, Americana — a beacon of truth and justice. This story has to be treated like a reality. It is its own reality, but it's a reality. It's bigger than life and yet has its own life."

Donner then pointed to a sign hanging on his office wall with the word *verisimilitude* printed above a drawing of Superman. "It means being true and real. It's the philosophy I live by. So I called my agent and said, 'I'd love to make this movie, but I hate the screenplay.' The producers let me bring in Tom Mankiewicz to rewrite the script, and he did a great job. I had been offered a million dollars to make that film with Marlon Brando and Gene Hackman. Imagine! In 1976 that was like all the tea in China. But I would have given it all up had they not let me rewrite the script. And so I was able to defend my childhood hero, Superman, and made a million bucks."

"How do you account for the success of the *Lethal Weapon* movies — pairing Mel Gibson and Danny Glover?"

"I had always wanted to do an action film, but all the scripts that came my way were nothing more than action. Then I read Shane Black's script, a great story about the growth of a relationship between two men. Not that it was so profound, but it was unusual for an action film, and that's the reason I took it. I think all of my films are predicated on relationships. Relationships make good material for movies."

"When you're filming a movie do you click into a particular frame of mind?"

"When I make a movie, it's like I put on a different pair of shoes. These shoes keep me moving and prevent me from slowing down or standing in one place. I become extraordinarily disciplined. The magnitude of decision making that comes down to you when you're making a film is mind-boggling. You have to decide on everything from whether or not to have sesame seeds on the morning rolls to whether or not to fly in a piece of equipment that costs $600,000 for a scene that only lasts a few minutes. You're constantly being inundated with questions and decisions. If you ignore or delegate them to someone else, you lose control of your movie."

"Have you gotten more confident as a director over the course of your career?"

"Because so much of what I do as a director is intuitive, I can't help but feel insecure. *Am I doing this right? Does this look right?* You doubt yourself all the time. And tremendous amounts of money are at stake. You want to tell a story in a certain way but have to contend with the opinions of many subjective stakeholders. So it comes down to, *Who do you make a movie for?* You make it for yourself. You've got to make yourself happy. And if you don't, then you're doing a movie by committee. Then you live and die by what the committee thinks. If you make a movie for yourself, you live and die by what you think."

"So what's next for you?"

"Well, I'm at the edge of deciding if I want to direct anymore. It's a different world out there now. Maybe I should leave it to the new crowd. Maybe I'll produce one of their films and push my traditions into their contemporary filmmaking. Maybe I can add just a little bit of enlightenment to something they're doing. Maybe I can help them make better films."

Lawrence Kasdan

After earning his reputation as a gifted screenwriter with The Empire Strikes Back *(1980),* Return of the Jedi *(1983), and* Raiders of the Lost Ark *(1981), Lawrence Kasdan went on to write and direct some of the most popular box-office hits of the 1980s and 1990s:* Body Heat *(1981),* The Big Chill *(1983),* Silverado *(1985),* Grand Canyon *(1991), and* The Bodyguard *(1992). I sat with him in the patio of his Beverly Hills home while his dog Mac, the subject of his most recent film,* Darling Companion *(2011), slept at his feet. We spoke about his life and the challenges of writing, directing, and creating meaningful work.*

"What does it feel like knowing that so many of your screenplays and films have been enjoyed by millions of moviegoers?"

"This is what you're always striving for as a filmmaker. It's enormously satisfying when people tell you they related to your film, were caught up in it, because it all comes from you—your personal experiences combined with your training. You take your life, transmute it, and hope that it connects with people. But even if people laugh in the theater, you don't really know what emotions you've tapped into. Comedy is especially misleading because people laughing at the jokes tells you nothing about whether or not the film will have any kind of residual impact. And therefore I tend to underrate the affect of my movies."

"What were your early influences as a screenwriter?"

"Cinema always had a great impact on me. I related to every kind of movie genre in a personal way, whether it was a human drama, an adventure, or a western. Growing up, I was completely struck by the Hollywood image of the world—the conventions and the moments of startling unpredictability that get at the truth of life. Hollywood movies have always been dictated by certain strictures—fantasies and rules and filtered through this kind of artifice that I found very powerful. *Lawrence of Arabia* (1962) and *Seven Samurai* (1954), two of the greatest films ever made, influenced me enormously because the good guys triumphed. I was twelve when I saw *The Great Escape* (1963), which formed my ideas of how men should act—heroism, sacrifice, generosity, all within this giant canvas and portrayed by five or six of some of the most impactful stars. These were the people who gave me a model of what men should do, what's courage, what's grace and lack of grace. Movies have always had unreachable standards for people in terms of having courage and being cool."

"What about characters like James Dean's in *Rebel Without a Cause* (1955)? He's not particularly heroic in the conventional sense, yet he became a role model for a whole generation of young men."

"The antihero was as important to me as any straight heroic character, and that describes about half the characters in Hollywood movies. The Bogart or Cooper models are about people who struggle through some horrible tragedy or failure that they work off the rest of their life, reluctantly. Indiana Jones reluctantly becomes a hero, overcoming his own selfish drives and finds a bigger purpose."

"Was it your intention for Luke Skywalker to be a great cinematic hero?"

"Han Solo is really the character that people find irresistible, not Luke. Luke is too good for people to invest in. Han is right out of the classic mold. He's William Holden. He's Jimmy Cagney. He's Humphrey Bogart. Han is the one who is compromised and reluctantly forced to be altruistic and heroic."

"When you script your characters, do you draw in part from your own personality, character traits, and behaviors?"

"As the writer you have to be everybody in your story. I certainly feel that way about the characters in *The Big Chill* and in *Grand Canyon*—the men, the women, and the children. When I wrote *Grand Canyon* with my wife Meg, it was very much our experiences in raising sons here in Los Angeles. The teenager in *Grand Canyon* is trying to figure out how he can navigate the streets, and his parents are trying to protect him from the things they can't protect him from. The world is chaotic, and they're fearful for him. In real life we're crazy in love with our children, but we have to let them loose, let them drive and go out into the world. It's terrifying for parents, and so we were referencing ourselves in the movie."

"Has telling human stories brought you closer to understanding your own life?"

"You don't get closer to understanding life. The older you get, the less you know. It may sound like a cliché, but it's true. The world just seems more complicated, not less. When I was younger, I thought I was pretty sophisticated. I remember being at my wedding, twenty-one years old and talking with a really smart friend of Meg's parents. He was one of the most sophisticated and insightful people I'd ever met. And yet I had this outrageous arrogance to think that my mind encompassed his. This was the 1960s and we thought, 'We get it and they don't.' Maybe that's necessary for one's progression. If you don't have that crazy misplaced confidence in yourself, maybe you can't make the journey. Today, young people who lack confidence find themselves lost. The ones that do make it have this sense of *I get it and the older people don't get it*. But then as you get older, you don't get anything."

"Would you say that the themes that run through your films— questioning conventional wisdom, pursuing truth, seeking happiness— are evidence of a personal quest?"

"Yes absolutely. In a commencement address at my alma mater, the University of Michigan, I encouraged the graduates to question every-thing and to accept the duality within themselves, that in our lives we feel both triumphant and defeated at the same time. I wanted them to accept what they're feeling rather than shun it. I tried to convey to them that life only becomes more confusing."

"In the YouTube video of that speech, you told graduates, 'There are two of you—the real you and the deeper you. Listen to the deeper you. Listen to your heart. Be who you are and let yourself know what you know.' That's powerful advice."

"That's right. The deeper you is very hard to get ahold of. I've never had the discipline to get ahold of the deeper me because I've allowed myself to be swamped by the many trivial or temporal concerns to hold on to it."

"It's more than twenty years since you addressed those graduating seniors, forty years since you graduated. Is there anything you would amend in that speech if you were to deliver it today?"

"I wouldn't want to say to them what I know now: that the world is dark, that the forces of good are not necessarily going to triumph, and that people's behaviors are often beyond comprehension. I don't think it would be the right thing to tell them this as they embark on a new life, but I do feel that. I sometimes think of life as being on a ship that goes down in a storm. You grab some refuse floating by and hang on to it for dear life, but you lose your grip. You get tossed about again and again. And then, luckily, something is thrown your way that you can hang on to. And in those relatively brief moments you feel, *Oh, I'm going to make it*. Those are the moments when you see with clarity how you should or want to live your life. But most of the time you're just tossed about."

"The entertainment business in particular can really toss you around, messing with your self-esteem, your confidence."

"Until you make it in this business, you're considered no good, rejected. Even when you've made it and been accepted, you're still thinking, *I'm a fraud. I'll be found out. That was the true me that was being rejected. I'll soon be found out and tossed out again.* Those two emotions are always working on you no matter how successful you become. I've just finished a screenplay that I've been writing for months and months. It's really hard to guess how people will react to it. People will either say, 'I was riveted by it' or 'I can't see this as a movie.' Unless you're incredibly arrogant, you believe both points of view. You think to yourself, *I knew what I was doing when I created it and it works* or *Ooops, they found me out!*"

"How did you break into the business and move into directing so quickly?"

"I had been taught conventional, classic dramatic structure by a wonderful teacher at the University of Michigan who had taught Arthur Miller, and that's why I went to school there. It took me about six screenplays before selling one—*The Bodyguard*—and then work started coming at an enormous rate, and I was able to become a director very quickly. Once I was on the inside, I asked myself, *Why am I doing so well?* I realized that I was satisfying the [demand for] classic dramatic structure that had been lost in Hollywood, and that made me valuable. But that way of thinking can be limiting because you become devoted to working that way. Your writing can lose some of the freedom that it should have. Instead of using those structures and hiding them, you can't hide them. You think too rationally, too conventionally; you think this is the classic way to do it. And that's never the road to creating something new."

"Have your films been an examination of your own life?"

"Absolutely. That's been my goal. François Truffaut said, 'When what interests you also interests an audience it's a miracle.' It almost never happens. I thought, *If I write* The Big Chill *about my true experiences, it'll find an audience.* When it did, it was a dream come true. It's amazing to think that you can write something so personal and have millions of people of all ages relating to it."

"What made it so popular?"

"It gives you a wonderful feeling about friendship, and that's enormously comforting. It's about a cocoon of people who come together for a weekend and care about each other in a scary world. The music was like a drug pumped into the theater, putting everyone in a great mood. People my age at that time had not yet been conveyed in the movies. And it was not just the film's music that resonated with audiences, but also the music of the dialogue. The characters talked the way real people talk to their friends, a voice not heard in the movies to that time."

"How is it that the more specific you are about examining your inner life the more universal its reach?"

"If you try to speak to everybody in a general way, you speak to no one. If you go from the details in your own life, working out the issues that mean something to you, there's a greater chance that others will be able to relate to the work. *The Big Chill* is really about the theme that runs through all my movies—finding a new family. One's own family is often difficult and unsatisfying or has left you damaged in some way. So we constantly go out to find new connections. *The Big Chill* is very explicitly about that search, and very powerful. *The Accidental Tourist* (1988) is also about creating a new family to replace a dysfunctional one. Almost everybody can say, 'My family is dysfunctional.'"

"So that's what defines a Lawrence Kasdan Film?"

"It may be. I think a lot of what I've done comes out of my own difficult childhood and home life. So in my work I've looked for something more stable or explored why growing up in my home was so upsetting. But I haven't been bold enough in looking at the darkness or a crazy mother or irrational family situation. And sometimes that's a failure. It was such a horrible part of my life that I didn't want to re-create it. So if anything, I haven't gone far enough in my films."

"Do you feel that the messages in your films come through clearly?"

"If you can say what a piece of art is about, it's probably not good. I have a great quote hanging on my wall near my desk. It reads, 'A work of art should not need to be explained.'"

"Do you enjoy the process of writing for the screen?"

"I don't like writing. It's a lonely process. Getting myself to start every day is a challenge, and it never gets easier. I recently wrote a screenplay and hated every minute of the struggle. Only occasionally did I think, *Oh this works! I whipped that thing!* Mostly I feel like I'm being defeated by the material."

"Is it difficult to maintain the original vision of a story once it goes from words on a page to the cinematic process?"

"Yes. You simply don't always have control over the telling of your own story. There are so many variables, and your control over them will vary enormously from day to day. Some days the location may not work out, or the actors can't do what you wanted them to do. Fortunately, you can work with the material in the editing, and some days that you thought were terrible turn around to be the best."

"Do you have the same level of passion, curiosity, energy that you had when you started out?"

"I do! You're writing something that concerns you, and then you go out and turn it into a movie. Making movies is a constant adrenaline rush, and it's addictive. That's why those of us who have done it and then can't do it anymore, meaning that they can't get the money, are in agony. There are only a handful of directors who can go movie to movie to movie. I was lucky for twenty years. I would write 'em, direct 'em, write 'em, direct 'em, and release a film about every two years without studio executives telling me what to do. That's almost twenty years of impunity. My God, that's unbelievable. It's unheard of now, even among our most successful auteurs, who usually have to wait five years between movies. Directors spend a lot of time in agony because in most cases their movies don't get made."

"Are you in a state of agony now?"

"Yeah. I feel terrible. When I'm not going through the process—the scouting, the casting, the shooting, the editing—I'm in agony. And when years go by and you don't do it, you become jealous of the person you once were, the person you got to be. It's terribly frustrating because you feel that you've failed yourself. I've been grateful for every second that I worked on movies. I remember this one night on location in New Mexico after shooting had wrapped. I was standing in this very isolated spot on the top of a hill. The sun was going down. I could see the red taillights of all the cars driving away. I thought to myself, *I'm the luckiest person on earth. All these talented actors and craftsmen were here just to help me. They've spent a lifetime getting good at their skills, whether it's pulling cable, recording sound, or designing light. All those skills have been put to work because of a story I wrote sitting alone in my room.* I've never taken it for granted."

Tim Van Patten

Tim Van Patten, the younger brother of actors Dick and Joyce Van Patten, struck gold when producer-creator David Chase hired him to direct The Sopranos *(1999–2007). Van Patten went on to direct a number of HBO's top hits, including multiple episodes of* Sex in the City *(1998–2004),* The Wire *(2002–2008),* Deadwood *(2004–2006),* Rome *(2005–2007),* The Pacific *(2010),* Games of Thrones *(2011–), and* Boardwalk Empire *(2010–), for which he also serves as executive producer. I spoke with Tim in his office at the Steiner Studios, the production site for* Boardwalk Empire *housed within Brooklyn's navy yard.*

"Can you point to anything in childhood that may have contributed to your becoming a director, a storyteller?"

"My mother died when I was twelve, and we found ourselves a family in crisis. My father was a highly literate man and understood that storytelling would take me and my siblings out of our misery and lift us up, which it did. He was a great storyteller with a vivid imagination and would embellish while he read to us and to the neighborhood kids. All my friends and my brother's friends would sit on the stoop outside our house, and he would read to us. And I read a great deal on my own. I loved classic comics, which are the great literary works boiled down to comic books. I was particularly interested in the composition of the animation in stories like *Moby-Dick*, *The Man in the Iron Mask*, *Kidnapped*, *Robin Hood*, and *Call of the Wild*. I had a dresser full of toy soldiers that I played with endlessly. I liked becoming a soldier or a cowboy or a knight. But for me acting it out wasn't enough, so I made up scenes and directed them. Directing spoke to all the things in me—the storyteller, the artist, the musician, the observer."

"Was there a particular path you pursued to become a television director?"

"The beauty of this business is that there is no one path. It's like the Gold Rush. The gold is out there, and everyone has to find their way to get it using their own tools and materials. It's a level playing field for everybody. But somebody has to stand up for you and lead you in. No one is going to just hand you a television episode to direct. That person in my

life was director-producer Bruce Paltrow. I would be mixing cement now if it weren't for Bruce. I moved to California right out of high school, and at seventeen he cast me in the role of Mario 'Salami' Pettrino on a television series called *The White Shadow* (1978–1981). He saw something in me, I don't know what. The role called for a tough kid, a transplant to California. The truth is that I had no business being on that series. I was barely an actor; I was just being me. Later, when I got parts that required my playing people other than myself, acting got a lot harder. I realized fairly quickly that I was more interested in what was happening behind the camera. To me the director is like the catcher in a baseball game. He has a view of the entire ball field. He's calling the pitcher's pitches and involved in every play of the game. The actor is like the right fielder— occasionally a ball comes out his way, and so he's only involved in the game intermittently. The actor is kept in a cubicle until his scene, and then afterwards he goes back to his cubicle. Three days can go by before he's called out again. Acting can be very isolating. I preferred the sense and spirit of the crew, which is always inside the action and engaged with other people. When you're working on a series, after ten months you become like a family. So early on I set my sights on becoming a director."

"Once you made the decision to shift from actor to director, how did you get there?"

"I figured that I'd have to stop acting because I didn't want anyone to be confused about what I wanted to do. I was passionate about becoming a director. I was not passionate about being an actor. So I went cold turkey—completely stopped acting. I started watching how directors worked and even directed some music videos for aspiring artists, none of whom became famous. To support myself in the interim, I did construction work, digging trenches and laying pipes. Ultimately it became a war of attrition. I was not going to give up. I jumped in my jeep and drove from the East Coast to L.A. in three days and vowed I wouldn't come back until I got a directing job. It took me five or six years, and then one day Bruce turned to me without any warning and said, 'I think I'm going to give you one. I think I'll let you direct episode 5 on *Home Fires*.'"

"You must have been thrilled."

"I was terrified! I had no safety net. And I remember something that he had once said to me: 'The Director's Guild of America is littered with the bones of first-time directors.' 'What if I fail?' I asked. 'You're not going to fail. You're going to succeed at this,' he told me. But it would take me another two years to get my next directing job. I went back to construction. Bruce then gave me my second and third job. I was so nervous in those early years I used to contemplate driving into a tree, not to kill myself, just to bang my head so I could get out of doing it. That's how terrified I was. After I worked on *Homicide* (1993–1999) things started to take off. I cut my teeth in terms of technical stuff on *Touched by an Angel* (1994–2003). I did thirty episodes and that became my film school."

"*The Sopranos* put you on the map. How did you land that series?"

"I met David Chase when he was about to do *The Sopranos*. He hired me in the show's first season, and I ended up doing a quarter of the episodes. And that was my first introduction to the quality of shows on HBO, which are highly cinematic and very feature-like."

"The stakes must have been high. The show became a landmark television series. By that point were you pretty confident in your skills?"

"I worried about all sorts of things in the beginning, like how to talk to the actors and how to stage scenes. I had a bunch of contingency plans. I would have a B plan if the A plan didn't work. I had a C plan if the B plan didn't work. But these sorts of concerns began to slowly disappear. What became more important were the subtle nuances of directing—the themes, tone, palette, the inner life of the characters, referencing. If *Touched by an Angel* was my big introduction to technical education, my storytelling education was on *The Sopranos*. And I learned a tremendous amount being around great writing and great acting. After *The Sopranos* I was hired to direct episodes of *The Wire, Deadwood, Rome, Pacific, Sex in the City, Game of Thrones*, and my current show, *Boardwalk Empire*."

"How's your level of enthusiasm and confidence today?"

"I'm still as enthusiastic as I ever was and quite possibly even more passionate. My confidence level is high, but it's never so high that I'm not worried about being knocked on my ass. I never look at shows once I've cut them because I'm afraid doing so might paralyze me. My gut still gets in a knot before I go out to direct, and I've directed over a hundred episodes of television."

"For the most part the stories you tell are excessively gritty, violent, and explicitly sexual in content."

"I'm not a particularly violent person or fixated on adult-themed material. It really comes down to being interested in good writing. It begins and ends with that. There comes a point when you have to become specific about what you take on. I found that after working on *The Sopranos* that I liked character-driven stories. For me, the characters have to be anchored in reality. That's the case even with a show like *Game of Thrones*, which is total fantasy but audiences can relate to the characters because they're real. The great thing about a television series is that you can explore the inner life of a character for, let's say, five years. That's like eighty hours of character exploration. You can really examine a life. A feature film only gives you roughly two hours to run the arc of a character. When you look back at *The Sopranos*, you might imagine that it was a very violent show, that someone gets killed in every episode. That's not the case. It was a much more internal story. The writing was oblique. There was no expositional storytelling at all. It was all from the inside out, and that's what was so appealing about it. If you look at Edie Falco's character, Carmela, you see that her story is about her struggle of knowing what her husband does for a living and the price she has had to pay for it. This inner conflict was great for dramatic storytelling. I'm also attracted to themes that speak to our American history and culture, like *Deadwood*, *Boardwalk Empire*, and particularly *The Pacific*, which meant a lot to me because of what it stood for—our American troops in World War II."

"Tony Soprano is a guy you should hate but can't. Why are we so drawn to this fictional character?"

"Jimmy Gandolfini is the only actor who could have played Tony. He's a deep thinker and an extraordinary talent. I've worked with so many great actors and sometimes you don't even see the fine nuances of their craft until you watch it in dailies. I remember walking with Jimmy after shooting a scene that he was struggling with, and I was thinking, *He missed it. He never got there.* Then I looked at the screen and it was all there—so much going on behind the eyes. It was an amazing performance. I've learned more about directing from great acting like his than anything else."

"*The Soprano*'s Tony Soprano and *Boardwalk Empire*'s lead character Nucky Thompson share some similar character traits. They can both be tender, loving, and generous and at the same time malevolent and brutal. What makes these men so compelling to watch week after week, season after season?"

"What draws you to these men is the internal conflict they're living with. They're not one-dimensional characters. Nucky Thompson is like Rick in *Casablanca*. He's benevolent. He's cruel. He's the smartest guy in the room. Same is true for Tony Soprano. It's almost like the writer's rule that no one can outsmart these guys, and we can't wait to see what they're going to do next."

"What's your process to get great performances out of your actors?"

"The essential ingredient is trust, always. And having been an actor, albeit not a great one, there's a common language. If an actor doesn't sense trust from the director, they're finished, there's no dialogue, no relationship between them. It's just shot-making. Every actor is different. For example, Jimmy Gandolfini and Edie Falco have different processes. Jim lives it, wears it, and comes in wearing it. Edie just walks in and—like that—becomes Carmela. She can sight-read. Jim has to get the dialogue deeply embedded. I don't have set rules that I make people adhere to. I adjust to the actor's personalities and to the characters they're playing. My job is to make sure that the scenes are delivered or imparted effectively, so the best thing is to have an understanding of what everyone wants to have in a scene. The actors on *Boardwalk Empire* don't get scripts in advance, and very often only get their own scenes, with the possible exception of the top three on the call sheet. We want them to be in the moment. The only tool I have in my toolbox is my bullshit meter. If I'm not sensing that someone's truthful in their performance, I quickly identify it."

"Do the actors usually know ahead of time what you expect of them?"

"Remember, the actors are working at home in a vacuum with the pages. And because of that sometimes they can't envision the overall meaning of a scene in a particular episode. I'll have prep meetings with the writers to discuss each of the scenes and how they come together, so I have the bigger picture. Sometimes the actors come in and need to explain to me how they see a scene. Sometimes it differs from how I see it. When that happens we have to work it out. In television you have to think quickly, but if what you're doing comes from an organic place, it will come together for the actors because it feels realistic and natural."

"What I notice about your directing in particular is your dramatic use of the camera: unusual and varied perspectives, tight close-ups, and selective focus to heighten the storytelling."

"I do everything from gut instinct. I start by trying to design each episode by identifying its themes, which then inform how I'm going to shoot it. I try not to shoot every episode the same way because each has its own story and its own themes. I think about lenses, lighting, and perspective as storytelling tools. Very often I'll use photography or paintings as references for the visuals, and I'll share those with the DP, and together we develop a plan to infuse them. I try never to make a shot that isn't telling the story. And I try to be lean because a lot of cutting and sizes [close-ups and long shots] are a distraction. Directing a television series, like directing a film, is like holding a paintbrush with a hundred hands. Remember it's a highly collaborative process."

"Marty Scorsese is the executive producer of *Boardwalk Empire*. What's it been like working with him, and has he influenced your directing?"

"Like every other kid from New York I worshipped Marty. His films inform much of my work. When I did my first episode of *The Sopranos*, I watched *Goodfellas* (1990) a hundred times, and I think in that first episode it shows. Going through the pilot process with him for *Board-walk Empire*—casting, production design, and wardrobe fittings—was unbelievably thorough. At one point he asked me and the show's creator, Terry Winter, to come over to his private screening room to watch a couple of movies for which he supplied the commentary. We saw *Some Came Running* (1958) and *Pete Kelly's Blues* (1955). 'Marty, why are we watching these films?' I asked. 'I wanted you to see this because of the carnival aspect of it,' he explained. He wanted us to relate it to the board-walk in Atlantic City. We watched *Some Came Running* for just the scene in which Frank Sinatra is riding on a train. Marty wanted us to observe Frank Sinatra's finely nuanced energy. Marty has an encyclopedic under-standing of this medium and is incredibly detail-oriented. He wanted us to observe those details and explained that the story's got to be present in all the shots. He directed the first season's episode, and I was to follow him. It was like having to bat after Babe Ruth! Since shooting the pilot, he's not here much, but he weighs in on every episode and sends us his notes. The guy is like a hawk; he sees it all. He's like precision bombing. He can identify the tiniest thing because he has such clear vision."

"You said you've directed more than one hundred television episodes. What are some of the important life lessons you've learned along the way?"

"Well, I learned how to triage a gunshot wound," he said with a laugh. "Making movies and telling stories is a deeply human experience. On *Boardwalk Empire* alone I work with around two hundred people a day. It teaches you about patience, honesty, trust, generosity, and responsibility. You become a better person. Directing is the experience of making things together with other people, not about the end product. I have a great fondness for the casts, crew, writers, and production staff I've worked with over the past thirty years. I'll never forget them."

"What advice would you give to someone who is desperate to break in, like you were?"

"Stay with it. Stay true to your vision and work to keep the dream alive. Don't falter for one second. If you get knocked down, get back up. Don't be afraid to fail. Read literature and explore the rich culture that surrounds you, see the world, and embrace life. YOU are the greatest asset that you're going to bring to this job. There are so many opportunities out there, enough for everyone. So do it. Do it one scene at a time."

Taylor Hackford

Taylor Hackford built his career telling stories about struggling working-class people with such films as The Idolmaker *(1980),* An Officer and a Gentleman *(1982),* White Nights *(1985),* Everybody's All-American *(1988),* Delores Claiborne *(1995),* The Devil's Advocate *(1997), and* Ray *(2004). During our conversation at his beautiful Hollywood hills home, I learned that he, like so many of his characters, came from humble beginnings. Hackford has become one of the most respected and accomplished filmmakers in Hollywood.*

"When did you first decide that you wanted to be a filmmaker?"

"It wasn't until after I graduated from USC and had joined the Peace Corps. While serving in Bolivia, South America, I began to think about the political quotient of film, particularly documentaries. I engaged in that sort of intellectual fermentation that one does as a young adult. I read Marshall McLuhan and books on cinema and went regularly to this little theater just outside of La Paz, where they showed European films. I observed the Indians in the Andes, became obsessed with how they operated and fascinated by their myths. I got a hold of a Super 8 camera and began to record them, even though I had no practical experience with film. For the first time I felt passion for something. I decided to become an artist instead of a lawyer. When I informed everyone that I wanted to be a filmmaker, they accused me of being self-destructive: 'You don't have any connections into the industry. You prepared yourself to be a lawyer. Why are you doing this?'"

"Why were you doing this?

"Filmmaking gave me a voice, a way to communicate my point of view to people. It was the late 1960s, the Summer of Love, the antiwar movement was raging, and big changes were happening around the world. It was a momentous time in our history. I wanted to be involved and believed that documentary films were a political tool that could have an impact on people's thinking."

"What made you think you could be successful at it?"

"When I was a student at USC, which in the 1960s was a very docile, upper-middle-class, conservative school, my liberal views were for the

most part out of step with both the faculty and students. That didn't stop me from being very active and vocal about the need for change. I was good at public speaking and, against the odds, was elected student-body president. In that role I created the first student-body evaluation of faculty and helped open a cooperative campus bookstore that was considered by some to be communist-slash-socialist. My ability to make student government an agent of change in line with my philosophy and politics was an indication that I could also express my views on a larger scale through film."

"How did you learn the ropes as a filmmaker?"

"By watching films of the great directors. Back in the late sixties and early seventies, there were about were six or seven good movie theaters in L.A., some for foreign films and others for American films. I would go out every night and see about twenty films a week by such masters as Fellini, Godard, Truffaut, Bergman, Ford, Hawks, and Raoul Walsh."

"So how did break into the industry?"

"I got hired by KCET, the public television station in Los Angeles at that time. I started in the mailroom. One day someone asked me, 'Can you shoot film?' I lied and said yes and became their on-air investigative reporter. I covered things that were going on at City Hall, the Hall of Administration, and in state government in Sacramento. I'd go out during the day, shoot the footage, come back, cut it, write the story, and then go on the air live with it. We also did cultural programming and pioneered rock and roll on television. I had deadlines and air dates, and when you work like that you learn very quickly. KCET became my film school. Our shows won Associated Press awards and a Peabody for journalism. I was eventually promoted to associate producer, and it was during that time that I made my first documentary film, *Bukowski* (1973), a documentary on the life of poet Charles Bukowski."

"What drew you to this subject?"

"I had read his poetry in college and thought his work was stunning. He was an uncompromising artist, real working-class guy who had been a postal carrier and wrote about the Los Angeles scene. He liked to describe himself as 'having the stink of L.A. in his bones.' I wanted to understand the key to his art because *I* was trying to become an artist myself. I met him through Liza Williams, a journalist I knew from the *L.A. Free Press*. She was having an affair with him and arranged for us to meet. Once he agreed to participate in the documentary, the film was green-lighted by the head of the cultural affairs department at KCET, and I was given a budget of $1,500.

"Around that time Lawrence Ferlinghetti, the famous American poet and the owner of City Lights bookstore in San Francisco, had published Bukowski's highly sexual and exploitative stories. He titled it *Erections, Ejaculations and Stories of Ordinary Madness*, and it became a huge best-seller in San Francisco. Ferlinghetti invited Bukowski to do a reading at his bookstore, and I thought documenting that would be a good way to open the film. My crew and I, along with Bukowski's other girlfriend, Linda, accompanied him on the trip. When we arrived, Bukowski was treated like royalty. Ferlinghetti told him, 'We're all set up to feed your legend. Between seven to eight hundred people are coming to hear you read. I hope you're ready.' The L.A. poet community in those days was very small, and Bukowski had never had more than thirty people attend his readings, which usually took place in some dimly lit coffeehouse. Bukowski is now drinking a lot. We get to the City Lights Book Store event and a terrified Bukowski is drunk. I'm shooting all this and talking with him on-camera about what he's feeling. He steps onto the stage and throws up. The audience is wild, rowdy, and ready to see him brawl on-stage. They're yelling his name, 'Come on Bukowski!' But instead of reading his sexually explicit stories, he reads his poetry and completely tames these lions. The reading turns out to be an unbelievable success. That night Ferlinghetti held a party in [Bukowski's] honor, and all the girls were coming onto him. Linda, still angry with him for flirting with the stewardesses on the airplane, was getting more and more pissed. Later that night they got into this horrible fight. She beat the living shit out of him, kicked her foot through the door, and left. The next morning I show up and find Bukowski all beaten up and bruised. 'She's crazy,' he says. 'I'm just a poor poet.'

"We get back to L.A. and I show the footage to the executives at KCET, and they say, 'How can we air this? They're using words like fuck!' Still, they let me continue filming and *Bukowski* went on to win the San Francisco Film Festival."

"How did some of the lessons learned from *Bukowski* inform your later work?"

"I learned that in order to tell a story you have to go behind the scenes and examine the motivations of your characters in order to truly reveal who they are. I got Bukowski to admit that he purposefully stirred things up and created angst in order to create material that he could later write about. After we came back from San Francisco, he wrote in his weekly *L.A. Free Press* column that he went up north with this idiot filmmaker, this young punk who didn't know shit. Then he described himself as being totally on top of things while everyone around him was incompetent. 'Hey, I read your story,' I told him. 'Oh yeah,' he said. 'What'd you think, baby?' 'It's full of shit,' I said. 'That's not at all what happened. You make me look like a dick and yourself as a conquering hero, when I've got the footage showing you drunk, puking onstage, and having the shit kicked out of you by your girlfriend.' He goes, 'Well, baby, that's just the way it is. I'm a writer. When I write, I'm the hero. I can write whatever I want. You're a filmmaker. You'll tell it your way and I'll tell it mine.' In that instance Bukowski gave me an incredible gift. He gave me carte blanche to show him the way I saw him—as a flawed human being—which was the way he really was. I think that's when I learned how to tell someone's story."

"What was your next career move?"

"After *Bukowski* I decided to leave public television and pursue a career as a filmmaker. I quit my job at KCET, and for a while I starved. Then I heard that this social organization, The Children's Home of Southern California, was looking for someone to make a film about the problem of teenage pregnancy. They understood that film was a great tool for teaching young people about sex education, and I signed on to the film, which I wrote, produced, and directed. *Teenage Father* (1978) won an Academy Award for best dramatic short. That was my ticket."

"Your first feature was *The Idol Maker* (1980), based on the true story of rock promoter Bob Marcucci. How did you maintain your vision for this story in such a highly collaboratively medium?"

"I realized on the second day that, for better or worse, I had to do it my way to please myself. My cinematographer, Adam Holendar, who had shot *Midnight Cowboy*, said to me after I set up a shot, 'If you want to do it like this you can, but it's very pedestrian. I would shoot from back here and let the light come in from there. I'd let the actors be over there and so on.' So I said, 'Okay.' Then I showed what we had done to my very accomplished assistant director, Clifford Coleman, who had worked for John Ford, Robert Wise, and Sam Peckinpah. He said, 'Jesus Christ! I can't believe how stupid that is. It doesn't make any sense.' So, I said, 'Okay, we'll do it your way.' I was totally deferring to my collaborators on how to make this film. The next day I watched dailies and thought, *That's not very good. I don't like that shot, or this one.* So I gathered around all my collaborators and said to them, 'The people who financed this film may have been wrong, but they asked *me* to make it. There is no question that all of you have much more experience than I do, but I'm going to do it according to my vision, not yours. I'll listen to your suggestions, but in the end, I'm going to do it my way.'"

"All your main characters—Zack Mayo, Gavin Grey, Kevin Lomax, Ray Charles, just to name a few—are flawed human beings. Why are you drawn to these types?"

"What interest me are stories about working-class people and their struggles to overcome obstacles and find their voices. Without a class pedigree, you have to struggle to get ahead. That was my ethos. I was raised in Santa Barbara by a single mother who worked very hard as a waitress to provide for us. The kind of roughness and toughness she needed to survive was evident in the Kathy Bates character in *Delores Claiborne*. I directed that film and dedicated it to my mother. My interest in these types may also come from my early experiences with Bukowski. I'm compelled to go behind the façade of complex characters who say, 'I'm going to say and do what I'm going to say and do regardless of where it gets me.' Driven people who struggle to express themselves really interest me. Look at Ray Charles. He didn't own a pair of shoes until he was seven years old, and he was blind and black! That was the story I wanted to tell [in *Ray*] and once I did, I ended the film. Ray Charles went on to have a hugely successful career, but I wasn't interested in telling that story. Someone who has his act together is boring to me."

"What's the key to telling a convincing story?"

"The key is the people you use to tell the story. In *White Nights*, Mikhail Baryshnikov plays a Russian ballet dancer and Gregory Hines an American tap dancer. At the time we made that film Baryshnikov and Hines were two of the world's greatest dancers in their own styles. They were also driven human beings. You don't get to their stature just because you've got a little talent. You push yourself to be the greatest. They completely understood how to embody their characters in *White Nights*, which was about two men defined by their art and who needed to be free to express it."

"How did Richard Gere bring Zack Mayo to life so convincingly in *An Officer and a Gentleman*?"

"Gere acted on Broadway in *Grease* (1972) and in films like and *Looking for Mr. Goodbar* (1977) and *American Gigolo* (1980). Everybody accepted Gere's façade, which was cool, macho, and beautiful. And that's what he projected. But that wasn't enough for me. To cast him as Zack Mayo, a young con man who decides that he wants to be an officer in the U.S. Navy, I wanted to see who this actor really was. So I told him, 'Everybody else has only used your surface talent; if you do this film, I want to get behind the façade.' I was essentially saying, 'I'm going to break you.' To his credit, Gere said, 'Bring it on.' And I did. In the story, his drill instructor forces him to face who he is and become a man. I devised all of these physically humiliating and exhausting exercises for him to do in the film. I felt that if I didn't get behind Gere's diamond-hard exterior, I wouldn't be able to tell the story I wanted to tell. When Sergeant Foley finally breaks Mayo and he gets up and cries, 'I've got nowhere else to go,' that was real! I took him there and he used it. He knew what I was going for, and he went there with me and delivered. After we finished that scene, he called me over and said, 'Taylor, come over here, you son of a bitch.' He pulled off his shirt and showed me that the skin on his back had completed rubbed off and was flowing blood. We both got what we wanted. It made his career. I made mine. So it's not just having a good story. It's about getting performances out of your actors that reveal real emotions."

"You go for stories with conflict and confrontation. Why?"

"I'm interested in making films about real-life drama. My concept for cinematic storytelling is that you become enmeshed with the people on the screen, and it takes you on a journey. I think conflict and confrontation bring you to that moment when you have to be true to who you really are. For example, in my film *The Idol Maker*, Ray Sharkey plays the role of Bob Marcucci, the man who discovered teen idols Fabian and Frankie Avalon. He's a guy who is very talented but not very good-looking. So he finds a couple of pretty faces and imbues them with his talent. They sing his songs, and he propels them to stardom. At the end of the movie they both leave him, and he's forced to sing his own songs and manage his own career. Now he's got to be himself. Conflict leads him to come to terms with who he really is. That makes a powerful story."

"What was the message you were trying to get across with Gavin Grey's character in *Everybody's All-American*?"

"*Everybody's All-American* is about an athlete who is blessed with a physical gift, the adoration and adulation of his peers, but who is ultimately doomed. Gavin Grey was very much like a friend I had in high school who was an incredible athlete. He was our school's all-American. He went on to get an athletic scholarship to USC for football. But he got injured in his freshman year and never played again. When I called him years later to come with me to attend our high school reunion he said, 'I can't. I can't go back. They expect me to be that guy, and I'm not that guy.' His is a tragic story because he reaches great heights, but then there's no place to go but down. That's Gavin Grey's story. That's real life. *Everybody's All-American* is an epic tragic tale."

"What was your intended takeaway from a film like *The Devil's Advocate*?"

"This film is an allegory for the millennium. It's about where the legal profession has taken this society. I used a phantasmagorical style to investigate the reality of our society today, the narcissism, the loss of ethics and integrity, and the fact that everybody will do anything for the right amount of profit. It's about temptation and the devil. It's intended to point out how our ethos has changed in recent years."

"All your films deliver a political or social message, but the messages are delivered with subtlety, masked beneath the storyline and your characters. Why do you take this approach?"

"My way of storytelling is not to wave the message of the film in your face. When I started out, my political documentaries tried to get people to act in a certain way.

"Later I realized that I could be more effective doing dramas about the human condition. I'm saying things that I hope will have an impact on people. I'm proud of the statements I made in films like *An Officer and a Gentleman*, *Devil's Advocate*, and *Ray*—statements such as life is a struggle, but it's worth it."

"Do you see yourself as an artist?"

"Yes. I'm an artist. John Huston was an artist. Howard Hawks was an artist. I believe directors are artists. I celebrate that term. When you use a medium to express yourself, and the medium involves storytelling, acting, cinematography, lighting, editing, [and] music, and you are orchestrating and molding all of these collaborative elements into a singular vision, you are an artist."

"Do most artist-directors have an Achilles' heel?"

"Yes, their egos! When you deliver your vision and it's received with overwhelming success and a lot of money is made, Hollywood lies down and spreads its legs. You begin to feel like, *I've accomplished the impossible. I am the Man!* But you've got to realize that that was luck, or inspiration, or timing. All of those things go into what makes something a success. And yes, it was your talent and your vision. But if your next vision isn't successful, you will be scorned in the same way that you were adored. In fact, it's more than scorn—you become a pariah. No one wants to look you in the eye, and you've got to get through it. Every film that you make might be your last. And if you continue to make films over a career, it's somewhat of a miracle. To be a director you've got to be tough enough to stand up and fight again and again."

Robert Towne

Robert Towne, one of Hollywood's most respected screenwriter-directors is credited with such notable films as Chinatown *(1974),* Shampoo *(1975),* Personal Best *(1982),* Tequila Sunrise *(1988),* The Two Jakes *(1990),* The Firm *(1993), and* Mission Impossible *(1996, 2000). He is also known as the industry's most reliable script doctor, having contributed dialogue and crucial scenes to many popular films, among them* Bonnie and Clyde *(1967),* The Godfather *(1972), and* Heaven Can Wait *(1978). Towne sat down with me at his Los Angeles home on a warm summer afternoon to talk about his life as a cinematic storyteller.*

"I read that you got your start working with Roger Corman, who also helped launch the careers of Francis Ford Coppola, Peter Bogdanovich, Jack Nicholson, and so many others."

"Yes, Corman gave a lot of people opportunities to get started. He allowed us to try, within certain parameters, our hand at acting, directing, or writing. But I don't know that he was an aesthetic influence on us. What he did was limited by the generic nature of the films he was doing, and we were limited in terms of our abilities. But yes, it certainly was a place to get started."

"Did you aspire to be an actor in those early years?"

"No. I wanted to be a screenwriter. I was always interested in dramatic writing, and when I was very young thought I might be a journalist or a playwright. I realized, in the words of screenwriter James Agee when comparing playwriting with screenwriting, 'I've often been bored by a bad play, but almost never been bored by a bad movie.' Bad movies, at least in my early experience, were energetic, and they'd keep me awake. What I wanted to do was bring the seriousness or the intensity to moviemaking that people normally thought of in terms of playwriting. That was my ambition."

"How did you train as a screenwriter?"

"I had a liberal-arts education. Training for a career as a screenwriter in the late 1950s was unheard of. The only place that you could study anything to do with movies was in acting classes. In the 1970s the idea of a class in screenwriting was a joke. Now, forty years later it's an industry."

"So you're basically self-taught."

"Yes. When Roman Polanski and I started working together on the rewrite of *Chinatown*, he gave me a book on screenwriting. I kept it because he had inscribed it, 'To my partner with fond hope,' but I've never read it."

"How then did you learn the craft?"

"You just have to try. I felt I could do it and started in television. In those days your writing was changed before it was shot. Rarely did anyone speak a line you wrote. The first time I wrote anything used as written was my rewrite of *Bonnie and Clyde*. That gave me a great feeling of confidence as a screenwriter."

"Were you confident that your original screenplay for *Chinatown* would find its way to the screen?"

"I figured because it was a detective story, a genre piece, that it would give me something of an edge, but nobody understood it. It was a complicated story about how the city of Los Angeles was formed. There were also complex personal relationships that wove through the story. Once it was in production, I kept thinking, *This is going to be a disaster*. All I could see were the things that didn't go the way I hoped they would. I was so convinced that it would be a disaster that when a reviewer came up to me after its initial screening and couldn't stop telling me how great it was, I thought to myself, *This fucking guy is crazy*. Then when all the other reviews came in full of praise, I was really shocked."

"It earned you your first Oscar. Did its success open doors and give you the confidence to try new things?"

"Yes. It made me feel that even though some people might have considered what I was doing not to their taste, I now had the confidence to say, 'To hell with you. I like it.'"

"What prompted you to turn to directing?"

"I had written a script called *Greystoke—The Legend of Tarzan, Lord of the Apes*. It was a traditional Tarzan story full of adventure about a child raised by animals. It had no dialogue for the first hour and a half. I had essentially written a silent movie. When you write a screenplay, you imagine each scene and shot, so in a way you've already seen the film in your mind. To extend that process to dozens and dozens of set-ups to shots, you realize that for better or worse you've already gone a long way into directing that movie before you go into production. So if you've seen it a particular way, it seems absurd to hand over a bunch of camera angles for someone else to direct and say, 'That's my work.' No matter how much you describe a camera angle there are ten thousand ways to do it. It seemed irresponsible to myself and to the work to let someone else direct it and risk having to say, 'You screwed it up.' I lost the ability to direct the Tarzan film due to lawsuits. A very bad version of it was done, which I've never seen. [Towne was so upset by the incident he had his screenplay credit shown as P. H. Vasak after his dog. The screenplay was nominated for an Oscar.] If I had to do it all over again, that wouldn't have happened. It was after *Greystoke* that I wanted to direct my own scripts. To this day I think it's the most interesting and personal script I've ever written."

"How so?"

"It's not because I fancy running around in the jungle. It's because of the ever-increasing tendency to view other life forms as less worthy of the respect we give human life. It's what has allowed all the brutalization of life in one form or another, like slavery. When the fighting was going on in places like Korea and Vietnam, the common view was, 'Well, the Oriental has a different philosophy of life than we do.' Basically, they were saying they don't feel as much as we do, so you can kill them with impunity. Telling this story about a child raised by another form of life that is summarily slaughtered was a serious attempt to dramatize this sort of brutalization and disrespect for life. No story has ever been more important for me to tell."

"Do great stories have to deliver a message?"

"I'm sort of in line with what Samuel Goldwyn once said: 'If I want to send a message I'll call Western Union.'"

"What makes a cinematic story appeal to an audience?"

"You owe the audience a hook in order for them to become engaged. You want them to spend their time in the world that you've created. Any story that makes the audience ask 'What's going to happen next?' is a cinematic story that works."

"I've heard you say that audiences respond to passion. How does a filmmaker communicate passion?"

"Well, you don't communicate *passion* as such. It happens because a filmmaker has passion for his subject, and that is communicated to the audience automatically. It's the level of engagement that the artist has for his material that communicates itself to the viewer. Studio executives drive themselves crazy trying to figure out what it is that an audience is going to like. The only sure way is when the storyteller is so engaged in the story that he creates the desire on the part of the audience to look over his shoulder to see what's going on: 'What is so interesting?' It's that. It doesn't matter so much what the subject is. What matters is the passion. Your passion is what gives you the ability to communicate and inspire."

"Have you ever worried about losing the ability to communicate your passion?"

"Of course! In the sixties and seventies there were many opportunities to do whatever kinds of films you could think up: 'Yeah, go ahead and do it.' But the restraints got greater over the years. Filmmakers who had asked, *What is it that I want to tell?* now have to ask, *What is it I want to tell that they'll let me tell?* That's a losing game, because if the only question becomes *What is it that they will let me tell?*, sooner or later you forget to answer the first question—*What is it that I want to tell?* And that's where I think you lose the ability to communicate your passion."

"I've heard artists speak about experiencing a kind of high, a rush that happens when things come together for them creatively. What's that experience like for you when you're writing a screenplay?"

"I experience that when something I have no idea will happen, actually happens. Discovery! *Oh, that's what I was trying to do.* I also experience it in the course of writing when something unanticipated happens that is right for the project. My reaction to those very rare moments is that I've been given a precious gift. I'm sitting there trying every which way to do this thing, and then suddenly it just works. That's a good feeling."

"Do you look for it to happen with each script?"

"I don't look for it. I hope for it."

"I assume this is also true for directing?"

"The possibilities of discovery are more dramatic in directing than anywhere else because of the variables. Everything is a variable: the actors, the crew, the weather that day. The possibilities for surprises are endless. And that's very exciting. You're in charge and responsible for making the best use of everyone's work. And there is a tremendous amount of work involved, from the actors to the cinematographer to all the various departments, whether it's sound or production design. Yet arguably, because of that, you're the only person on the set without a specific job. Your job is to appreciate everybody else's job. And that's quite a job."

"Do you always start out with a theme you want to explore?"

"I don't start out with a theme. I come to realize in the course of telling a story what the theme is. Then it sharpens itself as I work on it. *Oh, this is what I'm writing about!* I go in with what I think is the story, but it just changes and sharpens itself."

"You mean it takes on a life of its own? You're not guiding it? It's guiding you?"

"At its best, that's exactly right. It's like you start the dance and you stumble around on the floor, but sooner or later your partner steps in and you follow her."

"What was the theme that revealed itself in *Tequila Sunrise*?"

"This film touches on feelings of friendship and betrayal. Mac and Nick were boyhood friends from the age of eight or nine to about sixteen or seventeen, who saw each other every day. They couldn't have been closer. But as the years go by, they drift apart. What happens is that they think they know each other much better than they do. They are thinking of each other as they were, but they've been living for years without the knowledge of shared experience. The revelation is that they may have changed more than they think they have. I think it's particularly true in our business where you've worked with actors, grown up with them, and shared ambitions. You might work on one or two movies together, but years go by when you have little contact. You continue to think of them with the intensity of your former experiences as a certain kind of person, but perhaps they're not anymore. They've changed. With the vividness of your shared experiences, it's hard to realize they're now a different person."

"What have you learned about yourself from telling human stories?"

"I realized a few years ago that I've never written a story where a person's profession wasn't at the center of it. Gittes was a detective. George was a hairdresser. Steve Prefontaine an athlete."

"Is that because what we do defines who we are and how we behave?"

"I think so. I could never tell a love story in which people's professions are not involved. I think it comes from having been a child of the Depression. Just as influential was the question, 'What do you want to do when you grow up?' What would I become . . . a doctor, lawyer, fireman? It was automatic, thinking what you were going to do. I've said, not really in jest, that my enduring attitudes on this subject were probably shaped by Walt Disney cartoons. Mickey, Donald, and Pluto were professionals. Steamboat Willie was a boat captain, a furniture mover, or a plumber. As children we were able to identify with these characters and wanted to try different professions—skyscraper builder, detective, whatever it was. The scope of professions was quite extraordinary, and they lent themselves well to imaginative animation."

"What is your greatest challenge as a storyteller?"

"As I get older, I think my greatest challenge is to maintain my curiosity and my interest in life. Life's problems can sometimes interfere with your ability to fantasize."

"Most of your characters are highly driven individuals. Is that because you too are driven?"

"I suppose. I'm certainly driven enough to have done the work that I've done. Beyond that, it's a question that I don't know how to answer."

"What are the questions you'd like to have answers for?"

"Where have we come from? Where are we going? Does the journey begin at birth and end at death?"

"You know, I had this notion, I realize now probably a ridiculous one, that people who spend their lives telling stories about human experiences might have learned enough about what makes us tick to answer some of those big questions. But, sadly, it seems that nobody has answers. Storytellers don't know any more than the rest of us."

Robert laughed. At my naïveté, I assumed. "Have you ever seen the (1957) Ingmar Bergman film *The Seventh Seal*?"

"Yes."

"There is a scene when the knight is playing chess with Death. He's playing for his life. And he says to Death, 'Will you reveal your secrets to me?' And Death replies, 'I have no secrets.'"

Recommended Viewing

The following list of films, stage productions, and television shows served as research material for my conversations with the directors. This is not a complete listing of their work. I recommend viewing these films and shows, and particularly their celebrated works, for a greater appreciation of our conversations. All of these films and many of the stage shows and television series are readily available.

MICHAEL APTED
>*Up* series (1964–)
>*Coal Miner's Daughter* (1980)
>*Nell* (1994)
>*Gorillas in the Mist* (1988)
>*The World Is Not Enough* (1999)
>*Amazing Grace* (2006)
>*Chronicles of Narnia* (2010)

ROBERT BENTON
>*The Late Show* (1977)
>*Places in the Heart* (1984)
>*Kramer vs. Kramer* (1979)
>*Billy Bathgate* (1991)
>*Nobody's Fool* (1994)
>*The Human Stain* (2003)
>*Feast of Love* (2007)

JAMES L. BROOKS
>*Terms of Endearment* (1983)
>*Broadcast News* (1987)
>*As Good as It Gets* (1997)
>*Spanglish* (2004)
>*How Do You Know* (2010)

MEL BROOKS
>*The Producers* (1968)
>*The Twelve Chairs* (1970)
>*Young Frankenstein* (1974)

Blazing Saddles (1974)

High Anxiety (1977)

History of the World: Part 1 (1981)

Life Stinks (1991)

JAMES BURROWS

Taxi (1978–1982)

Cheers (1982–1993)

Fraiser (1993–1997)

Friends (1994–1998)

Will and Grace (1998–2006)

Mike and Molly (2010–2012)

JOHN CARPENTER

Assault on Precinct 13 (1976)

Halloween (1978)

The Fog (1980)

Escape from New York (1981)

The Thing (1982)

Christine (1983)

Starman (1984)

Big Trouble in Little China (1986)

Village of the Damned (1995)

JOSEPH CEDAR

Time of Favor (2000)

Campfire (2004)

Beaufort (2007)

Footnote (2011)

RICHARD DONNER

"Nightmare at 20,000 Feet" (*Twilight Zone* episode) (1963)

The Omen (1976)

Superman (1978)

Inside Moves (1980)

Ladyhawke (1985)

Lethal Weapon 1, 2, 3 (1987, 1989, 1992)

Maverick (1994)

JONATHAN FRAKES

Star Trek: The Next Generation (1987–1994) TV Series

Star Trek: Deep Space Nine (1994–1995) TV Series

Star Trek: First Contact (1996)

Star Trek: Insurrection (1998)

Leverage (2009–2012) TV Series

NCIS: LA (2010–2012) TV Series

Castle (2012) TV Series

LESLI LINKA GLATTER

Tales of Meeting and Parting (1985)

Twin Peaks (1990–1991) TV Series

ER (1995–2008) TV Series

Law and Order: Special Victims Unit (1999–2001) TV Series

The West Wing (2002–2006) TV Series

Mad Men (2007–2010) TV Series

Homeland (2012–2013) TV Series

The Newsroom (2012–) TV Series

TAYLOR HACKFORD

Bukowski (1973) Short Film

Officer and a Gentleman (1982)

White Nights (1985)

Everyone's All-American (1988)

Delores Claiborne (1995)

Devil's Advocate (1997)

Ray (2004)

WALTER HILL

Hard Times (1975)

The Warriors (1979)

48 Hrs. (1982)

Crossroads (1986)

Johnny Handsome (1989)

Wild Bill (1995)

Undisputed (2002)

Deadwood (2004)

ARTHUR HILLER

The Americanization of Emily (1964)

Love Story (1970)

The Out of Towners (1970)

The Hospital (1971)

The Man in the Glass Booth (1975)

Silver Streak (1976)

Author, Author! (1982)

DOUG HUGHES

Frozen (2004) Broadway

Doubt (2006) Broadway

Inherit the Wind (2007) Broadway revival

Oleanna (2009) Broadway

The Big Knife (2013) Broadway

LAWRENCE KASDAN

Body Heat (1981)

The Big Chill (1983)

Silverado (1985)

The Accidental Tourist (1988)

Grand Canyon (1991)

French Kiss (1995)

JOHN LANDIS

Animal House (1978)

The Blues Brothers (1980)

An American Werewolf in London (1981)

The Twilight Zone: The Movie (prologue and segment 1) (1983)

Trading Places (1983)

Coming to America (1988)

BARRY LEVINSON

Diner (1982)

Tin Men (1987)

Liberty Heights (1999)

Avalon (1990)

Bugsy (1991)

Good Morning, Vietnam (1987)

Rain Man (1988)

You Don't Know Jack (2010)

EMILY MANN

Having Our Say (1995)

The Search for Signs of Life in the Universe (2000)

Anna in the Tropics (2004)

Translations (2007)

A Streetcar Named Desire (2012) Broadway

KATHLEEN MARSHALL

Wonderful Town (2005), Broadway revival

The Pajama Game (2006), Broadway revival

Grease (2009) Broadway revival

Anything Goes (2012) Broadway revival

Nice Work If You Can Get It (2012) Broadway

ROB MARSHALL

Annie (1999)

Chicago (2002)

Memoirs of a Geisha (2005)

Nine (2009)

Pirates of the Caribbean: On Stranger Tides (2011)

MICHAEL MAYER

A View from the Bridge (1998) Broadway revival

Thoroughly Modern Millie (2004) Broadway

After the Fall (2004) Broadway revival

Broadway Spring Awakening (2009) Broadway

American Idiot (2011) Broadway

On a Clear Day You Can See Forever (2012) Broadway

PAUL MAZURSKY

Bob & Carol & Ted & Alice (1969)

Blume in Love (1973)

Harry and Tonto (1974)

Next Stop, Greenwich Village (1976)

An Unmarried Woman (1978)

Down and Out in Beverly Hills (1986)

Enemies: A Love Story (1989)

MIRA NAIR

Salaam Bombay (1988)

Mississippi Masala (1991)

Kama Sutra: Tale of Love (1996)

Monsoon Wedding (2001)

The Namesake (2006)

The Reluctant Fundamentalist (2012)

HAL PRINCE

Cabaret (1969) Broadway

Follies (1972) Broadway

A Little Night Music (1974) Broadway

Candide (1996) Broadway revival,

Sweeney Todd (1980) Broadway

Evita (1983) Broadway

The Phantom of the Opera (1988–) Broadway

Kiss of the Spider Woman (1995) Broadway

BRETT RATNER

Rush Hour 1, 2, 3 (1998, 2001, 2007)

The Family Man (2000)

Red Dragon (2002)

X-Men: Last Stand (2006)

Tower Heist (2011)

GARY ROSS

Pleasantville (1998)

Seabiscuit (2003)

The Hunger Games (2012)

MARK RYDELL

The Cowboys (1972)

Cinderella Liberty (1973)

The Rose (1979)

On Golden Pond (1981)

The River (1984)

Intersection (1994)

For the Boys (1991)

JAY SANDRICH

He and She (1967–1970)

The Mary Tyler Moore Show (1970–1977)

The Bob Newhart Show (1972–1978)

Soap (1977–1979)

The Cosby Show (1984–1992)

Seems Like Old Times (1980)

SUSAN STROMAN

The Music Man (2000) Broadway revival

Contact (2002) Broadway

The Producers (2007) Broadway

Young Frankenstein (2009) Broadway

The Scottsboro Boys (2010) Broadway

JULIE TAYMOR

The Lion King (1997) Broadway

Frida (2002)

Across the Universe (2007)

Titus (1999)

Tempest (2010)

Spiderman: Turn Off the Dark (2010) Broadway

ROBERT TOWNE

Personal Best (1982)

Tequila Sunrise (1988)

Without Limits (1998)

Ask the Dust (2006)

TIM VAN PATTEN

The Sopranos (1999–2007)
The Wire (2002–2004)
Sex in the City (2003–2004)
The Pacific (2010)
Boardwalk Empire (2010–2014)

Bibliography

Bergman, Ingmar. *An Autobiography: The Magic Lantern*. New York: Viking Press, 1988.

Brody, Richard. *Everything Is Cinema: The Working Life of Jean-Luc Godard*. New York: Henry Holt, 2008.

Cohen, Robert. *Theatre*. Mountain View, CA: Mayfield Publishing, 2000.

Christie, James. *You're the Director . . . You Figure It Out: The Life and Films of Richard Donner*. Duncan, OK: BearManor Media, 2010.

Director's Guild of America Quarterly. Winter 2010, fall 2010, fall 2011, winter 2011, spring 2012.

Eichenbaum, Rose. *The Actor Within*. Middletown, CT: Wesleyan University Press, 2011.

Freer, Ian. *Movie Makers: 50 Iconic Directors from Chaplin to the Coen Brothers*. London: Quercus, 2009.

Gray, Susan, *Writers on Directors*. New York: Watson-Guptill Publications, 1999.

Kagan, Jeremy. *Directors Close Up*. Maryland: Scarecrow Press, 2006.

———. *Directors Close Up: Interviews with Directors Nominated for Outstanding Directorial Achievement*. Boston: Focal Press, 2000.

Kazan, Elia. *A Life*. New York: Da Capo Press, 1988.

Hirsch, Foster. *Harold Prince and the American Musical Theatre*. Cambridge, MA: Cambridge University Press, 1989.

Le Blanc, Michelle, and Colin Odell. *John Carpenter*. Herts, UK: Kamera Books, 2011.

Lipton, James. *Inside* Inside. New York: Dutton, 2007.

Long, Robert Emmet. *Broadway: The Golden Years*. New York: Continuum, 2003.

Lumet, Sidney. *Making Movies*. New York: Vantage Books, 1995.

Mamet, David. *Theatre*. New York: Faber and Faber. Inc. 2010.

Mazursky, Paul. *Show Me the Magic*. New York: Simon and Schuster, 1999.

Mordden, Ethan. *Beautiful Mornin': The Broadway Musical in the 1940s*. New York: Oxford University Press, 1999.

Prince, Hal. *Contradictions: Notes on Twenty-six Years in the Theatre*. New York: Dodd, Mead, 1974.

Suber, Howard. *The Power of Film*. Studio City, CA: Michael Wiese Productions, 2006.

Taymor, Julie. *Playing with Fire*. New York: Harry Abrams, 1995.

Thompson, David. *Levinson on Levinson*. New York: Faber and Faber, 1993.

Tirard, Laurent. *Moviemakers' Master Class*. New York: Faber and Faber, 2002.

Index

ABOUT THE AUTHOR

Rose Eichenbaum is an award-winning photographer
and photojournalist. Her work has appeared in several national
magazines and has been the subject of numerous exhibitions, including
a national tour hosted by the Smithsonian Institution. A respected educator,
Eichenbaum is a professor at Woodbury University in the School of Media,
Culture and Design and directs the dance photography workshop at Jacob's
Pillow. She also teaches photography at the Los Angeles Center of Photography.
Eichenbaum is the author of four books and lives in Encino, California.

Aron Hirt-Manheimer is the editor of numerous books and articles,
including Eichenbaum's *The Dancer Within* and *The Actor Within*.